Data Flow

Visualising Information
in Graphic Design

—

gestalten

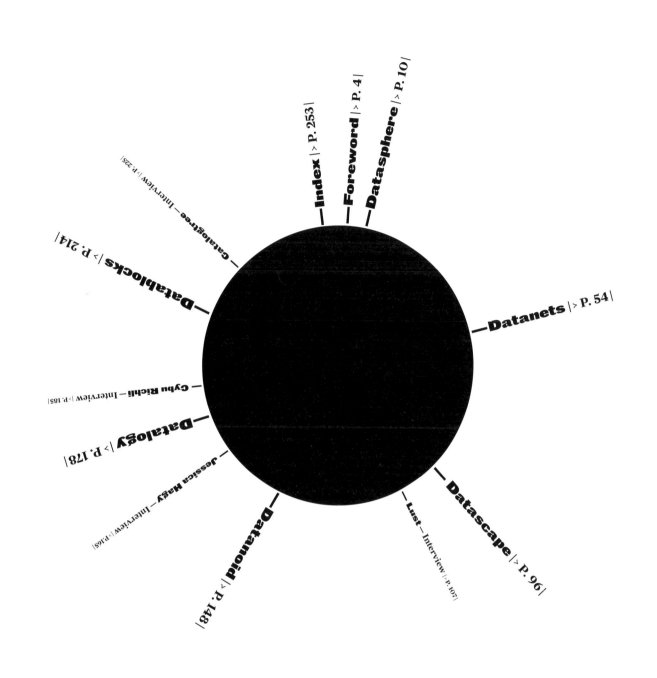

Foreword

—

Visual metaphors are a powerful aid to human thinking. From Sanskrit through hieroglyphics to the modern alphabet, we have used ciphers, objects, and illustrations to share meaning with other people, thus enabling collective and collaborative thought. As our experience of the world has become more complex and nuanced, the demands to our thinking aids have increased proportionally. Diagrams, data graphics, and visual confections have become the language we resort to in this abstract and complex world. They help us understand, create, and completely experience reality.

—

As more and more aspects of our lives become connected in the webbed environments of urban landscapes, the information that we generate and consume collects into massive databases. As Daniel and Joris from Catalogtree put it, 'By just going about our daily routines, we become part of a large and unseen ornament'. But this ornament is unformed and mutable, subject to the imagination and intent of the data designer. By giving shape to data, we not only provide access and insight to the hidden patterns of meaning it could reveal; we also give shape to the potential for creative collaboration between individuals.   We live in a world where every idea has been thought of before, and it becomes too easy simply to use the Microsoft® template for presenting our data. The visual form we adopt becomes driven by the tool or the topic we are presenting, rather than the usefulness of the data or the insight it gives us. 'This is business data, so it must be a bar chart' may be an easy way to approach the subject of presenting information, but it is a far less satisfying and provocative route for the designer of human thinking and intent.

—

The visual form we adopt becomes driven by the tool or the topic we are presenting

—

————— **Patterns of Intent** — Design has been described as 'patterns with intent'. The information designer shapes an experience, or view, of the data with a particular aim in mind. To clarify, confuse, inspire, redress, and connect—all of these are legitimate intents for design, towards which the chosen visual presentation can be directed.   The marriage between visual metaphor and intent is exactly what makes the examples in this book inspirational and fascinating. A pinpoint in space spreads out to become a sphere of meaning. A structured space is manoeuvred to reveal connection, energy, hierarchy, and context. As multiple data points spread out to occupy coordinates in a matrix, we see a network of contextual values that derive sense from their relationship with each other. We travel through semiotic and scientific landscapes that communicate through colour, shape, pattern, and emotion.

Imagining data as a cloud, a river, or even as perfume profoundly changes the choices we have for observing it, in terms of directing attention or placing emphasis. Inspired by this approach, *Data Flow* examines the various visual metaphors used in design to capture data in an accessible way. All infographics are an imposition upon the raw material, yet by borrowing from the cultural, emotional, and contemporary world of the viewer, a multi-layered symphony of expression can be created. If we can show data as blocks, spheres, rivers, nets, or landscapes, we open up a new and rich visual language through which the external world is brought into our internal world of understanding. In other words, we communicate.   This approach places a premium on human accessibility. The design is a potent semiotic signal cutting through the filters of relevance to connect with the viewer as a coherent, visceral expression of meaning. The message contained in the data is not weakened by process or cliché. The simplistic formulas of 'business = pie chart' can be subverted and playfully re-engineered in a considered exchange with the end-user. By presenting the data in a form dictated by the viewer's needs, rather than the needs of the originator or even the data itself, a connection is drawn between viewer and data. And it is the designer who makes this connection possible, by turning his or her inspiration into a form that opens up new meaning.

—

The information designer shapes an experience, or view, of the data with a particular aim in mind

—

————**Simplexity** — Design is not just about making things simple. In fact, there is a complementary relationship between simplicity and complexity that influences design choices to produce surprising and informative data diagrams. By shaping their view on data, designers can choose to introduce a level of complexity that allows just the right amount of contrast to drive profile, focus, and definition. The choices determining this delicate balance—called simplexity—are highly dependent on the context and audience for the resulting data presentation.

—

Illumination and knowledge flow together

—

A professional, visually literate audience will relish a higher sophistication and subtlety that can be delivered with sublime elegance. However, access to ever larger databases can seduce the designer into placing complexity, and the challenge of bridging the gap between information and its expression, at the very forefront. Software tools such as Processing have made it possible to give shape and meaning to massive amounts of information, yet in many cases the tool becomes the message. As with the early days of Photoshop, a designer's fascination with the tool does not necessarily lead to a better elucidation of complex data. It can obscure meaning and hide behind style, besides leading to an overconsidered analysis. In the words of Cybu Richli (see interview), 'Abstract and reduced visualisations can easily put distance between the viewer and the subject. Although aesthetics are taking on an increasingly important role, we must always ensure that visualisations make things easier to understand. This is the big challenge facing information designers today.' Compositions must ensure comprehension; that is the simple and elegant mantra in the design of complex data explanations.   Inevitably, however, designers will stamp a part of their personality on the way the data is presented. It is the cerebral filter of abstraction that distils, contorts, and reveals a new insight or profound conclusion from the heart of the data. Each designer has an inherent cultural 'operating system' through which he or she turns meaning into expression, yet the language of data and science is open-ended and culturally neutral. By using well-designed, pertinent data graphics, we achieve a kind of universal dataflow—the ability to transcend narrow and individual experience and elicit meaning beyond ourselves. We look at the tourist guides developed by Tube Graphics and understand their meaning without reading the text. We see the analysis of languages in a meta-language of clarity. Through this artful imposition, the designer also imparts meaning, in a form where illumination and knowledge flow together.

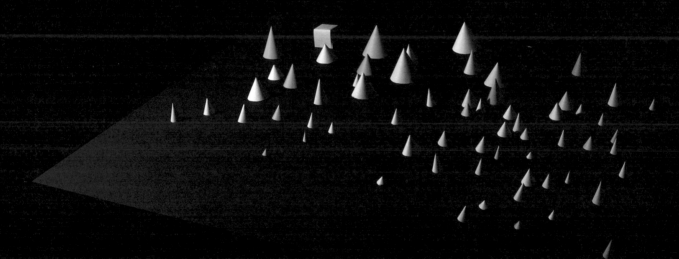

Datasphere

—

The circle is the first, perfect shape. The equidistant arrangement of the outer points from the centre, defining and ideal, are impossible to achieve by human hand. The space speaks of potential — the tension between what is achieved and what could be achieved. From the circle, we derive ideals and focus, both the halo of saints and the cross-haired target in gun sights.

—

In design, the whole equals complete, while fractured equals potential. The design of infographics can use the metaphor of a circle or sphere as the starting point for many different forms of visuali-

—

'Shares of a whole'

—

sation. The most simplistic and recognisable—pie charts—are quite a crude tool for exact comparison, yet offer an easy way to highlight the effect of large differences—sales volume at face value, for instance. But designers have taken the two-dimensional nature of pie charts a step further, blending layer upon layer to construct the stories behind the data in a cumulative fashion.

— The Shape of Family | > P. 47 | CHRISTINA VAN VLECK

The simple sectioning of cylindrical space—the 'sliced and diced' approach—leads to an intuitive understanding of 'shares of a whole', in a simple side-by-side comparison. Christina van Vleck interprets genealogy as the sections of a stem, exposing the influence of patriarchs across generations, in a sectional, assembled history. Individual sections find context in the clear definitive shape of the whole: the 'O' of one. The ubiquitous use of the pie chart has led to 'the messenger becoming the message'. Where the designer wishes to make a subtle

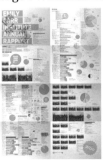

— Woo, issue 3: Emily Carr Institute Annual Rapport | > P. 40 | ABI HUYNH

reference—either pointed or ironic—to 'serious analysis', pie-charts are shorthand for 'business'. Fun can be had by turning pie charts from the Emily Carr Institute's annual report into fizzy bubbles, expressly subverting the ubiquity of the form to add a student personality to the document. Alternately, the sphere can take on a representational quality, both as a unit or as part of a collective. The self-contained completeness of circles often leads to their being used to stand for individual human beings. Dots on a page become deaths or human rights. The individual is at once secluded and distinct from the whole, yet, within the arrangement, becomes part of a larger tapestry of directional

intent. Individual spheres reach out to form a gestalt that ultimately reveals their significance. Where the framework for arrangement is familiar, meaning is transposed onto landscapes, as growth, decline, and differentiation are painted with pointillist precision. The flickering dots are cities in 1kilo's presentation of the Ruhr industrial region, growing and shrink-

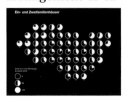

— Das Ruhrgebiet im demografischen Wandel | > P. 33 | 1KILO

ing as their economic fortunes rise and fall. The pattern of the arrangement may be familiar, but the insights revealed are surprising. The well-being of cities in the region is delineated by the size and shape of individual spheres.

Stepping inside the sphere unlocks a mutable field of potential when it is viewed, more subtly, as ordinal space. The imposition of ranking adds relativity, direction, and energy to the data points as they spread out from a central focus or deliberate locus. A position further from the centre means something different from being closer. Clusters and diffusion exist in a zone of meaning. An arc becomes

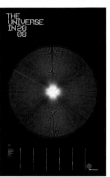

— Universe In 2008 | > P. 68 | JEFFREY DOCHERTY

reach, the hue becomes frequency. The fractured radii extending from the centre provide a rooted matrix from which we can read progression, cycles, and time, contained in an understandable unit. From Jeffrey Docherty's 'Universe in 08' calendar of scientific events, to image now's conception of the Ali v. Foreman 'Rumble in the

—

Dots on a page become deaths or human rights

—

Jungle', the inexorable march towards conclusion finds its structure in the certainty of the sphere. Whether contained, connected, or fractured, spheres—with their transparency and deliberate nature—lead to focus, value, and clarity. By layering and connecting within known constraints, we can illuminate cycles that are driven by the energy expanding from a fixed point in space.

PREVIOUS PAGE —— **The Rain Project**
|›P. 45| THANKS EVERYBODY

—— **SearchClock** CHRIS HARRISON — Google's search revenue and profitability are now expected to surpass that of Microsoft Windows, one of the best-established and well-known monopolies of the IT universe. This meteoric rise in corporate fortunes is driven by billions of people around the world riding the keyword rodeo. Google can open up the universe of meaning hidden among billions of web pages, but this universe cannot be seen or experienced without the all-important keywords. As the internet has evolved, so has what people look for from, and within, it. By tracking the most popular search words for each hour of the day from 1997 to 2000, we get an intimate and profound insight into the evolution of the web. Ironically, the earliest searches were dominated by a desire for contact with people. User-generated content was delivered through chats. Over time, the trend has moved towards information, pre-packaged content edited and refined for mass consumption, as the web has become more akin to a corporate pamphlet. The shift has been accelerated by the spread of e-commerce. This snapshot of the web's history highlights the irony of the Web 2.0 debate. As twitter, newsvine, and other social messaging networks embed the web in daily life, we return to its very essence: the need to connect with other people.

—— **One week of the Guardian: Wednesday** |›PP. 59, 70| DESIGNING THE NEWS — The purpose of this project was to present the news in a way that people seldom experience. It attracts the viewer's attention with deliberately beautiful and unexpected graphics, then holds this attention with a deeper investigation of the information that viewers see every day. The concentric circles rank and categorise stories, placing them in sequence like tracks on an old analogue LP. Each colour band represents a category of news, ordered according to total news contribution. The word counts of individual articles are scattered across the surface, according to the category under which they appear.

This forced reassessment of the news clearly encapsulates the Guardian's role as a critical reporting voice in the UK.

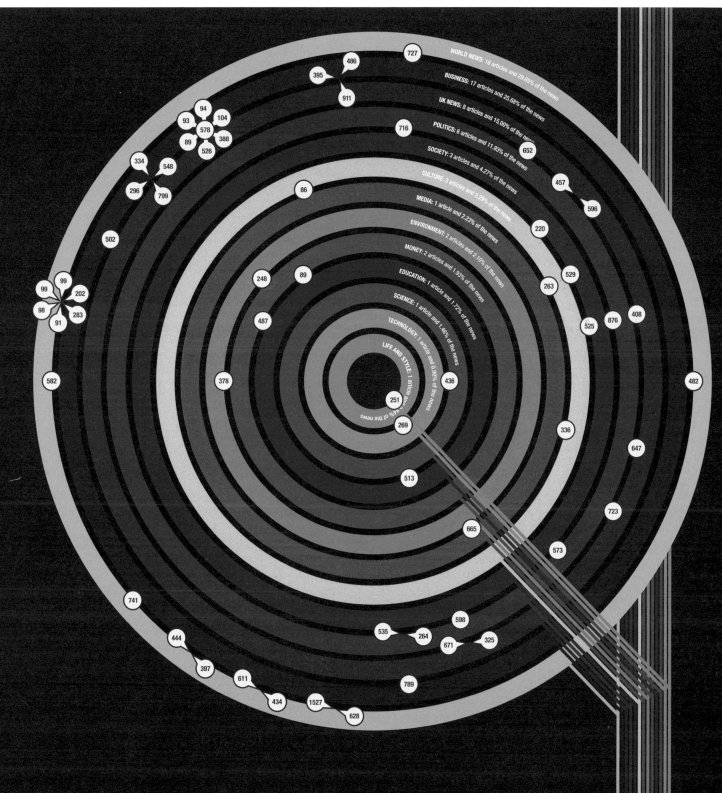

WORLD NEWS: 18 articles and 29.65% of the news

BUSINESS: 17 articles and 25.68% of the news

UK NEWS: 8 articles and 15.00% of the news

POLITICS: 6 articles and 11.93% of the news

SOCIETY: 3 articles and 4.27% of the news

CULTURE: 3 articles and 2.29% of the news

MEDIA: 1 article and 2.23% of the news

ENVIRONMENT: 2 articles and 2.10% of the news

MONEY: 2 articles and 1.93% of the news

EDUCATION: 1 article and 1.72% of the news

SCIENCE: 1 article and 1.46% of the news

TECHNOLOGY: 1 article and 0.90% of the news

LIFE AND STYLE: 1 article and 0.44% of the news

£7bn Barclays profit soothes investors
A safer ride on the rollercoaster
A website fit for heroes: 14m first world war medals recorded on line
Anger at gap between rich and poor - ICM poll
Art traffickers suspected as looted treasures found
Asda gives Wal-Mart a British boost
Banksy works on sale at new exhibition
Barclays director lands £14.8m bonus
Boost for micro power studied
Broadcasters face spot checks on phone lines
Bush shaken by memorial to 800,000 Rwanda dead
Celebration tempered by caution
China faces renewed criticism as dissident's subversion trial starts
Coroner urges action on armoured vehicles
CPS admits disc of suspects' DNA was 'mislaid' for a year
Credit Suisse suspends traders for over-pricing
Debt market scuppers Cadbury windfall
Democrat rivals tackle ailing US economy - and each other
Disney foothold in India
DJ Grooverider jailed for four years in Dubai
Domino's delivers bigger profits with new menu and on line ordering
Fear that China will push up world inflation after prices rise 7%
Fishermen missing after warship and boat collide
GSK cuts HIV drug prices for developing countries
Homeless man lived at Gatwick
Hutton accused of U-turn on flexible working for parents
Illness forces Castro to quit after half a century in power
Insurer ousts boss and may hive off risky business
Intercontinental hits targets and aims high
iPod users get BBC shows on the move
Litvinenko was traitor seeking conflict, says murder suspect
Migrants must earn citizenship, says Brown

Monsters of the deep
Move to link unemployment benefit to new work scheme
MPs demand more detail as Darling rushes through Northern Rock bill
MPs question home secretary's ingredients
Much aped chocolate advert scores with public
North Korea hosts US musicians
Older label's new look
Opec worries drive oil price to $100 close
Papers reveal how alleged war criminal escaped UK arrest
Police capture 'supreme one' in crime syndicate in Italy
Porsche threatens legal action on £25 congestion fee
Rivals close in as Musharraf suffers Pakistan poll rout
Rock report to reveal Darling's delays
Royal Mail is urged to rethink London closures
S&N expects recovery after a difficult year for beer
Schoolboy, 12, killed in fall during skiing trip
Serbian convoy enters Kosovo amid fears over partition of new state
Signs of protest from patient children of the revolution
Smith regrets failure to win over 42-day critics
Stem cell jabs reverse damage after strokes, doctors claim
Stop Blair: ambition to lead Europe hits fierce opposition
Study links baby diet in first weeks with adult IQ
Suspected suicides in Bridgend area reach 17 as schoolgirl found hanged
Thomson gets qualified approval to buy Reuters
Three lenders scrap 125% mortgage deals as criticism increases
Tokyo's advice to US should be saved for home consumption
Tommy Sheridan's wife and father-in-law charged with perjury during libel trial
Toshiba withdraws from high definition market
University dropout steady at 22%
Vulnerable removed from streets to foil insurgents
White House rejects calls for an end to embargo
Whitehall amateurs hold purse strings for £678bn spending

Information
The categories of news are represented by coloured concentric circles, expanding from least to most total word counts per category. The individual word counts of each story are plotted on the corresponding concentric circle, on a spoke of the corresponding page. All headlines in the paper are categorised and listed alphabetically.

One week of
The Guardian
February 20th 2008

Talkshow 03-09-07

MAPPING A TALKSHOW BETWEEN AARON KOBLIN, WILFRIED HOUJEBER AND CATALOGTREE
ON 03-09-2007 AS PART OF THE INFO AESTHETICS SYMPOSIUM ORGANIZED BY LUST, THE HAGUE, NL.
DESIGN: CATALOGTREE IN COLLABORATION WITH KIM HOYER / PROGRAMMING: LUTZ ISSLER

—— **Talkshow** CATALOGTREE in collaboration with Lutz Issler — Aaron Koblin is an established pioneer of data visualisation, aiming to transform social and infrastructural data into artwork. Some of his pieces form part of the permanent exhibitions at the Museum of Modern Art in New York. —— **Rhythm Textures Poster** |> PP. 72, 78| STEFANIE POSAVEC — Just as the rings of a tree tell us about the seasons — their length, intensity, and the heat and coldness accompanying climatic shifts — Stefanie Prosavec takes us on a journey through the rhythm and flow of text. Every exclamation, every pause is reflected by changes in the thickness of the rings, or in their absence altogether. The density and potential of text are living entities, growing around the source.   The intuitive feeling we get for the text makes the comparison between passages more compelling, as we feel the pace speed up or slow down. At both a micro and a macro level, we develop a new appreciation of Jack Kerouac's style, as selected passages are compared and contrasted, like organic structures that expand to support themselves as they grow in richness and complexity. —— **mapping:ch** |> PP. 21, 103, 230| LORENZO GEIGER — Here, power, prosperity, and contentedness are shown as multivariate islands, scattered outwards from individual countries. Denmark, China, and Luxembourg are the unexpected, densely-encircled islands claiming the top spot for contentedness, number of troops, and gross domestic product. The use of concentric circles to show both data type and ranking allows multiple rankings to be shown simultaneously. The additional loosely formal grid, its coordinates determined by the unexpected opposites of money/happiness and innovation/prettiness, leads us to re-evaluate our assumptions about national success.   Would you brave the cold waters to swim from the 'island' of Switzerland to the United States, if you had to leave behind happiness and beautiful surroundings?   The colour coding also reveals interesting clusters and contrasts. Why do so few countries have a multiple top ten ranking? Why do the powerful countries not migrate towards contentedness?

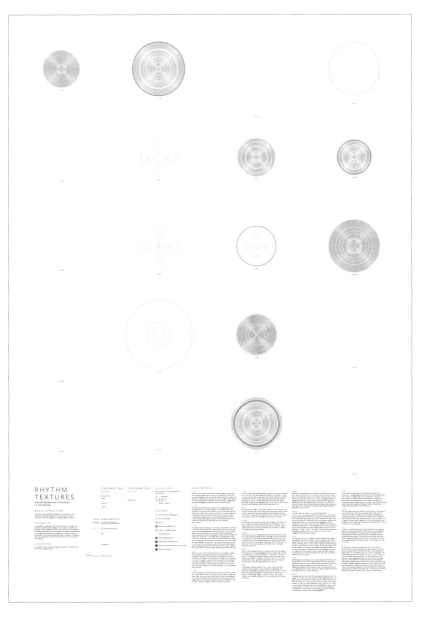

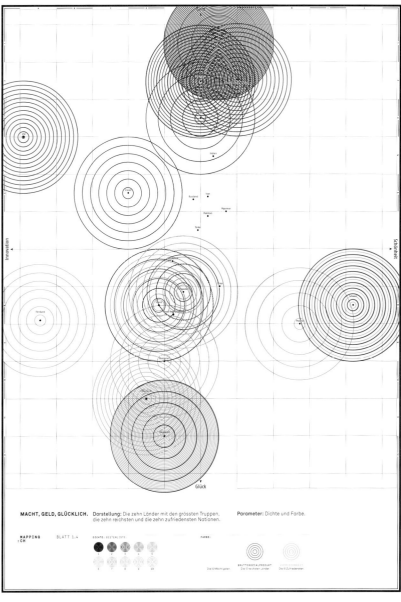

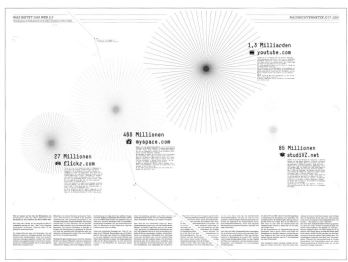

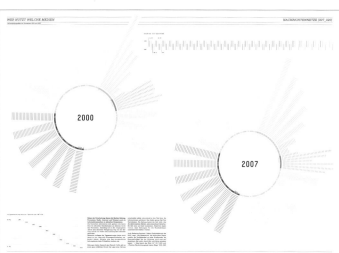

— Overnewsed but uninformed

|> PP. 75, 242| STEFAN BRÄUTIGAM — Price is energy, according to this piece. Like a gigantic firework display at midnight on New Year's Eve, the cash values of company acquisitions are visualised as stellar explosions. Starbursts represent the land grab for influence in the Web 2.0 media sphere. The €1.3 billion detonation of YouTube's change in ownership creates the pinnacle of a loosely drawn company lifeline. This was the day when its founders turned their dream into cash, celebrating the arrival of the new internet with an explosion of media interest.   The energy and space inside the stars also reflect the nature of Web 2.0, with its participative, user-generated nature. YouTube, flickr, and myspace exist because of the contribution of multiple individuals, connected through the random distribution of free functionality. The energy potential of the different sites is reflected in the latticework of radii, reaching out from the central idea that binds users together. ——— Diffusion, projection, and influence in the media age are all examined in this work. In terms of the preferred media by which Germans keep themselves abreast of world events, there is a clear shift towards the internet. The histograms radiating out from the central source refract through the lens of chronological age to show how different groups of people gravitate towards a preferred medium.

The radius (or length) of each bar becomes an automatic reference to media 'reach', a key factor in determining advertising costs. Influence is artfully quantified to show where media power will lie in the future.

The shift between 2000 and 2007 shows not only a change in preference for a specific medium, but also a change in the age profile of newspaper readers and internet users.

——— A news event spreads through the blogosphere, like roots from a tree. This study of the changing importance of blogs as a news source specifically compares German- and English-language coverage of the collapsing bridge in Minneapolis in 2007.

One would naturally expect an American event to receive more coverage among American bloggers, but even so, the sparse nature of the German coverage in this piece is very striking.   The field of potential for blogging as a social medium is presented through the buzzing lines of text, which connect, intersect, and create new meaning as lines converge. In this way, they are expressing the true nature of social news coverage.

——— A B peace & terror etc.
The computational aesthetics of love & hate

PLUSMINUS — One man's freedom fighter is another man's terrorist. On the geopolitical stage, there are two sides to every story. Rarely has that message been captured to such striking effect as in this double-sided poster, which expresses quantitatively the contribution to peace and terrorism made by UN member states. Printed on semi-transparent paper stock, the two sides blend into one artistic whole when held up to the light.

Three levels of data are presented in concentric circles, with the scores per country reduced to three line weights representing high, medium or low.   For peace, the global peace index scores are shown in the inner ring, while the happy planet index and global subjective well-being index scores are shown in the outer ring. For terrorism, the measures are extracted from the political terror scale (shown in the inner ring) and from weapon holdings and military expenditure per capita, seen in the outer ring.

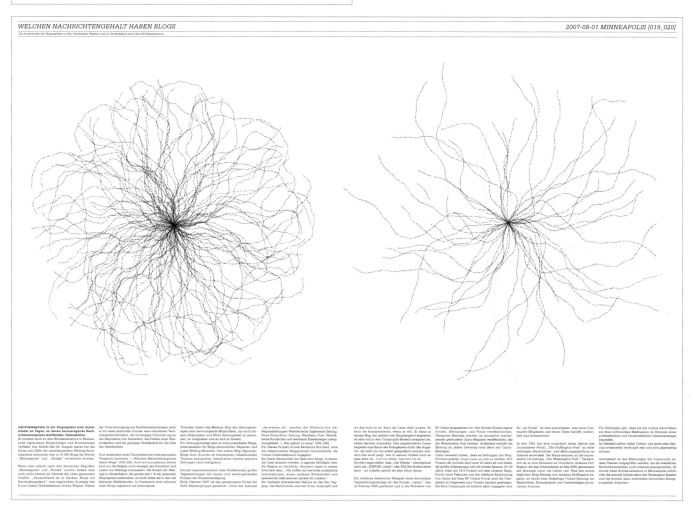

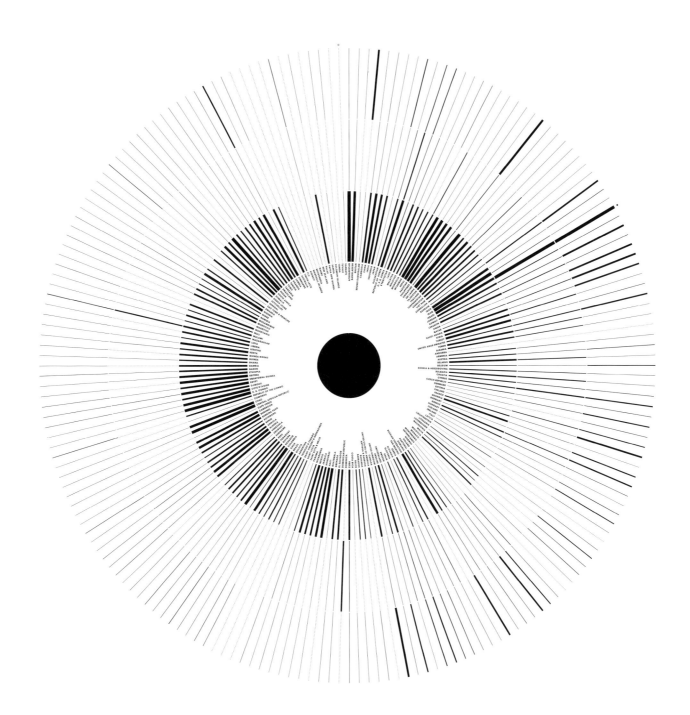

B_

TERROR ETC_the computational aesthetics of hate

INNER RING_POLITICAL TERROR SCALE_http://www.politicalterrorscale.org/

The Political Terror Scale represents a numerical measure of a states' political
violence and human rights violations. The index allows scholars and advocates
to monitor, report, study, and evaluate a states' human rights record against
prevailing norms and in comparison to one another.

MIDDLE RING_WEAPON HOLDINGS PER CAPITA_http://www.bicc.de/

Weapon holdings Per Capita is a measure that estimates the national per
capita holdings of light and heavy military, paramilitary, law enforcement and
civilian weapons. It stands in contrast to the Small Arms Survey that estimates
the arsenal of privately held weapons amongst civilians.

OUTER RING_MILITARY EXPENDITURE PER CAPITA_http://www.sipri.org/

Military Expenditure Per Capita data from SIPRI are derived from the NATO
definition, of current and capital expenditures on the armed forces, including
peacekeeping forces, defense ministries and other government agencies
engaged in defense projects, paramilitary forces and military space activities

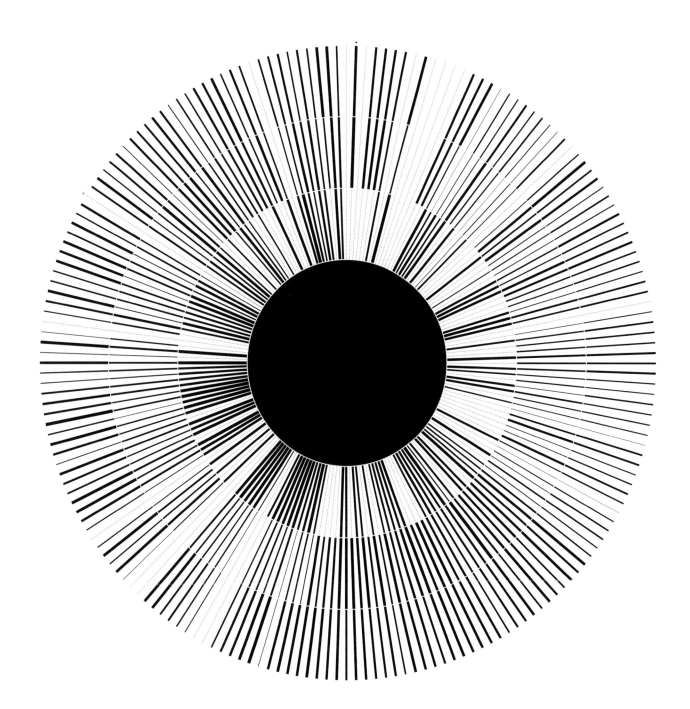

_A

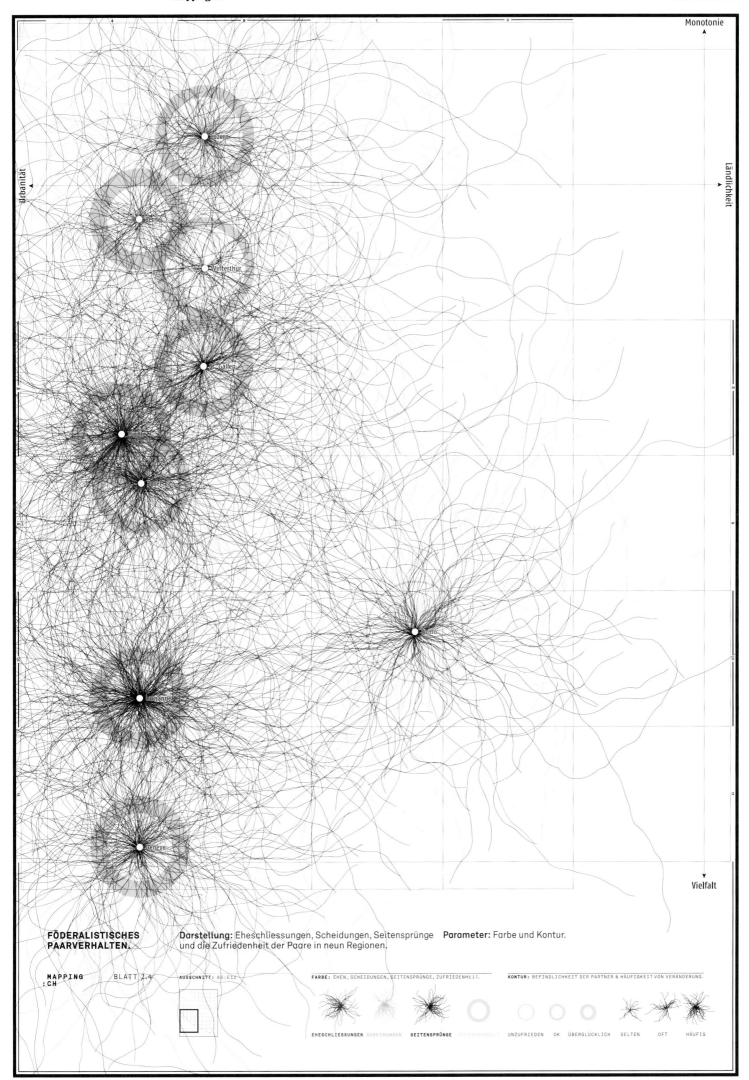

Monotonie

Urbanität

Ländlichkeit

Vielfalt

**FÖDERALISTISCHES
PAARVERHALTEN.**

Darstellung: Eheschliessungen, Scheidungen, Seitensprünge **Parameter:** Farbe und Kontur.
und die Zufriedenheit der Paare in neun Regionen.

**MAPPING
:CH**   BLATT 2.4   **AUSSCHNITT:** A8:E12

FARBE: EHEN, SCHEIDUNGEN, SEITENSPRÜNGE, ZUFRIEDENHEIT.   **KONTUR:** BEFINDLICHKEIT DER PARTNER & HÄUFIGKEIT VON VERÄNDERUNG.

EHESCHLIESSUNGEN   SCHEIDUNGEN   SEITENSPRÜNGE   ZUFRIEDENHEIT   UNZUFRIEDEN   OK   ÜBERGLÜCKLICH   SELTEN   OFT   HÄUFIG

PREVIOUS PAGE ———— **mapping:ch**
|▷ PP. 103, 230| LORENZO GEIGER — An imaginary landscape emerges from the intersection of data spheres. Key cities are ranked according to their diversity, and the degree to which they are rural or urban. Circles and spheres then playfully illustrate the relationship between fidelity and happiness. The aesthetic reinforces the complexity of human nature, defying a simple interpretation. Is Ticino less happy than other cities because it is more rural? Or is it because infidelity is more common?

The different densities of colour suggest arbitrary ranking and proximity, which, once again, imply that there is no simple explanation for the data.

— Research in the Visualisation of Financial Data |▷ PP. 25, 186, 232, 233|

CYBU RICHLI, Silo (Richli / Moser) — Risk literally takes shape, as the composition of investment portfolios from different asset classes is visualised in terms of benchmark versus actual allocation. The traditional five components of an investment portfolio form the axes showing their relative proportions in the portfolio. The curving outlines of the actual allocation are distinct and obvious compared with the ideal circular target. Risk profiles are transparently shown and easy to elicit, since over- or under-allocation is given a visual clarity that is not obvious in traditional data tables.

— Logos / Diagrams Generator

ADVANCE DESIGN — Time can be seen as identity. Advance Design's project underlines the function of the Brno House of Arts as a showcase for contemporary art. The Moravian city's unique geographical location has always placed it at the crossroads of cultural influences. Acting as a bridge between the four corners of Europe, this cultural centre becomes a lens through which time (as history) and space (as geography) are refracted to shape the moment. By using time as the key data source for generating a constantly changing identity, the march of time becomes less significant, superseded by the impact of a specific moment on our perceptions. With over 2.5 million permutations of the identity, each moment becomes unique and all the more powerful for its observation, captured within the identity. In the words of the designers, the circle represents the ideal of art, distorted in multiple ways, as a metaphor for the process of coexistence of artists and cultural institutions. The whole is enclosed by an everyday time loop. The notion of individual typography should follow the idea of a constant transformation of art through the sign of the logo. The twenty-four hours of the day are represented by twenty-four different colour hues. Two inner circles combine and reshape themselves in unique configurations for each minute and second. Colour and shape converge in dynamic spheres that continuously shift and change, just as the House of Art's identity is shaped by its artistic content.

An interview Koblin gave at the Info Aesthetic Symposium in The Hague has, fittingly, been turned into a real-time artwork. All the words in the discussion have been captured as data and transformed into a visual experience. Concentric rings expand like waves when a word is repeated, thus emphasising the central topics. The artwork also applies real-time coding and processing in a way that underlines the aesthetic nature of Koblin's creativity.

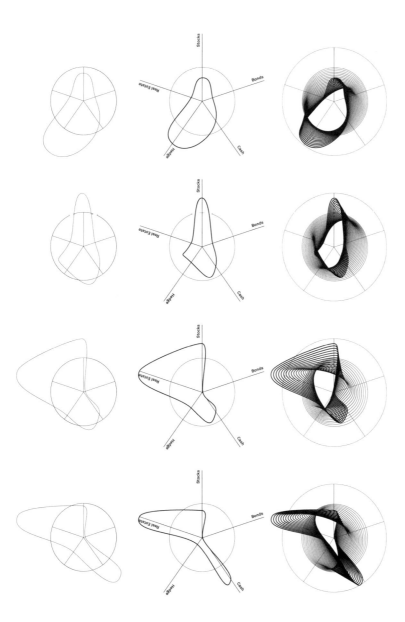

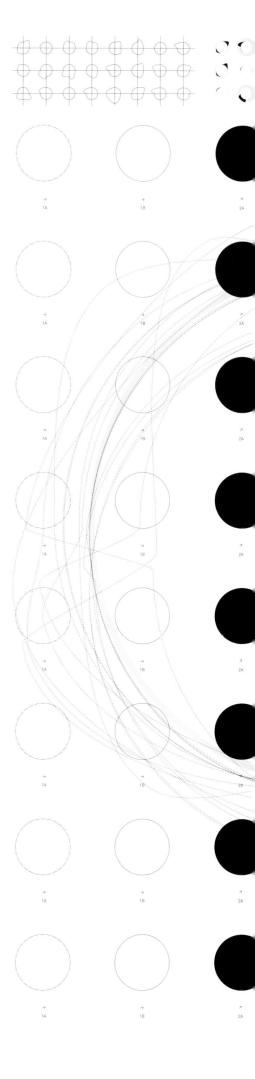

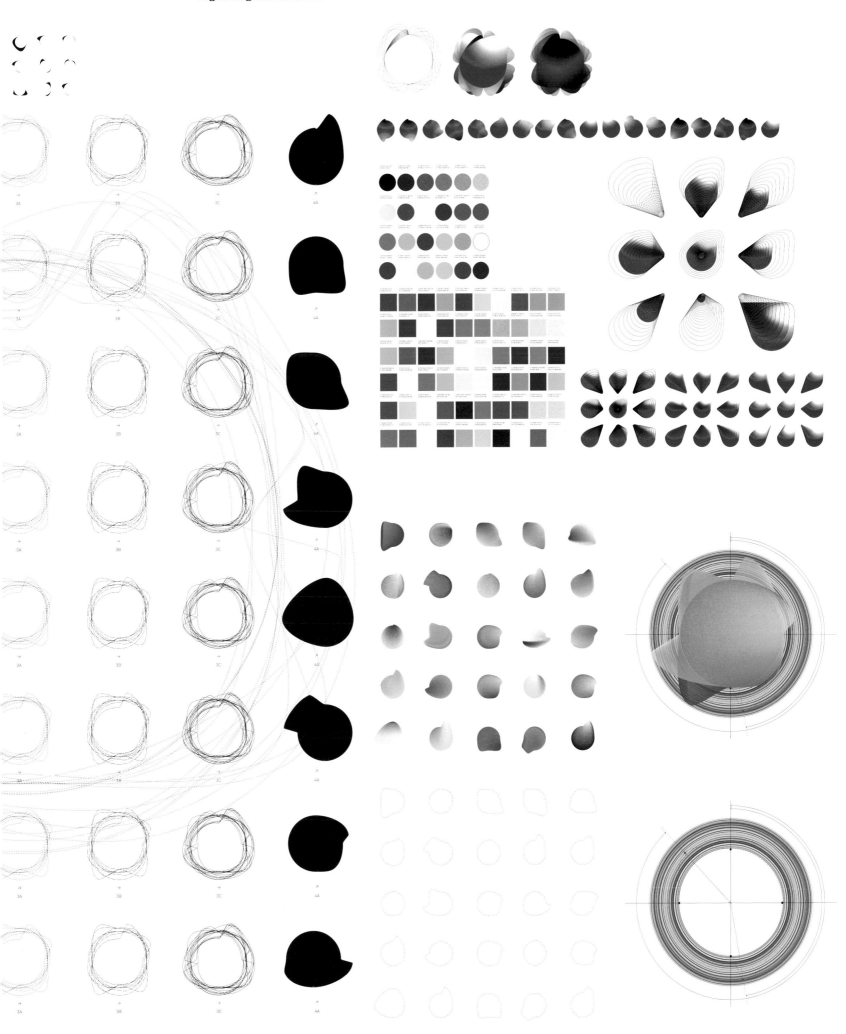

—— Anatomie der Datengrafik

|▷ PP. 182, 221| TOBIAS NUSSER & TOM ZIORA — In this piece, we see a poster summary of six sections in this book. The core objective—to show how widely the presentation of the same data can differ—is dramatically achieved. Applying a consistent colour palette to the varying aspects of spheres and circles, the same data set is repeatedly visualised, yet at first glance the different entities all seem radically different. This stark effect calls into question how regularly our opinion of 'the facts' is shaped by design choice, rather than by the substance of the data itself.

—— The networked digital age has made data an integral part of our everyday experience. The way in which data is presented is a design choice. As with every choice, we consciously include and exclude certain realities by committing to one specific form. In this extensive project, Tobias Nusser investigates this topic by assuming that the form in which data is presented is independent of the data itself, and that visualisation can be decided at will. The form influences the data to the same extent as the data influences the form.

By comparing various ways of presenting the same data, it quickly becomes apparent how design shapes the meaning, understanding, and emphasis of what is being said. Just as the digital manipulation of images using Photoshop® has changed the way people view reality, the way in which data is presented shapes opinion. The importance of this manipulation in meaning is significant in a society where, more than ever before, pervasive data shapes public debate. **—— Research in the Visualisation of Financial Data** |▷ PP. 186, 232, 233| CYBU RICHLI, Silo (Richli /

Moser) — Simple and reduced, the essential elements of the sphere are used to indicate quantity, style, and sector in financial data. Surface area, colouration, and orientation are used to provide specific meaning. Quantity is quickly defined through the discrete division of area, as unit quantities can be varied by their distance from the centre. Style can be shown by a combination of binary coding and locational indicators, while sector is shown by nuanced elements of the colour wheel. Depending on the level of analysis, the highly-reduced abstract visualisation can be expanded to provide more information.

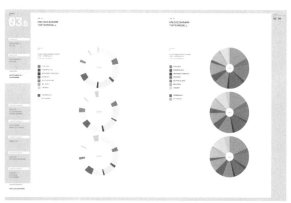

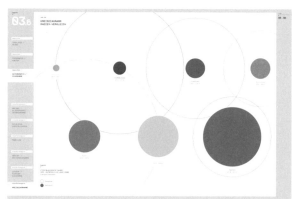

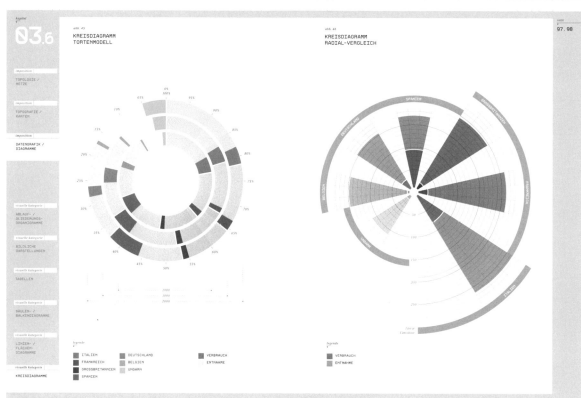

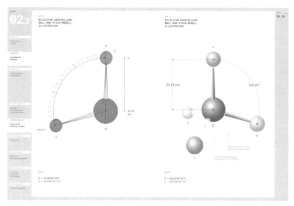

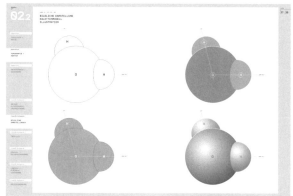

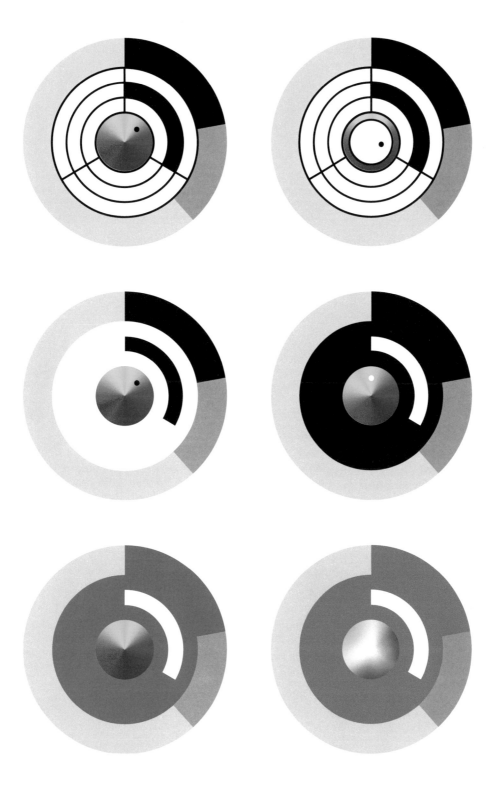

Timecircle 24 hours week day in connection to the activity of technologies

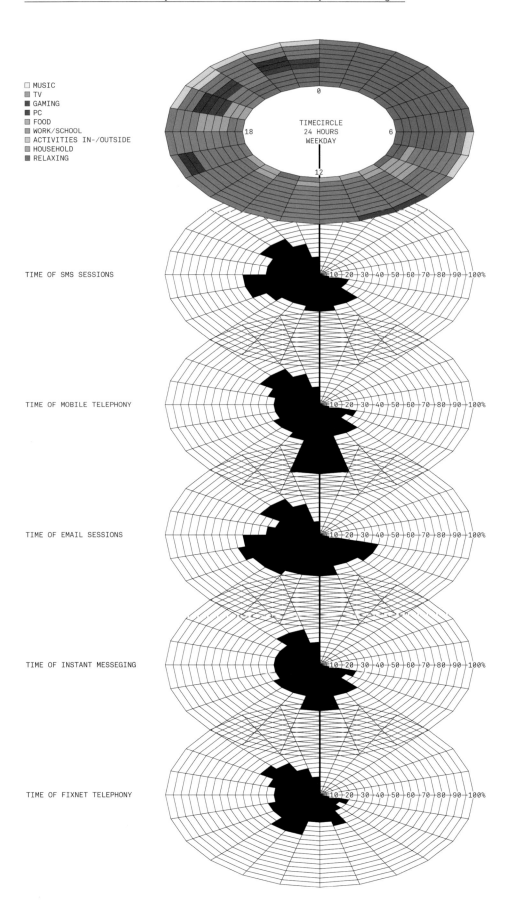

□ MUSIC
▨ TV
■ GAMING
■ PC
▨ FOOD
▨ WORK/SCHOOL
□ ACTIVITIES IN-/OUTSIDE
▨ HOUSEHOLD
■ RELAXING

TIMECIRCLE
24 HOURS
WEEKDAY

0

18   6

12

TIME OF SMS SESSIONS   10 20 30 40 50 60 70 80 90 100%

TIME OF MOBILE TELEPHONY   10 20 30 40 50 60 70 80 90 100%

TIME OF EMAIL SESSIONS   10 20 30 40 50 60 70 80 90 100%

TIME OF INSTANT MESSEGING   10 20 30 40 50 60 70 80 90 100%

TIME OF FIXNET TELEPHONY   10 20 30 40 50 60 70 80 90 100%

—— **Research in the Visualisation of Technology and Communication Data** CYBU RICHLI — Communication is an enabler for both work and play. The activities we engage in determine the content of the conversations we have, but do they also change the vehicle for engagement? An exploded view of a daily cycle reveals the successive use of various types of communications technology. It not only serves as a quick and effective comparison between different forms of communication, but also allows comparisons between the various activities that may have a bearing on the communication. It shows e-mail, IM chat, SMS, and phone calls as the skeleton of conversations and dialogue, the structure upon which the flesh of meaning and exchange is built. —— SMS texting was a huge consequence of the boom in the mobile phone market, as unexpected as it was unintended. As with other innovations in social technology, industry pundits speculate about the impact on productivity and other activities that is brought about by the ability to 'chat'. This piece uses fictitious data to compare and contrast the time allocated to different daily activities, and the encroachment of texting upon these activities. The spider figure at the centre spreads out towards the waking cycle, which is colour-coded for each specific activity. By comparing areas of intense SMS activity with the nature of the activities shown on the outer ring, we can quickly see not only which activities are particularly prone to the text-message assault, but also how strongly they are affected. —— **LimaDeltaRomeo** LIMADELTAROMEO, Lorenz Tschopp, Dorian Minnig, Reto Bürkli — The coordinates of a personal topology are sketched out. As the designers depict the routes that circumscribe their daily lives, roads, passages and byways are catalogued and mapped. The sphere of activity gains texture and context as forest fields, rocks, and building types are injected upon the stream of traffic.

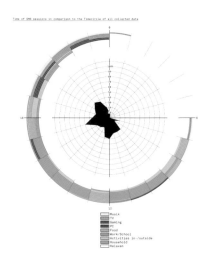

Time of SMS sessions in comparison to the Timecircle of all collected data

Musik
TV
Gaming
PC
Food
Work/School
Activities in-/outside
Household
Relaxen

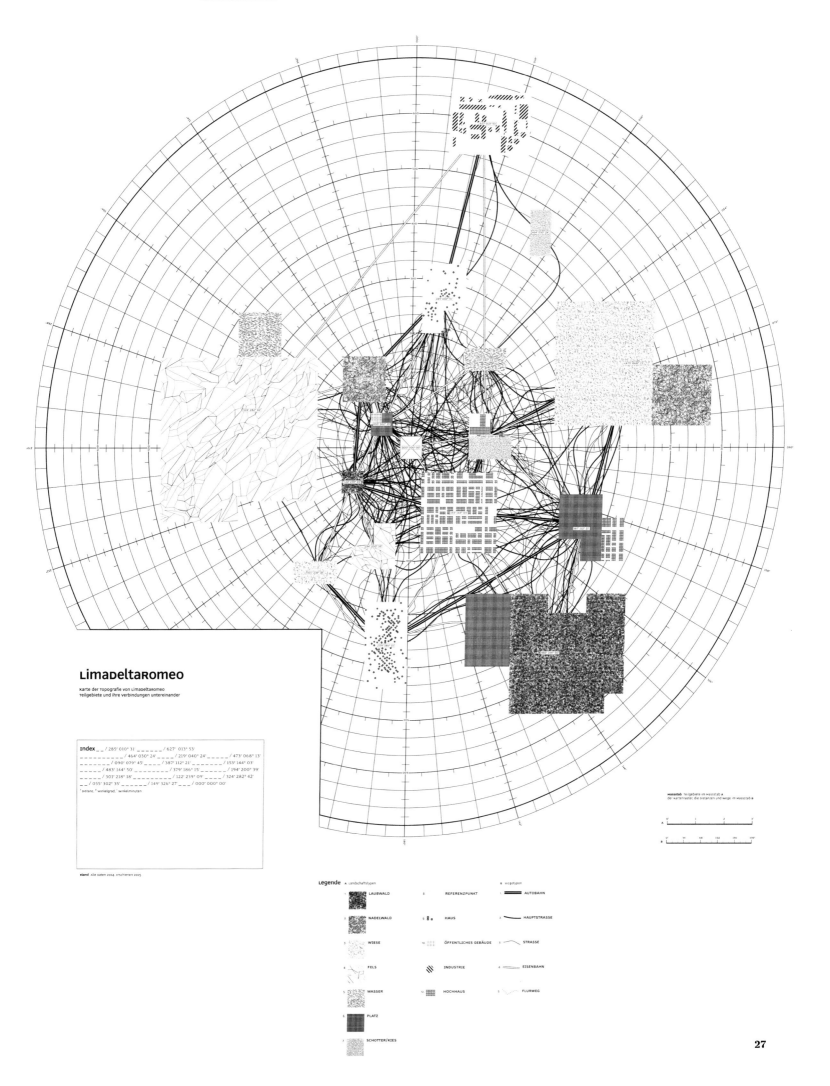

LimaDeltaRomeo

Karte der Topografie von LimaDeltaRomeo
Teilgebiete und ihre Verbindungen untereinander

Index _ _ / 285' 010° 31' _ _ _ _ _ _ / 627' 013° 53'
_ _ _ _ _ _ _ _ _ / 464' 030° 24' _ _ _ _ / 219' 040° 24' _ _ _ _ _ / 473' 068° 13'
_ _ _ _ _ _ _ / 090' 079° 45' _ _ _ _ / 387' 112° 21' _ _ _ _ _ _ _ / 153' 144° 01'
_ _ _ _ / 483' 144° 50' _ _ _ _ _ _ / 379' 186° 15' _ _ _ _ _ _ / 194' 200° 39'
_ _ _ _ _ / 301' 218° 18' _ _ _ _ _ _ _ _ / 122' 239° 09' _ _ _ / 324' 282° 42'
_ _ / 055' 302° 35' _ _ _ _ _ _ / 149' 326° 27' _ _ _ / 000' 000° 00'

' Distanz, ° Winkelgrad, ' Winkelminuten

stand alle Daten 2004, erschienen 2005

massstab Teilgebiete im Massstab A
der Kartenraster, die Distanzen und Wege im Massstab B

Legende A Landschaftstypen   B Wegetypen

1 LAUBWALD   8   REFERENZPUNKT   1 —— AUTOBAHN
2 NADELWALD   9   HAUS   2 —— HAUPTSTRASSE
3 WIESE   10 ÖFFENTLICHES GEBÄUDE 3 —— STRASSE
4 FELS   11 INDUSTRIE   4 —— EISENBAHN
5 WASSER   12 HOCHHAUS   5 —— FLURWEG
6 PLATZ
7 SCHOTTER/KIES

http://www.aec.at
http://www.convivionetwork.net
http://www.densitydesign.org
http://www.desphilosophy.com
http://www.designresearchsociety.org
http://www.digicult.it
http://www.doorsofperception.com
http://www.experimenta.org
http://www.forumforthefuture.org.uk
http://www.hexagram.ca
http://www.idonline.com
http://www.ijdesign.org
http://www.informationdesign.org
http://www.interaction-design.org
http://www.mediamatic.net
http://www.neural.it
http://nextd.org
http://www.noemalab.org
http://nova.ilsole24ore.com
http://rhizome.org
http://www.sciam.com
http://sigchi.org
http://siggraph.org
http://www.stockexchangeofvisions.org
http://www.ted.com
http://www.viridiandesign.org
http://www.wired.com
http://www.xcult.ch

http://www.apple.com/iphone
http://www.frogdesign.com
http://www.design.philips.com
http://www.global.yamaha.com/design/index.html
http://www.ideo.com
http://www.interactiondesign-lab.com
http://www.laptop.org
http://lawsofsimplicity.com
http://www.loewe.de

OGGETTI COLLOQUIALI
COLLOQUIAL OBJECTS

http://www.maedastudio.com
http://www.media.mit.edu
http://safe.mercedes-benz.co.uk
http://www.nintendo.com/ds
http://www.nose.ch
http://www.soundbug.biz
http://www.alistapart.com
http://www.bfgf.de
http://hello.eboy.com
http://www.ertdfgcvb.ch
http://infosthetics.com
http://www.oneone-studio.com
http://sodaplay.com
http://www.visualcomplexity.com
http://www.yugop.com
http://www.mutado.com
http://www.warprecords.com

MASTER OF ARTS SUPSI IN

—INTERACTION DESIGN

Esplora il mondo dell'interaction design visitando la collezione di alcuni dei riferimenti più significativi e attuali.

Explore the world of interaction design by visiting the collection of some of the most significative and updated references.

http://www.colourlovers.com
http://www.designerblog.it
http://www.designtaxi.com
http://www.eff.org
http://www.idearium.org
http://www.dataisnature.com
http://www.generatorx.no
http://www.gizmodo.it
http://www.itsnicethat.com
http://www.kloonigames.com/blog
http://makezine.com
http://www.newitalianblood.com
http://www.pixelsumo.com
http://www.shapeshifters.net
http://spamnation.info
http://swissmiss.typepad.com
http://www.we-make-money-not-art.com

http://developer.apple.com
http://www.docomolabs-usa.com
http://www.research.ibm.com
http://www.meri.com
http://research.microsoft.com
http://www.incx.nec.co.jp/robot
http://research.nokia.com
http://www.parc.com
http://www.research.philips.com
http://techresearch.intel.com
http://www.telecomitalia.com
http://www.w3.org
http://www.artemide.com
http://www.bang-olufsen.com
http://www.bticino.com
http://www.lge.com
http://www.jamo.com
http://www.microvision.com
http://www.motorola.com
http://www.nintendo.it
http://www.nttdocomo.com
http://www.osram-os.com
http://www.samsung.com
http://www.sonyericsson.com

PROGETTARE IL FUTURO
DESIGNING THE FUTURE

http://www.arduino.cc
http://artsoftware.org
http://www.cycling74.com
http://www.dynamicdiagrams.com
http://www.makingthings.com
http://onecm.com/sketches
http://www.processing.org
http://www.tinker.it
http://www.troikatronix.com/Isadora.html
http://vvvv.org

PROTESI COMUNICATIVE
COMMUNICATIONS PROTHESES

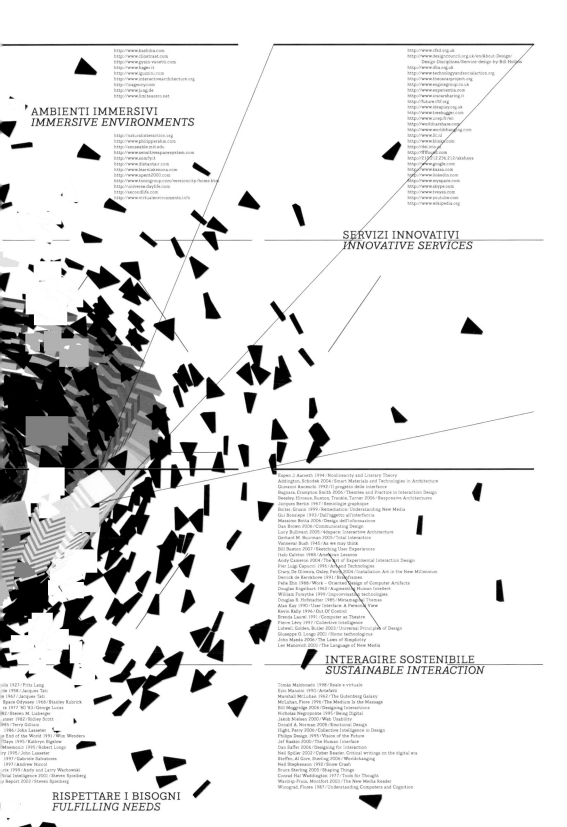

http://www.bashiba.com
http://www.cliostraat.com
http://www.gysin-vanetti.com
http://www.hager.it
http://www.iguzzini.it
http://www.interactivearchitecture.org
http://www.ioagency.com
http://www.jung.de
http://www.limiteazero.net

AMBIENTI IMMERSIVI
IMMERSIVE ENVIRONMENTS

http://naturalinteraction.org
http://www.philipperahm.com
http://senseable.mit.edu
http://www.sensitivespacesystem.com
http://www.somfy.it
http://www.distantair.com
http://www.learnlakenona.com
http://www.spent2000.com
http://www.tonicgroup.com/versioncity/home.htm
http://www.universe.daylife.com
http://secondlife.com
http://www.virtualenvironments.info

http://www.cfsd.org.uk
http://www.designcouncil.org.uk/en/About-Design/
 Design-Disciplines/Service-design-by-Bill-Hollins
http://www.dba.org.uk
http://www.technologyandsocialaction.org
http://www.theoscarproject.org
http://www.enginegroup.co.uk
http://www.experientia.com
http://www.icscarsharing.it
http://future.iftf.org
http://www.ideaplay.org.uk
http://www.treehugger.com
http://www.unep.fr/en
http://worldcarshare.com
http://www.worldchanging.com
http://www.2c.nl
http://www.blink.com
http://del.icio.us
http://ffffound.com
http://210.212.236.212/akshaya
http://www.google.com
http://www.kazaa.com
http://www.linkedin.com
http://www.myspace.com
http://www.skype.com
http://www.tveyes.com
http://www.youtube.com
http://www.wikipedia.org

SERVIZI INNOVATIVI
INNOVATIVE SERVICES

Espen J. Aarseth 1994 / Nonlinearity and Literary Theory
Addington, Schodek 2004 / Smart Materials and Technologies in Architecture
Giovanni Anceschi 1992 / Il progetto delle interfacce
Bagnara, Crampton Smith 2006 / Theories and Practice in Interaction Design
Beesley, Hirosue, Ruxton, Trankle, Turner 2006 / Responsive Architectures
Jacques Bertin 1967 / Semiologie graphique
Bolter, Grusin 1999 / Remediation: Understanding New Media
Gui Bonsiepe 1993 / Dall'oggetto all'interfaccia
Massimo Botta 2006 / Design dell'informazione
Dan Brown 2006 / Communicating Design
Lucy Bullivant 2005 / 4dspace: Interactive Architecture
Gerhard M. Buurman 2005 / Total Interaction
Vannevar Bush 1945 / As we may think
Bill Buxton 2007 / Sketching User Experiences
Italo Calvino 1988 / American Lessons
Andy Cameron 2004 / The Art of Experimental Interaction Design
Pier Luigi Capucci 1996 / Art and Technologies
Crary, De Oliveira, Oxley, Petry 2004 / Installation Art in the New Millennium
Derrick de Kerckhove 1991 / Brainframes
Pelle Ehn 1988 / Work – Oriented Design of Computer Artifacts
Douglas Engelbart 1962 / Augmenting Human Intellect
William Forsythe 1999 / Improvvisation technologies
Douglas R. Hofstadter 1985 / Metamagical Themas
Alan Kay 1990 / User Interface: A Personal View
Kevin Kelly 1996 / Out Of Control
Brenda Laurel 1991 / Computer as Theatre
Pierre Lévy 1997 / Collective Intelligence
Lidwell, Golden, Butler 2003 / Universal Principles of Design
Giuseppe O. Longo 2001 / Homo technologicus
John Maeda 2006 / The Laws of Simplicity
Lev Manovich 2001 / The Language of New Media

INTERAGIRE SOSTENIBILE
SUSTAINABLE INTERACTION

Tomás Maldonado 1998 / Reale e virtuale
Ezio Manzini 1990 / Artefatti
Marshall McLuhan 1962 / The Gutenberg Galaxy
McLuhan, Fiore 1996 / The Medium Is the Massage
Bill Moggridge 2006 / Designing Interactions
Nicholas Negroponte 1995 / Being Digital
Jakob Nielsen 2000 / Web Usability
Donald A. Norman 2005 / Emotional Design
Hight, Perry 2006 / Collective Intelligence in Design
Philips Design 1995 / Vision of the Future
Jef Raskin 2000 / The Human Interface
Dan Saffer 2006 / Designing for Interaction
Neil Spiller 2002 / Cyber Reader. Critical writings on the digital era
Steffen, Al Gore, Sterling 2006 / Worldchanging
Neil Stephenson 1992 / Snow Crash
Bruce Sterling 2005 / Shaping Things
Conrad Hal Waddington 1977 / Tools for Thought
Wardrip-Pruin, Montfort 2003 / The New Media Reader
Winograd, Flores 1987 / Understanding Computers and Cognition

olis 1927 / Fritz Lang
cle 1958 / Jacques Tati
e 1967 / Jacques Tati
Space Odyssey 1968 / Stanley Kubrick
rs 1977 '80 '83 / George Lucas
82 / Steven M. Lisberger
nner 1982 / Ridley Scott
985 / Terry Gilliam
1986 / John Lasseter
e End of the World 1991 / Wim Wenders
Days 1995 / Kathryn Bigelow
Mnemonic 1995 / Robert Longo
ry 1995 / John Lasseter
1997 / Gabriele Salvatores
1997 / Andrew Niccol
rix 1999 / Andy and Larry Wachowski
cial Intelligence 2001 / Steven Spielberg
y Report 2002 / Steven Spielberg

RISPETTARE I BISOGNI
FULFILLING NEEDS

—— Master of Interaction Design CYBU RICHLI, in collaboration with Fabienne Burri — Intended primarily to stimulate rather than inform, this work builds layers of meaning around the world of interaction design. This catalogue of influences shapes an info-sphere, showing loosely connected fields and sources that converge, blend, and form new interpretations in the area of interaction design. Data labels, columns, and shapes cluster dynamically to form a loose definition of the field, by reference rather than deduction.

—— **Fortune 500** CATALOGTREE — *Fortune* magazine's top 500 list of public corporations is the enduring bellwether of corporate success. The stability of the list belies its dynamic jostle and bustle, as companies move up and down the ranking, or disappear altogether. Anyone looking at the list for 1955 would be hard-pressed to predict the top 100 companies fifty years on. This swarming flock of companies, each with its revenue, and profit or loss neatly noted, is catalogtree's rendition of the 2008 list. The energy of commerce almost takes on the radiance of a sun, as the best managerial talents in the world steer their charges towards the gravitational centre where Walmart pips Exxon to the top spot — or, in this case, centre stage. —— **Work Year 2007** LÁRUSSON — Days spread out, spilling into clouds of work. Each dot in this piece swells to represent the number of e-mails received (as a proxy for work). The colour spectrum is distributed evenly across the year to provide every month with its own colour. Is work seen as pollution, or as growth? The reduced state of the presentation makes no comment on the nature of the work being performed, but shows how its frequency builds a topography of effort.

FORTUNE 500

← **2007 REVENUE**
(SURFACE RELATES
TO $ MILLIONS)

← **2007 PROFIT**
(SURFACE RELATES
TO $ MILLIONS)

← **2007 LOSS**
(SURFACE RELATES
TO $ MILLIONS)

CMP ← **COMPANY I.D.**

—— The Universal Declaration

PLUSMINUS — Following their project to commemorate the bomb blasts at Hiroshima and Nagasaki, plusminus have used whole circles to suggest the fragility and interdependency of human beings. The Luxury of Protest is a graphical call to arms. It aims to overcome the middle-class tendency towards laziness and to fulfil the obligations of all citizens in a liberal democracy—that is, to rebel against falsehoods and oppression.

In this series of five posters, plusminus use a combination of quantitative suggestion and qualitative interpretation to represent the Universal Declaration of Human Rights. Looking specifically at the rights both to protest and to free speech, each poster contrasts the single and unusual hand-coloured graphite dot with a varying number of black dots, arranged to suggest these fundamental rights. In each poster, the individual dot becomes a reflection of the individual human being's struggle in the context of each specific right. The single dot surrounded by the rest becomes the right to live free of persecution. In this way, a quantitative approach is used in an abstract fashion to represent the culturally complex concepts of human rights. —— **Das Ruhrgebiet im demografischen Wandel** 1KILO, in collaboration with Philipp Oswalt, Carsten Grosse Starmann, Petra Klug, Matthias Ritter, Urs Hofer, Frank Fietzek — Like all living things, cities have no guarantee of eternal life. They can be thought of as spheres, each one with its life-cycle of growth and decline, glowing in the dark and then fading away. The social and economic changes that have swept across the Ruhr area, and will continue to dictate its destiny, are depicted through white spheres which grow and contract, rendered to provide different insights into the financial, economic, and migration figures. Each dot relates to a specific city in the region, the Ruhr itself providing a neutral black backdrop where the changing fates of individual communities are graphically made clear. As time passes, communities shrink or move elsewhere, leaving the old cities to wither to unobtrusive dots like dying lights.

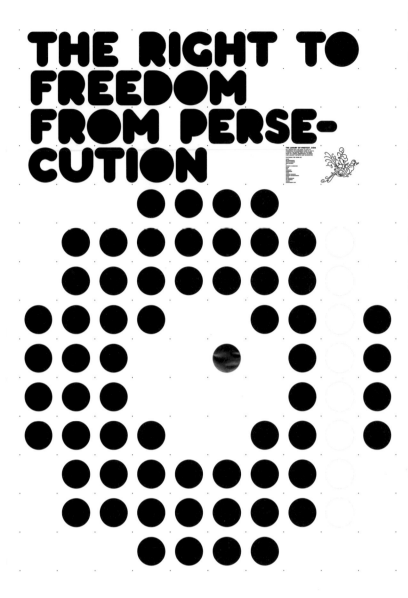

THE RIGHT TO FREEDOM FROM PERSE-CUTION

THE RIGHT TO FREE ASSEM-BLY & ASSOCI-ATION

THE RIGHT TO FREE THOUGHT & CON-SCIENCE

THE RIGHT TO FREEDOM OF MOVEME-NT

THE RIGHT TO REBELLION AGAINST TYR-ANNY

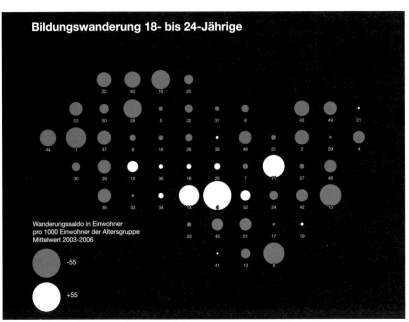

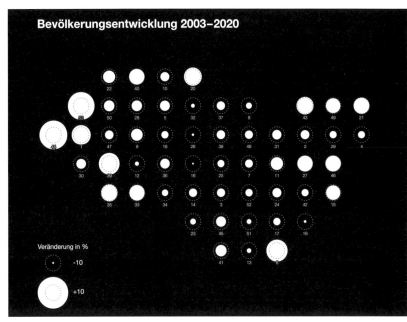

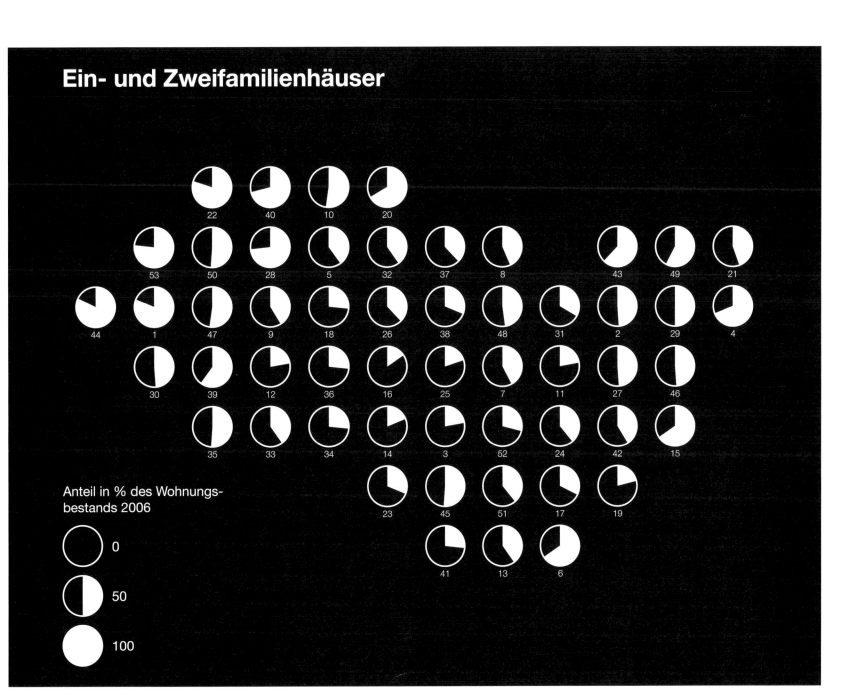

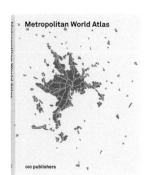

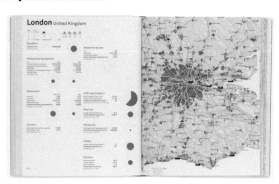

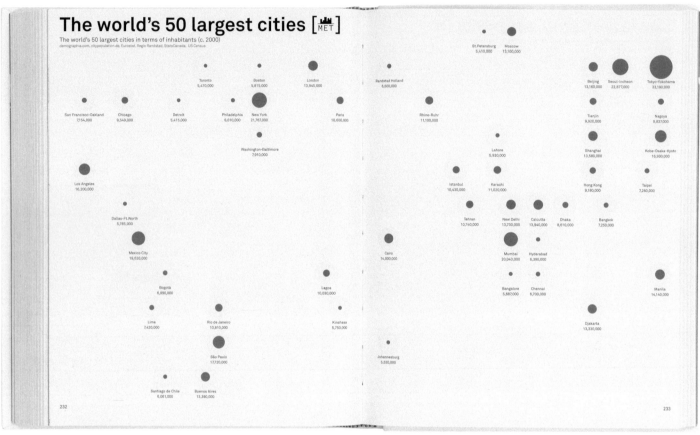

The world's 50 largest cities [MET]

The world's 50 largest cities in terms of inhabitants (c. 2000)
demographia.com, citypopulation.de, Eurostat, Regio Randstad, StatsCanada, US Census

St.Petersburg 5,410,000 · Moscow 13,100,000 · Randstad Holland 6,600,000 · Beijing 13,160,000 · Seoul-Incheon 22,877,000 · Tokyo-Yokohama 33,190,000

Toronto 5,470,000 · Boston 5,815,000 · London 13,945,000 · Rhine-Ruhr 11,100,000 · Tianjin 9,920,000 · Nagoya 8,837,000

San Francisco-Oakland 7,154,000 · Chicago 9,549,000 · Detroit 5,415,000 · Philadelphia 6,010,000 · New York 21,767,000 · Paris 10,600,000

Washington-Baltimore 7,910,000 · Lahore 5,920,000 · Shanghai 13,580,000 · Kobe-Osaka-Kyoto 16,930,000

Los Angeles 16,200,000 · Istanbul 10,430,000 · Karachi 11,020,000 · Hong Kong 9,180,000 · Taipei 7,260,000

Dallas-Ft.Worth 5,785,000 · Tehran 10,740,000 · New Delhi 13,730,000 · Calcutta 13,940,000 · Dhaka 8,610,000 · Bangkok 7,250,000

Mexico City 19,620,000 · Cairo 14,000,000 · Mumbai 20,043,000 · Hyderabad 6,390,000

Bogotá 6,990,000 · Lagos 10,030,000 · Bangalore 5,887,000 · Chennai 6,700,000 · Manila 14,140,000

Lima 7,420,000 · Rio de Janeiro 10,810,000 · Kinshasa 5,750,000 · Djakarta 13,330,000

São Paulo 17,720,000 · Johannesburg 5,530,000

Santiago de Chile 6,061,000 · Buenos Aires 13,390,000

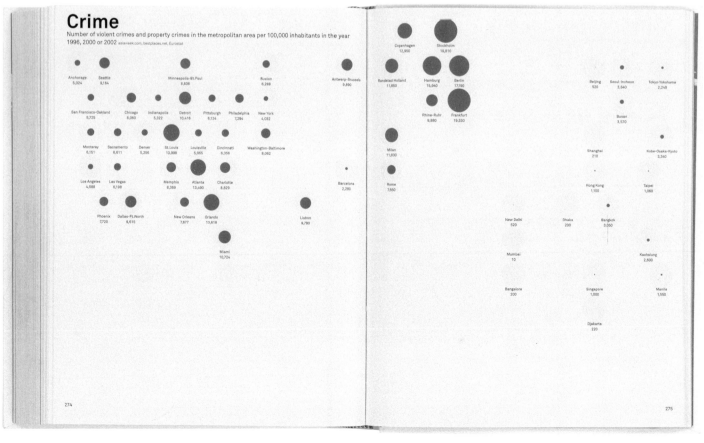

Crime

Number of violent crimes and property crimes in the metropolitan area per 100,000 inhabitants in the year 1996, 2000 or 2002 asiaweek.com, bestplaces.net, Eurostat

Copenhagen 12,950 · Stockholm 19,810

Anchorage 5,024 · Seattle 9,184 · Minneapolis-St.Paul 8,636 · Boston 6,288 · Antwerp-Brussels 9,890 · Randstad Holland 11,850 · Hamburg 16,940 · Berlin 17,190 · Beijing 520 · Seoul-Incheon 3,540 · Tokyo-Yokohama 2,240

San Francisco-Oakland 5,725 · Chicago 8,060 · Indianapolis 5,322 · Detroit 10,416 · Pittsburgh 6,124 · Philadelphia 7,294 · New York 4,032 · Rhine-Ruhr 9,880 · Frankfurt 19,530 · Busan 3,570

Monterey 6,151 · Sacramento 6,611 · Denver 5,256 · St.Louis 13,998 · Louisville 5,065 · Cincinnati 6,356 · Washington-Baltimore 8,062 · Milan 11,830 · Shanghai 210 · Kobe-Osaka-Kyoto 3,340

Los Angeles 4,588 · Las Vegas 6,198 · Memphis 8,369 · Atlanta 13,490 · Charlotte 8,829 · Barcelona 2,280 · Rome 7,660 · Hong Kong 1,100 · Taipei 1,060

Phoenix 7,720 · Dallas-Ft.Worth 9,615 · New Orleans 7,677 · Orlando 13,619 · Lisbon 9,780 · New Delhi 520 · Dhaka 200 · Bangkok 3,050 · Kaohsiung 2,600

Miami 10,724 · Mumbai 10 · Singapore 1,000 · Manila 1,550

Bangalore 200

Djakarta 220

—— Metropolitan World Atlas
JOOST GROOTENS — A system of orange dots accompanies the reader's journey through this analysis and comparison of 101 capital cities around the world. Through constant comparison with the top benchmark, the reader develops an intuitive understanding of where a metropolis fits. The prominent orange dots, sized according to comparative data, communicate information, which may be compared with the redundant, faded reference circle.

The strict grid and the repetition throughout the book develop into a type of three-dimensional chart, as successive pages of circles are 'stacked', allowing a quick flip through to reveal the changes in pollution, density, public transport, and other statistics. **—— The Shape of Globalization: The World Auto Industry** |▷ PP. 47, 241| CHRISTINA VAN VLECK — These cogs and gears richly illustrate the interdependency of different components in the global automobile industry. Joint ventures feed into shared ownerships, as the industry propels itself ever forward to meet increasing global demand for mobility. The need for a machine is serviced by the machine of a structural industry. Colour-coded by region, corporate structures are added like new components, or upgrades, in a finely tuned engine, to drive market reach and expansion into the all-important developing regions of China and India.

The Shape of **Globalization**

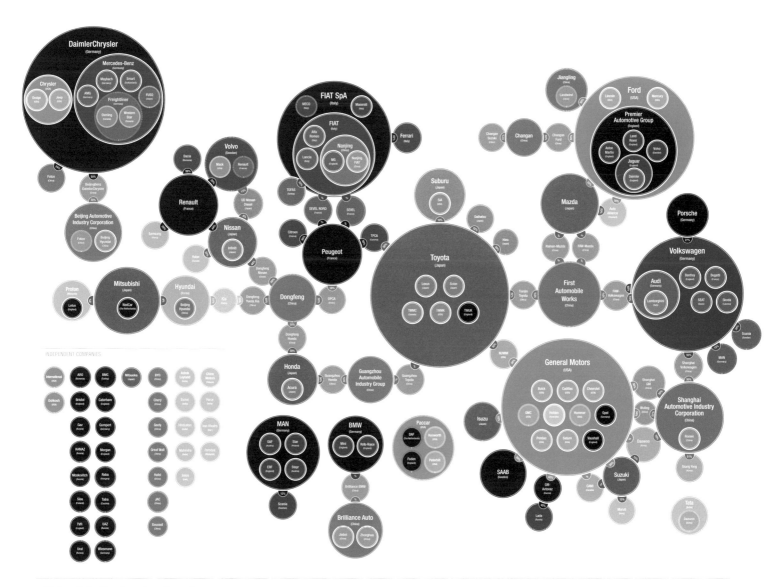

World Auto Industry

———— **Flags by Colours** SHAHEE ILYAS — National flags are the expression of arbitrary political will. They represent the division of the world into nation states, populated by human beings with more things in common than differences between them. By reducing the wide variety of national flags to their component colours, in proportion, and showing these as pie charts, the flags are no longer assertions of national identity, but choices on a colour wheel. The dense concentration of pie charts, each with its angular sections, creates random patterns, alive with connectivity as colours converge or intersect sharply across spheres. This artwork brings the whole world alive on the page, its people busy with debate and exchange. ———— The first pictures of Earth taken from space radically shook mankind's confidence in its own position as master of its universe. The solitary, lonely island of life floating in a desolate sea of emptiness triggered mass concern for the sustainability and health of the planet. In a sense, this pie chart by Shahee Ilyas is the planet as a political entity. Each country's flag is reduced to its colour components, forming its own slice of the global pie chart, in combination with all the others. Not sized according to population or income, each flag carries equal weighting. With an increase in the total number of nation states over the past forty years, it will be interesting to see whether the diversity of colour increases or falls over time. ———— **19/02/08** |›**P. 234**| SOCKET STUDIOS — Discrete elements of this layout combine to indicate class, quantity, and orientation. Arranged around the familiar clock face, this depiction of the designer's activities on 19 February 2008 is clear and open to various interpretations. The cumulative bar chart presents the same information as the pie chart; however, representation of the same data in circular form provides focus, and places it in context.   With the hours of sleep providing a sharp slice of the pie, blended into the background, the tension always falls between the designer's entry into, and exit from, the day.

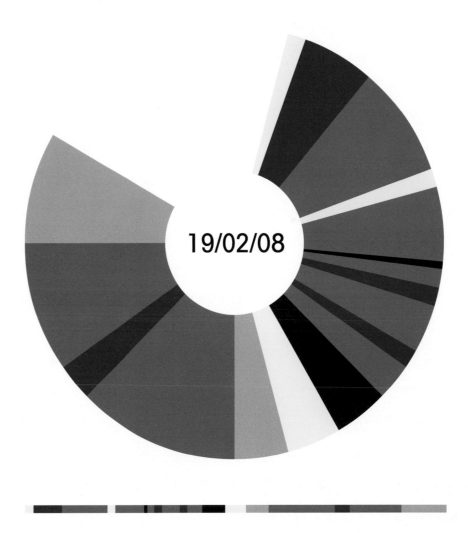

19/02/08

| Food | Online | Work | Misc | Pool |

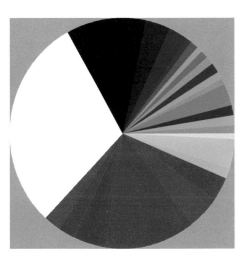

Pie ALAN WOO — Alan Woo's experiment in processing creates a benchmark for comparing various films by specific directors. Each frame is analysed according to its inherent colours, and is plotted against the sphere as it becomes visible. Mood, pace, and narrative are abstracted to a one-dimensional figure. The transition from darkness to light is an abstracted reference that relies on the viewer's own memory of the film to create meaning. Viewed as a triptych, it conveys a sense of the director's approach, without revealing or judging the film's artistic merit.

Metropolis, 1927.
Directed by Fritz Lang. Cinematography by Karl Freund, Günther Rittau and Walter Ruttmann. 153 minutes.

Soylent Green, 1973.
Directed by Richard Fleischer. Cinematography by Richard H. Kline. 97 minutes.

Bronenosets Potyomkin, 1925.
Directed by Sergei M. Eisenstein. Cinematography by Vladimir Popov and Eduard Tisse. 75 minutes.

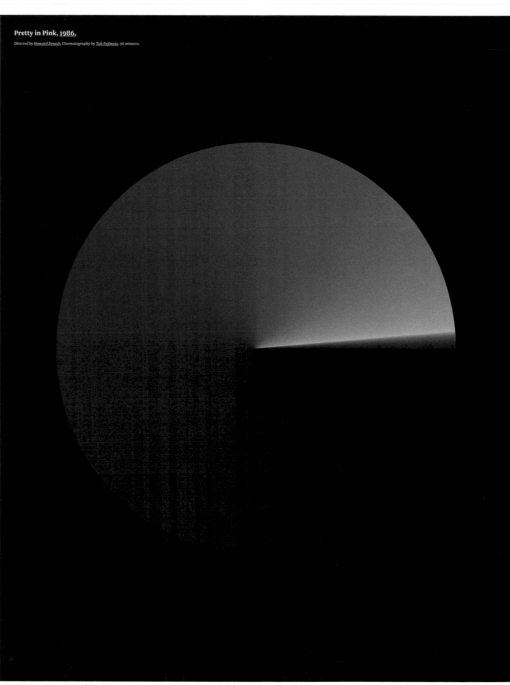

Pretty in Pink, 1986.

Directed by Howard Deutch. Cinematography by Tak Fujimoto. 96 minutes.

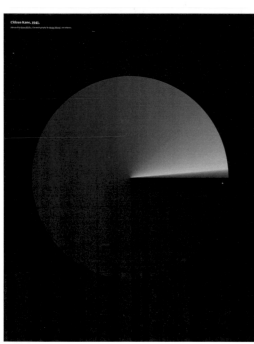

Citizen Kane, 1941.
Directed by Orson Welles. Cinematography by Gregg Toland. 119 minutes.

A Clockwork Orange, 1971.

Directed by _Stanley Kubrick_. Cinematography by _John Alcott_. 136 minutes.

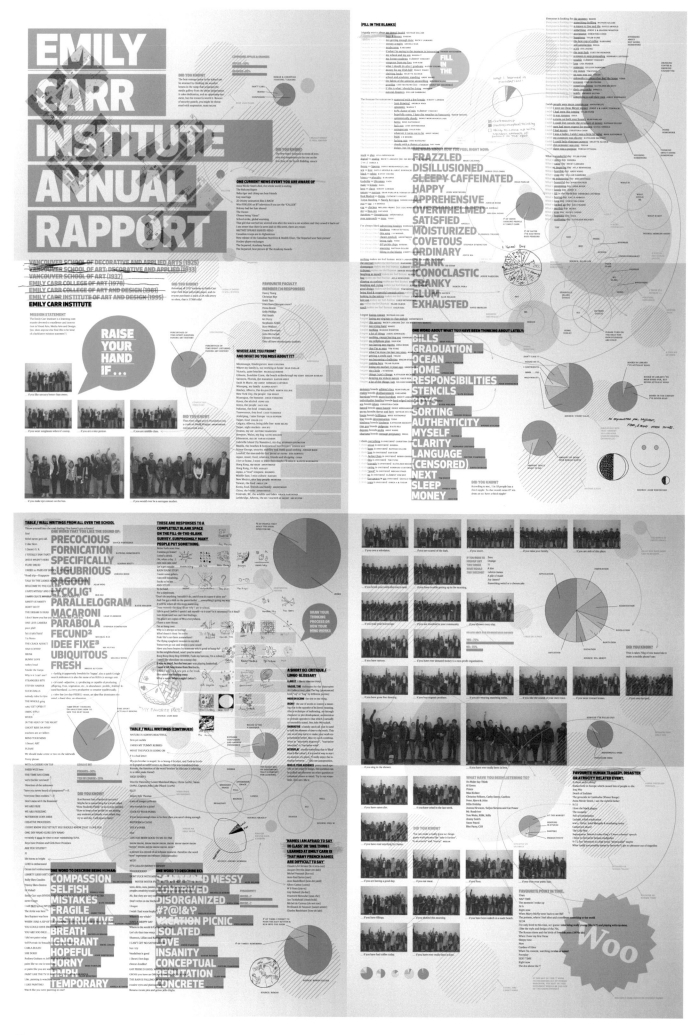

——————————— Woo, issue 3: Emily Carr Institute Annual Rapport
ABI HUYNH, in collaboration with Ross Milne Easton West & Todd Takahashi — Pie charts are well established as a succinct way of conveying information, but they are usually seen as dry and lifeless. In this mash-up, green pie charts of different sizes and hues pop and fizz, intersect and dissolve to surprise us with their exuberance.

Bubbling and effervescing across the page, this expression of student data acquires an apt, emotional quality, transformed into an annual report of spirit and attitude.
—— Feltron 2007 Annual Report
|> **P. 91**| NICHOLAS FELTON — In an ongoing project, Nicholas Felton (otherwise known by the nickname 'Feltron') investigates ways to encapsulate a year graphically. In this third edition, the increased use of data mash-ups

and eclectic elements deliberately evokes the open-source world of the web. Spheres are applied as a way to map, section, and zone diverse categories of data. Bar charts, area charts, and pie charts collaborate to fill in the textures and experiences of a complex and diverse life. It is an open-ended approach to analyzing, capturing, and depicting a personal experience of New York. References to this project are found throughout *Data Flow*.

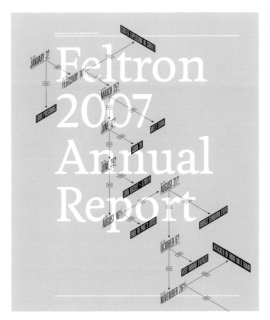

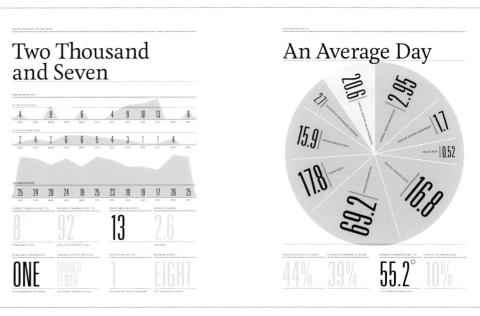

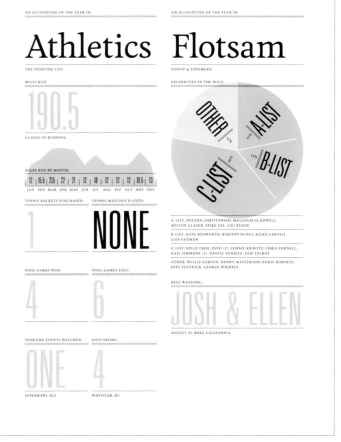

——— **Mondriaan Foundation Annual Report** LUST — The cover illustration of the Mondriaan Foundation's annual report not only reflects the foundation's aim of stimulating and promoting artistic endeavours, but also acts as a summary of its financial statements. It gives full disclosure of investments and revenues, and shows how the €26 million entrusted to the foundation has been received and spent. The foundation supports artistic communities from South Africa to South Korea, giving amounts ranging from a hundred dollars to many millions. From the inner ring, which shows income sources, to the outer ring, which shows the events and projects supported, the chart uses twenty different colours to display over a thousand projects. The structure shown on the cover provides a visual storyline of the foundation's work, percolating through the subsequent pages as a metaphor for the financial contribution that filters down from different benefactors. Meanwhile, specific details of the projects funded are revealed within the pages of the report.

As a contribution by the foundation towards sustainability, all copies of the report were printed on odd left-overs from the printers'. Because of this, no two documents are the same, as pages were inserted and swapped at random during the printing process. Each annual report thus becomes an individual work of art. The report's cover depicts the art world as both a sphere of financial activity and the very incarnation of aestheticism. In this way, the foundation's objectives coincide in both form and expression, achieving synergy between goals and results.

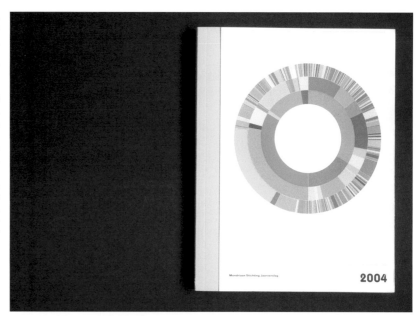

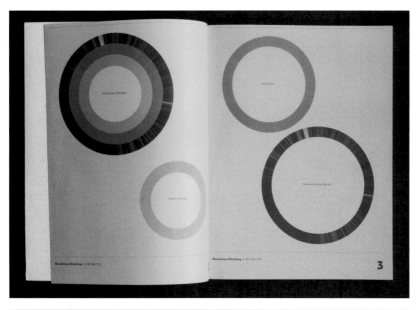

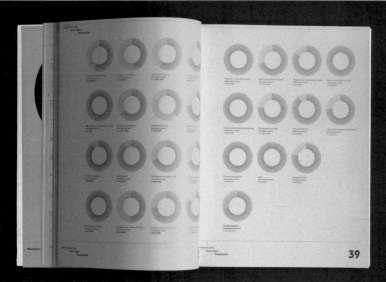

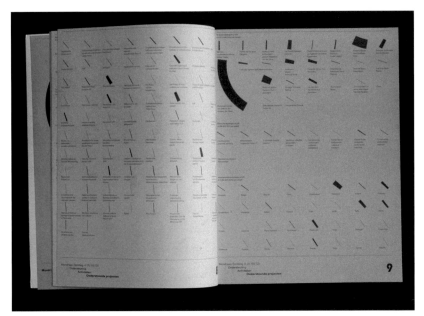

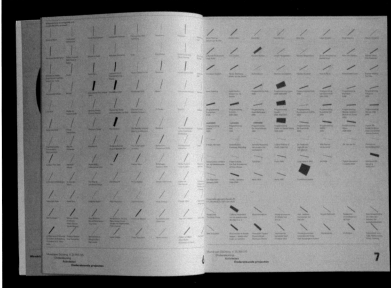

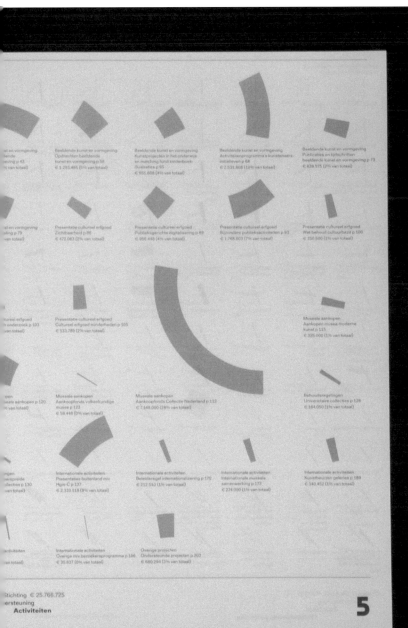

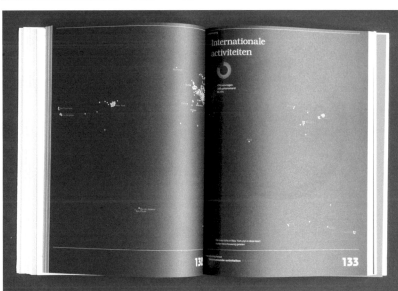

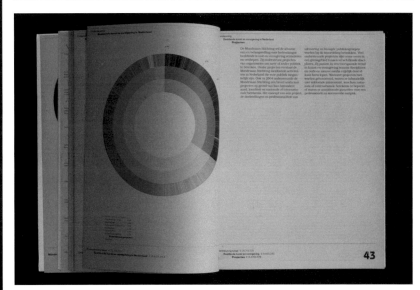

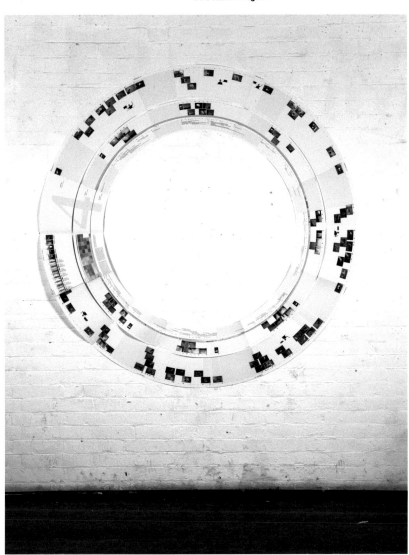

— **La représentation des statistiques** |>PP. 181, 200| XAVIER BARRADE, in collaboration with Arnaud Dupont — **The Rain Project** THANKS EVERYBODY — By placing himself at the centre of this work of art, Jake Hobart shows how the weather has influenced his personal choices in terms of 'healthy' and 'unhealthy' activities. Arranging the time sequence as a circle of human dimensions, he places the observer in the midst of these activities, which project outwards as determined by atmospheric conditions. The presentation becomes a metaphor for the finding that our environment influences who we are. Place us in another sphere of influence, and we will make different choices.

— Invisible journeys YESYESNONO — Pins have long been used to signify points of interest on maps. Pins on the globe can mark progress across an otherwise undefined space. Here, the four concentric spheres represent journeys through the urban landscapes of London (outer ring), Vescemont, Belfort, and Barcelona (inner ring). The red pins represent unencrypted Wi-Fi access nodes, while black pins represent nodes that are encrypted. Here, real space is subverted and re-presented in a way more fitting for travellers of dataspace. Moving through spheres of access, the journey is defined by the richness of that access, enhancing the otherwise inscrutable cityscapes. **— The Shape of Family: Extroverted** | ▹ P. 241 | CHRISTINA VAN VLECK — In a work that deliberately emulates the rings on a tree rather than the more conventional branches, families are represented by their successive generations down the years. The single colour for progeny is blended and layered with each new descendant. The spread of ideas, support, and attention across the generations, shaping the family's strength and continuity, is shown as layers of vellum building on the genealogical foundation — slices of a kindred history divided equally according to individual descent. The multi-layered pie charts of legacy take on individual shapes, prompting new questions about our own families and how special grandparents, uncles, or aunts have shaped our lives. Parents with an only child, parents who outlive their children, and all other personal histories evolve to show the shape of a family. **— The Shape of Family: Introverted** | ▹ P. 241 | CHRISTINA VAN VLECK — This piece represents the collective as a unit, and individuals as the sum total of social and evolutionary success. The analysis of evolutionary DNA has shattered the view that man is the apex of a long line of development geared towards delivering this particular pinnacle of design. The tree model of evolution implied specific directional and power structures. MitoWheel, one of several contemporary representations, places man in a circle of blended and residual DNA combinations. Some are redundant, some are active, and some are unexplained. In a similar vein, this spherical visualisation of the common family tree represents the designer as the centre of a unique combination of forces. The sphere is blended and shaded without any specific design or intent, resulting from a profusion of potential and purpose.

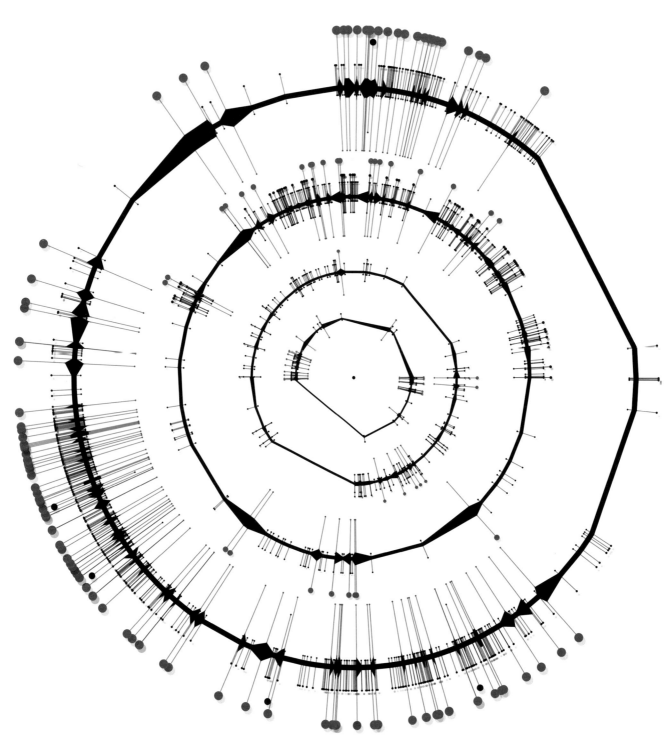

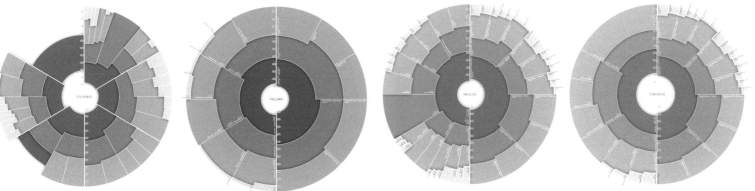

The Shape of **Family**

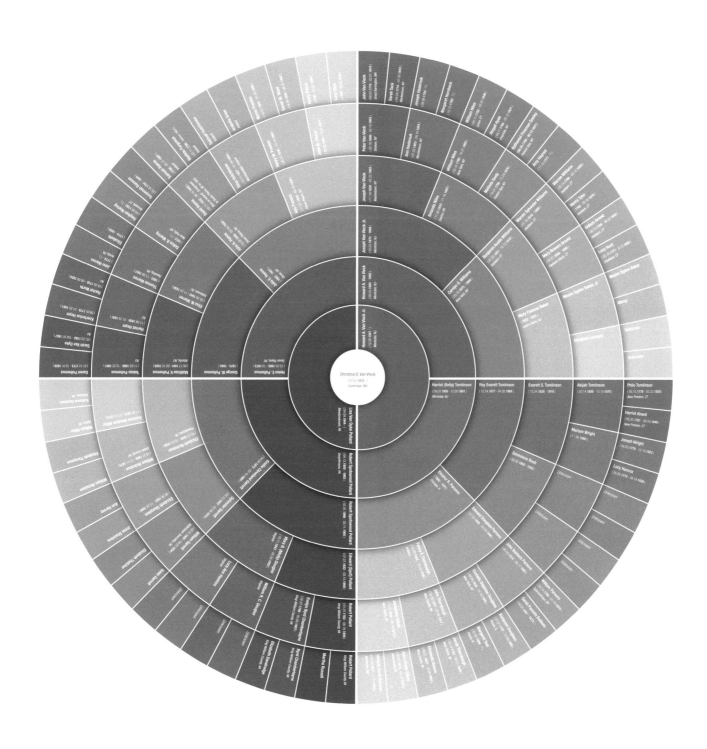

—— Total Interaction PROJEKT-
TRIANGLE, Jürgen Späth, Magnus Rembold,
Zurich University of the Arts — In developing
the layout for this book on interaction design, it was felt there was a need to enhance
the narrative by the visual explanation of
thematic links. By using a combination of
subjective, manually generated keywords
and automatically generated metadata, the
designers were able to create a scheme of
visuals. These enable the reader not only
to quickly assess the content and significance of a specific article, but also to
navigate its context within the book.
The book in its entirety acts as a spherical
container, inside which keyword clouds
cluster afresh for every article. The space
within the circle accordingly operates on
two levels, providing contextual locus and
substantive texture. **—— 1 – An exhibition in mono** IMAGE NOW, Aiden
Grennelle & Adam Gallacher — A mere 180
seconds can be a universe, inverting expectations, and leading to new insights and
discoveries. The epic 'Rumble in the Jungle'
that took place between Muhammad Ali
and George Foreman in October 1974 led
to just such a reversal of fortune. With the
underdog Ali pitted against Foreman, the
reigning world heavyweight champion and
hot favourite, it is said that Foreman's team
prayed beforehand that he would not kill his
opponent.   The 180 seconds of each
round develop into an ever-tightening series of arcs, as Foreman is ground down,
punch by punch. The dashed lines indicate
the exact moments at which Ali makes contact, versus the solid lines of his opponent.
The final blow, two minutes and forty-seven
seconds into the eighth round, strikes a dramatic and definitive line through Foreman's
supposed supremacy.

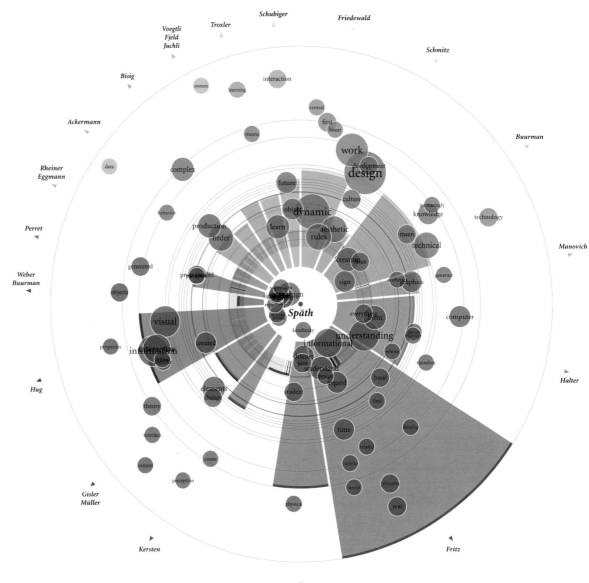

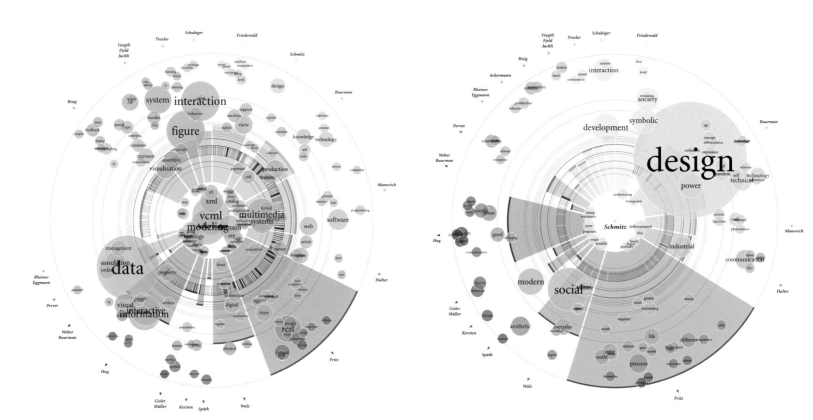

Muhammed Ali v George Foreman   30.10.1974   Kinshasa, Zaire

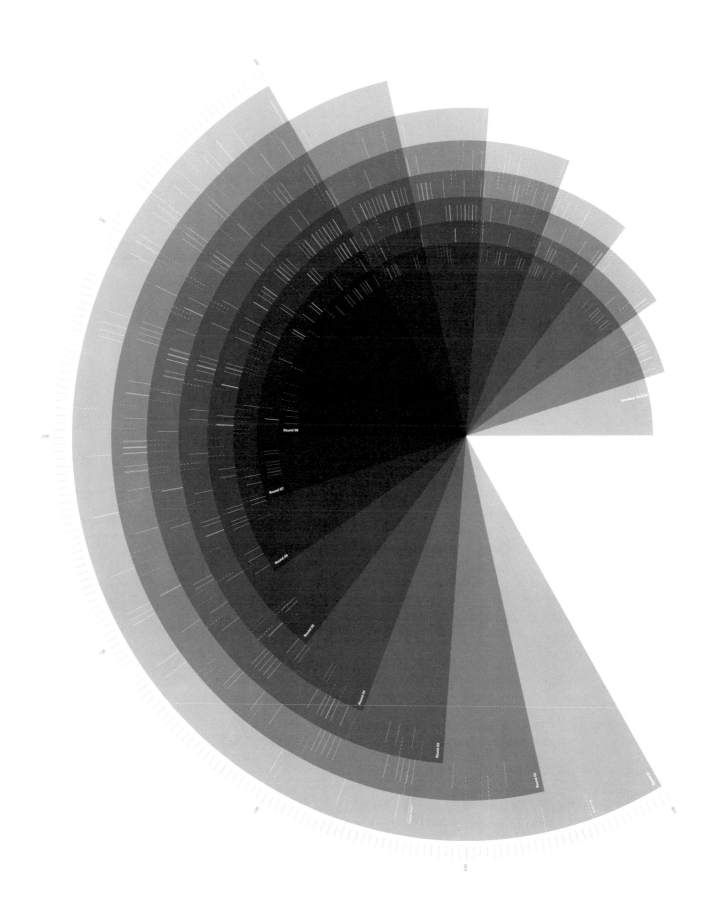

Measure by Image Now, 1 – An exhibition in mono.
24 of 28 designs for Blanka 09/06, edition of 100 only.

THE UNIVERSE IN 20 08

WWW.SEEDMEDIAGROUP.COM

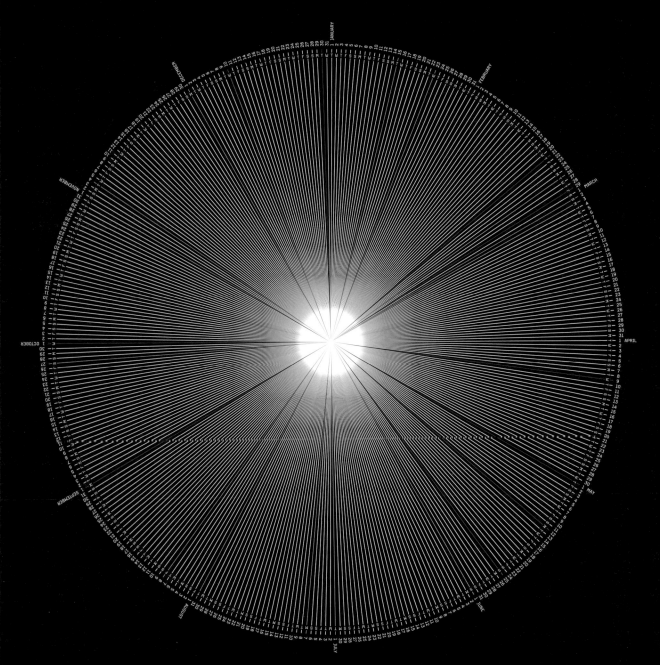

DISCIPLINE
COSMOLOGY
SOCIAL SCIENCES
ENVIRONMENTAL SCIENCES
NEUROSCIENCE
BIOLOGY
CHEMISTRY
PHYSICS

JANUARY
1 The UN names 2008 the International Year of Planet Earth
15 Filming begins on *The Stanford Prison Experiment,* a movie based on Zimbardo's famous study
23 The World Economic Forum Annual Meeting is held in Davos, Switzerland

FEBRUARY
21 A total lunar eclipse is visible over the Americas, Europe, Africa, and Western Asia
26 The Svalbard Global Seed Vault begins storing seeds for nearly 1.5 million crop strains
29 2008 is a leap year

MARCH
2 Russia elects its third president
3 Will Wright's much-anticipated game *Spore* hits shelves
20 International Earth Day is celebrated on the Vernal Equinox

APRIL
9 India launches its lunar orbiter Chandrayaan-1

MAY
1 The Large Hadron Collider starts operations
12 Cassini has its closest encounter with Enceladus
25 NASA spacecraft Phoenix lands on Mars

JUNE
1 The *Encyclopedia of Life* launches web pages for 50,000 species

JULY
1 New York City restaurants must eliminate all trans fat from their foods by this date
7 The G8 conference takes place in Hokkaido, Japan
31 Bill Gates steps down from his position as the head of Microsoft

AUGUST
8 The Beijing Olympics marks the 100th anniversary of women competing in the modern Games

SEPTEMBER
1 China launches Shenzhou 7 carrying three taikonauts into low Earth orbit
27 The Model T was introduced 100 years ago today

OCTOBER
1 NASA celebrates its 50th anniversary
14 The Athens Summit is the first international conference focused on the new paradigm of climate and energy security as exemplified by the UN Security Council
31 A prototype of the "solar impulse," a plane powered by solar energy, is expected to make its first piloted flight this fall

NOVEMBER
4 The United States elects its 44th president

DECEMBER
1 World AIDS Day is observed for its 20th year
10 The Nobel Prize Award Ceremonies take place in Sweden
30 Burj Dubai, predicted to be 1,922 feet, becomes the world's tallest building
31 By this date, EU nations must recover 60 percent of packaging waste

seed media group.

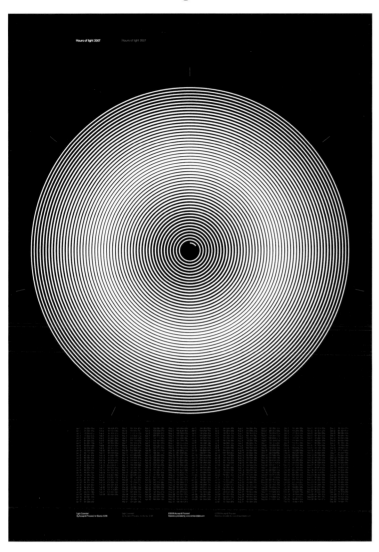

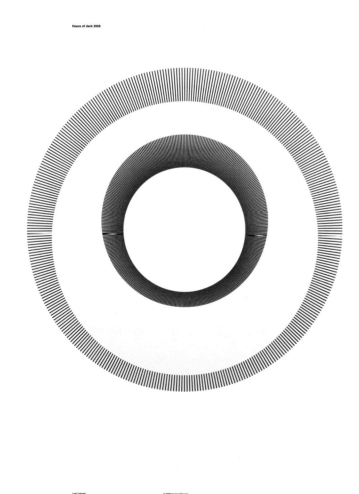

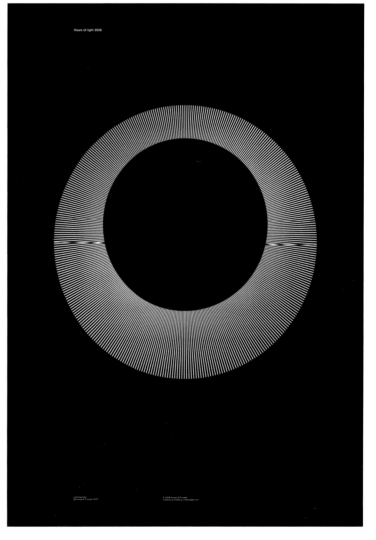

—— **Universe in 2008** JEFFREY DOCHERTY — As we stare straight into the refracting lens of scientific illumination, we see coloured lines that indicate specific events, colour-coded by individual scientific disciplines. The metaphor of science as light radiating out becomes even sharper as the contrast between non-event days and event days becomes clear. This work powerfully symbolises *Seed* magazine's mission to create and distribute original 'Science is Culture' content that communicates the fast-changing role of science within our culture to an international audience.

The title is a provocative reference to the role played by science in explaining the purpose of culture in time and space. Just as the Earth circles the sun to complete the year, or the hands of a clock march around its face to mark time, this graphic shows the progress made throughout a year of scientific discovery, revealing the entire universe through the prism of individual disciplines.

—— **Light Calendars 2007 and 2008** |› P. 203| ACCEPT & PROCEED, David Johnston & Stephen Heath — The process of unveiling the inner beauty of data is a theme that crops up frequently in the work of the Accept and Proceed design studio. This project, which was initiated by the studio itself and is updated every year, sets out to be both scientifically accurate and aesthetically pleasing as a work of art. Using fluorescent inks to represent the hours of daylight over the year ahead, the graph is a faithful reflection of its subject. The graph may be read in both light and dark conditions, the eccentric, overlapping spheres reminding us of the Earth's slightly tilted orbit and rotation, which creates the variation between the light and dark periods of night and day.

——— **Revolving Door NL** LUST
— The Netherlands is balanced delicately at the axis of a revolving door, caught between the flows of immigration and emigration. This artwork reminds us that migration statistics are not just numbers, but people. Each dot represents a life full of potential and challenges faced at the individual level.   As the twentieth century progresses, the density of inflows is clearly seen to increase, emphasising the fears that immigration will put pressure on local infrastructure. Net immigration is finely sliced within a segment of the circle, showing how the Netherlands is 'growing' with the influx.   Cultural diversity is implicitly shown by splitting the different regions of the world that immigrants come from into different tracks.   Rather than the faceless volume that is so regularly quoted in histograms of immigration statistics, this piece highlights concentration, density, and flow.

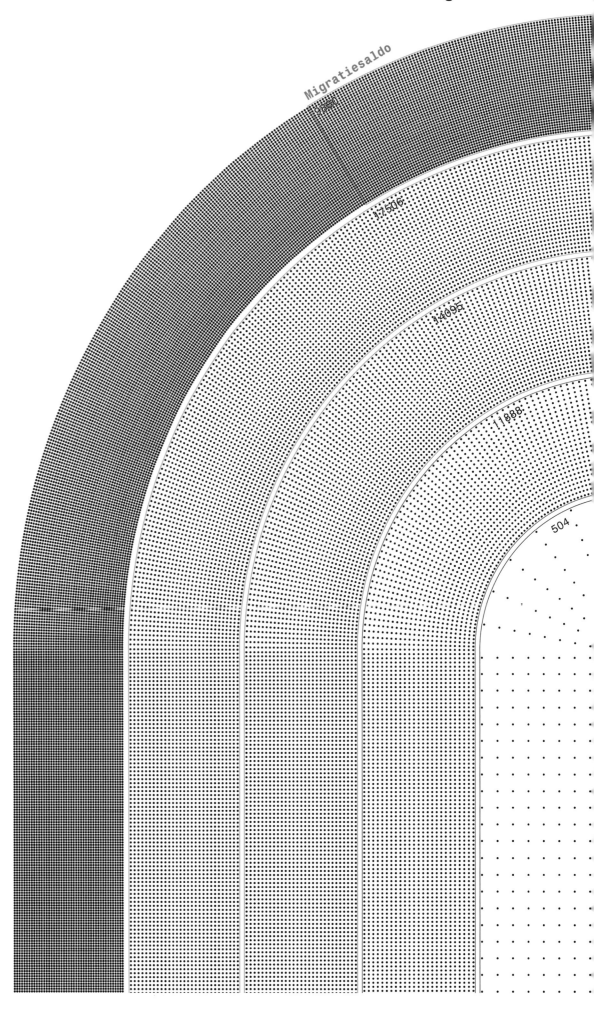

Immigratie Nederlan

migratie Nederland

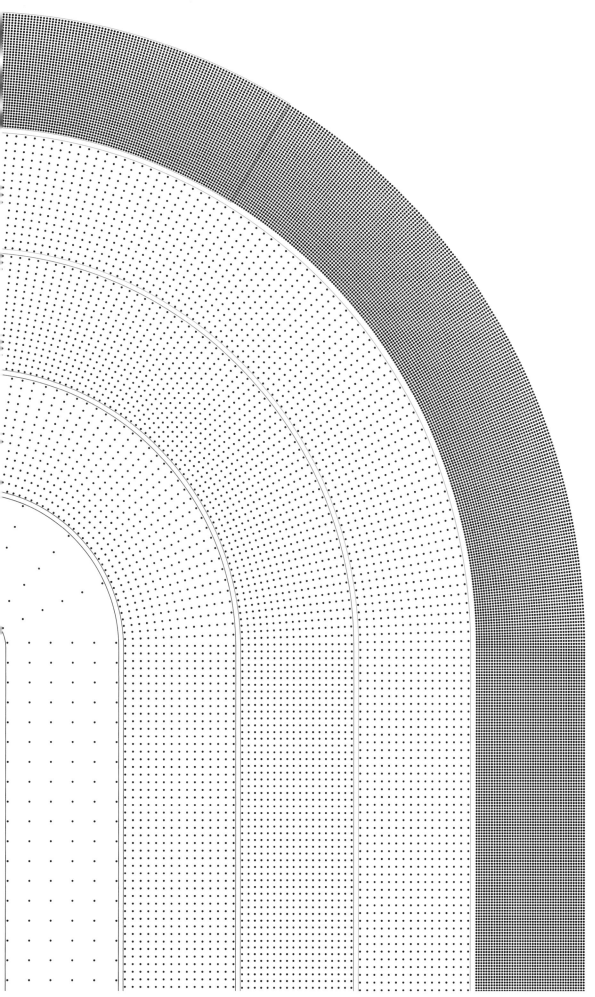

—

Datanets

—

—

When individual data points develop tension and connection with each other, the resulting structure becomes an entity in its own right—the network. It draws life essentially from connection and connectedness, and it is these qualities that are directed explicitly by the designer to show cause, context, or collaboration.

—

Woven together with artful intent, the structure of meaning is revealed by the links more than by the nodes themselves. Marian Bantjes's elegant

depiction of early influences takes this to the extreme, the content becoming entirely subjected to the shape of the connections. The connections here are the end product—the artistic handwriting that was developed from all of her influences.

—Influence Map |>P. 72|
MARIAN BANTJES

An overt network begins to impose a semantic structure of 'subject', 'verb', and 'object' on the data, as the reader decodes the functional relationship between nodes. These relationships vary in

strength, as line weights, hierarchy, and locus are used to filter and refine connections, distributing power through the interlaced assertion. By adding the aesthetics of alchemy to this model, Suzan Treister's clever depiction of the news raises pertinent questions about the vested interests behind the modern media. The

— Alchemy |>P. 79|
SUZANNE TREISTER

forces within the network dominate and shape its content. Paradoxically, the artefacts of the internet as a data network have all but disappeared from the interface we have with its

content. However, the nature of the web does shape our experience, since connection has a decisive impact on inclusion. The invisibility of the medium has led to a profusion of attempts to visualise the impact of the web on people and their relationships. Bestiario inves-

— Informational City
Distances |>P. 95|
BESTIARIO

tigate the virtual distances between places on the globe. Clear red lines of varied thickness indicate the semiotic proximity of physical places in a virtual space. Felix Heinen highlights the vi-

ral potential of social media penetration in Germany as a marketing force. In both these examples, designers are acknowledging the qualities of the network to shape experience and contribution.

— Data Visualisation of
a Social Network |>P. 66|
FELIX HEINEN

At the other extreme, the density and layering of content can become so overpowering as to hide the underlying links that bind the network together. Projekttriangle investigate

these invisible forces in their graphical studies of RFID tag usage. Their penetrating view through the content links concepts and discussions together in a way that a superficial reading cannot. Mirroring the invisible, intelligent web created by this artifice, the purposeful linking of the data reveals the true power of a connected society. Taking

— RFID-SYSTEME
|>P. 71|PROJEKTTRIANGLE

the metaphor of content over structure even further, Media A anticipates the future life of a designer by creating a dense forest of experiences, strange and unusual to the present-day viewer. The links between topics serve only as a slight suggestion for the reader to follow a narrative through the catalogue of invention. With affiliations that are

— A Day in the Life of a
Networked Designer |>P. 82|
MEDIA A

now almost incidental to the theme, the network becomes a conceptual construct rather than an organisational device. Yet in all these examples, the power of the network lies in elevating node to nexus, a humble contributor to

—

The forces within the network dominate and shape its content

—

a new level of meaning through association. The association can be ethereal rather than overt—a function of the gaps between units, rather than the units themselves.

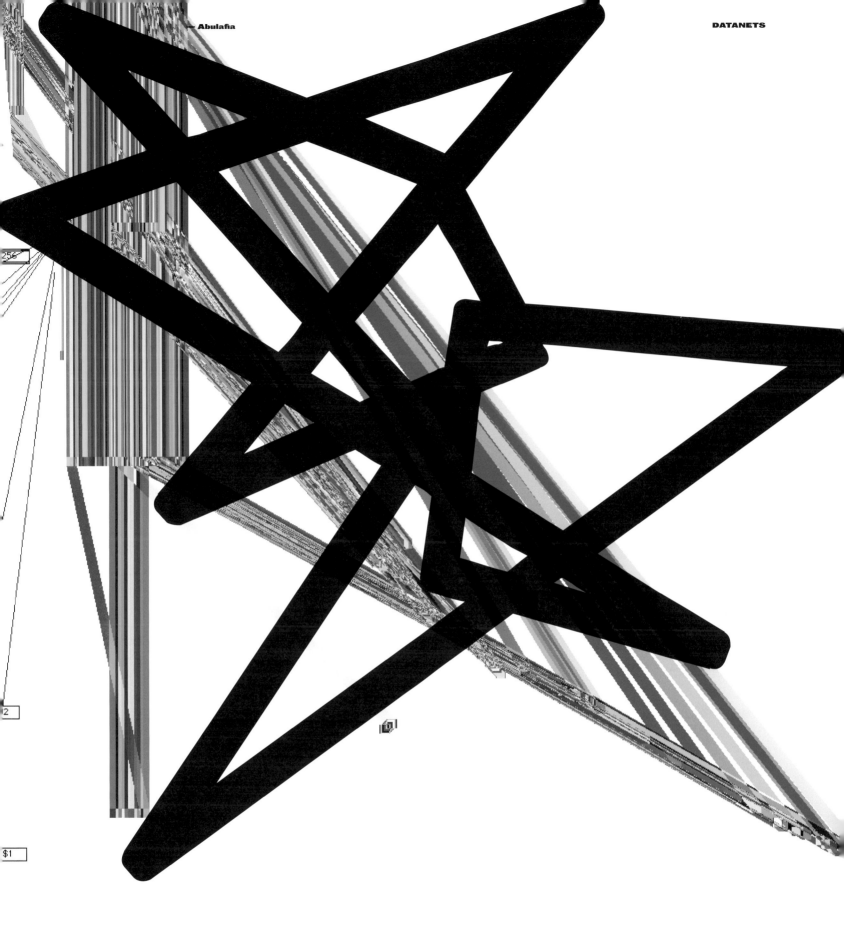

PREVIOUS PAGE ———— **Abulafia**
|▷ **P. 91**|
ADVANCE DESIGN — Here, music is experienced as a visual expression. The nuances of pitch, resonance, and tempo struggle against the constraints of the Prague flatland to emulate the richness and dynamic range of feelings evoked by sound. Advanced design codes and reduced musical notes were used to develop this visual language and, ultimately, the logo for the 2008 Sperm Festival.

— Love Will Tear Us Apart Again PLUSMINUS, Peter Crnokrak — The impact of a song transcends national and personal boundaries. As time rolls on, the songs that touched us most intensely get covered, reinterpreted, and cherished again. Joy Division's 1980 hit 'Love will tear us apart' provokes memories of personal and raw moments in love, moving successive artists to develop their own individual version of this song.   PlusMinus have created a data-rich chart that captures the stark emotional rawness of the song and its meaning for the artists who have performed it, as conveyed by their different interpretations.   Over and above the factual references to year, duration, artist, and studio, which are outlined in a circle, the network of thin lines shows how artists have been drawn to the song over the years, in heartfelt expressions of the impact it has had on their personal lives.

— One week of the Guardian: Thursday |▷ **P. 71**| DESIGNING THE NEWS — This is another poster in the series that embodies the *Guardian*'s role as a critical reporting voice in the United Kingdom. The newspaper's content is analysed, categorised, and presented afresh in a visually evocative manner. In this particular diagram, headlines, writers, pages and categories are all spread out evenly over the circular graph. The colour-coding of news categories becomes the semantic web displaying the breadth and diversity of topics covered by the newspaper. The relationships between date, writer, headline, and category are strengthened according to word count to provide distinction and weighting.

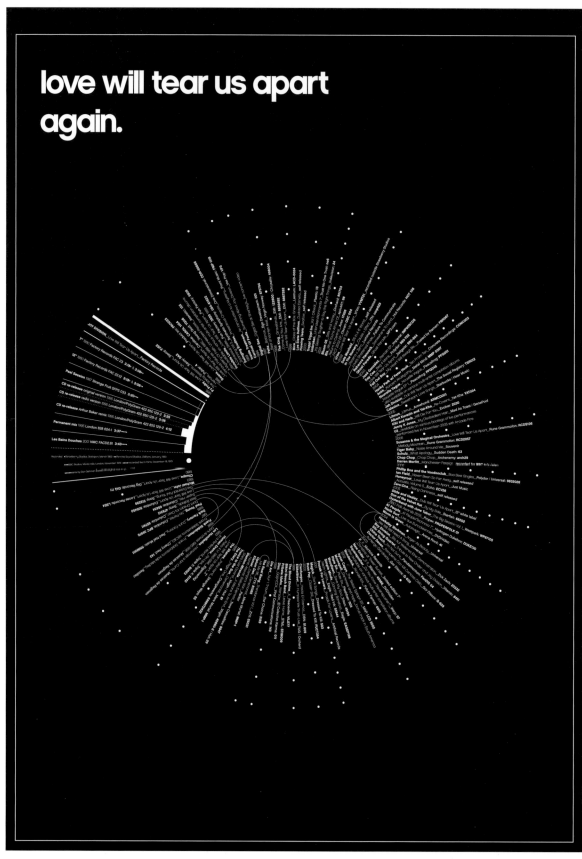

Business
Education
Environment
Science
Technology
Society
Politics
Life and Style
Culture
UK News
World News

£4bn windfall gives Darling a much needed budget boost
A&L brings down shutters
Academics back Bridgend families in blaming media
Afghan farmers' opium income rises to $1bn
After 10 straight victories, Obama's camp claims wide lead and urges Clinton to quit
Amsterdam looks underground to ease congestion
Anglo-American puts Tarmac sale on shelf
Arctic Monkeys lord it again
Arman's cutting remarks show rogue editor
Asda warned suppliers it will clamp down on price rises
Audit office launches inquiry into rescue
Balkan murder plot denied at Diana inquest
Banned party vows to enter politics despite arrests
Bizarre barracking outbreak
BP goes back to petroleum
Celebrity chefs back hard-pressed farmers
Closed hearing and a secret ruling: how the word Israel was deleted
Concerns grow for nine-year-old girl missing for two nights
Conservatives would criminalise forced marriages, says Cameron
Crocs shares sink despite 130% sales leap
Cubans cling to socialist dream
Fertility clinic boosts safety and success
From West Wing to the real thing
How Labour used the law to keep criticism of Israel secret
Husband denies ordering wife's murder
Industry enjoying period of sustained demand
Inquiry as Tories attack DNA failure
Islamic scholars to hold talks at Vatican
Israel's weapons - a diplomatic no-go area
It's brickbats time for the housebuilders
Kosovo border secured as Serbs turn up heat
Major disease outbreaks around world becoming more common
Mayor's aide cleared of fraud
Merkel challenges Liechtenstein over tax evasion
Michelle and Cindy compete for patriotic crown
Migrants to earn citizenship during probationary period
Miliband blocks release of key Lockerbie files
Minister's cure for 'sicknote culture'
Mortgage costs to rise, A&L warns, as shares hit all-time low
Musharraf pushes Swiss to prosecute Zardari
MySpace seeks joint ventures for iTunes rival
Nintendo launches Wii to get couch potatoes fit
No counterbid for S&N
Northern Rock nationalisation in turmoil over offshore trust
Opposition warns of more street demonstrations
Paisley to bow out of politics after pressure from party
Party donations hit midterm record of £56m
Rate setters fear manufacturers will push up inflation
Renault wins race to supply Sarkomobile
Rhys Jones murder weapon found among 108 guns taken off streets
Sarkozy struggles to contain worker unrest
Shuttle return clears way for navy to blast satellite
SocGen report finds lax controls of rogue trader's activities
Stamp duty soars to £31bn in 10 years of Labour
Standard Chartered drops plan to rescue SIV
Stiffer sentences urged for 'happy slapping' attacks
The elusive G spot really does exist, say researchers
The FO's case to the information tribunal
Three countries in pact to save mountain gorillas
Three killed as houses collapse in earthquake
Vernalis to shed half its staff
Viacom starts black entertainment channel
White middle-class children not held back by poorer state schools
Why the money ran out

30
29
28
27
26
25
24
23
22
21
20
19
18
17
16
15
14
13
12
11
10
09
08
07
06
05
04
03
02
01

X.Rice
V.Dodd
T.Macalister
S.Jones
S.Goddenberg
S.Carrell
S.Bosely
S.Bates
R.Wray
Riddell
R.Smithers
R.Norton-Taylor
R.Batt
P.Booth
P.Wintour
P.Curtis
P.Hodgson
N.Watt
N.Pratley
M.Milne
M.Barnoux
L.Wroughton
L.Elliot
K.Connolly
J.Tuckman
J.Treanor
J.Freedland
J.Finch
J.Carvel
J.Carter-Morley
I.Sample
I.Black
H.Carter
D.Walsh
D.Leigh
D.Hencke
D.Gow
C.Dyer
AP
A.Travis
A.Gillan
A.Clark
A.Chrisafis

No. 002 / 002   Subject «Data visualisation of a social network»   Version 02a v. 04022007

Wo?

Geographische Datenvisualisierung

Ein Vorteil des Online-Netzwerks ist die Möglichkeit, große Distanzen zu überwinden um Kontakt zu seinen Freunden zu halten. Dadurch erstreckt es sich über eine erhebliche geographische Ausdehnung. Zudem ist durch die Pflichteingabe der Postleitzahl bei jedem Mitglied eine eindeutige örtliche Zuordnung festgelegt. So können alle preisgegebenen Informationen im Bezug zu dem Wohnort dargestellt werden.
Ausgangspunkt sind alle Städte in Deutschland, Österreich und der Schweiz. Dabei werden die hundert mitgliederstärksten Städte herausgegriffen und für sie alle benutzerspezifischen Angaben zusammen gefragen.

Dadurch könnte man «ausbaufähige» Städte und «Lokalisierzentren» aufzeigen und dementsprechende ortsbezogene Maßnahmen ergreifen um den Bekanntheitsgrad zu steigern.

Stand: Februar 2007   Datenquelle: http://94.97.153.77   Autor: Felix Heinen

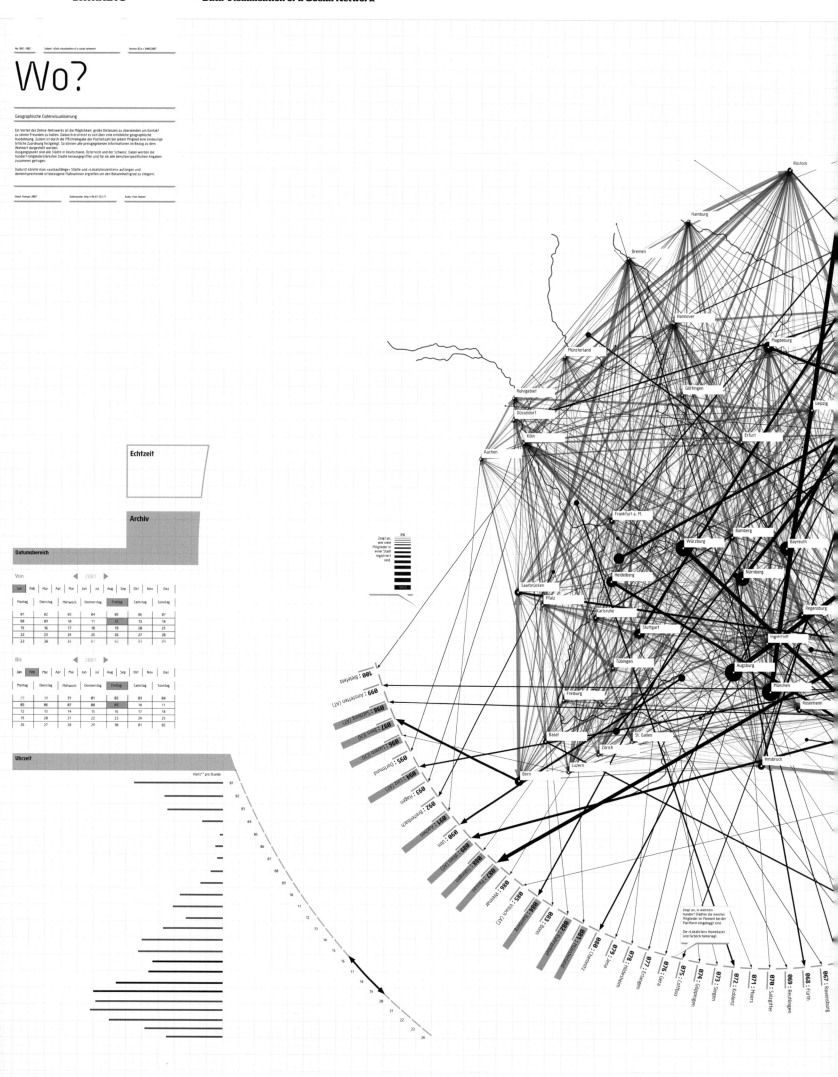

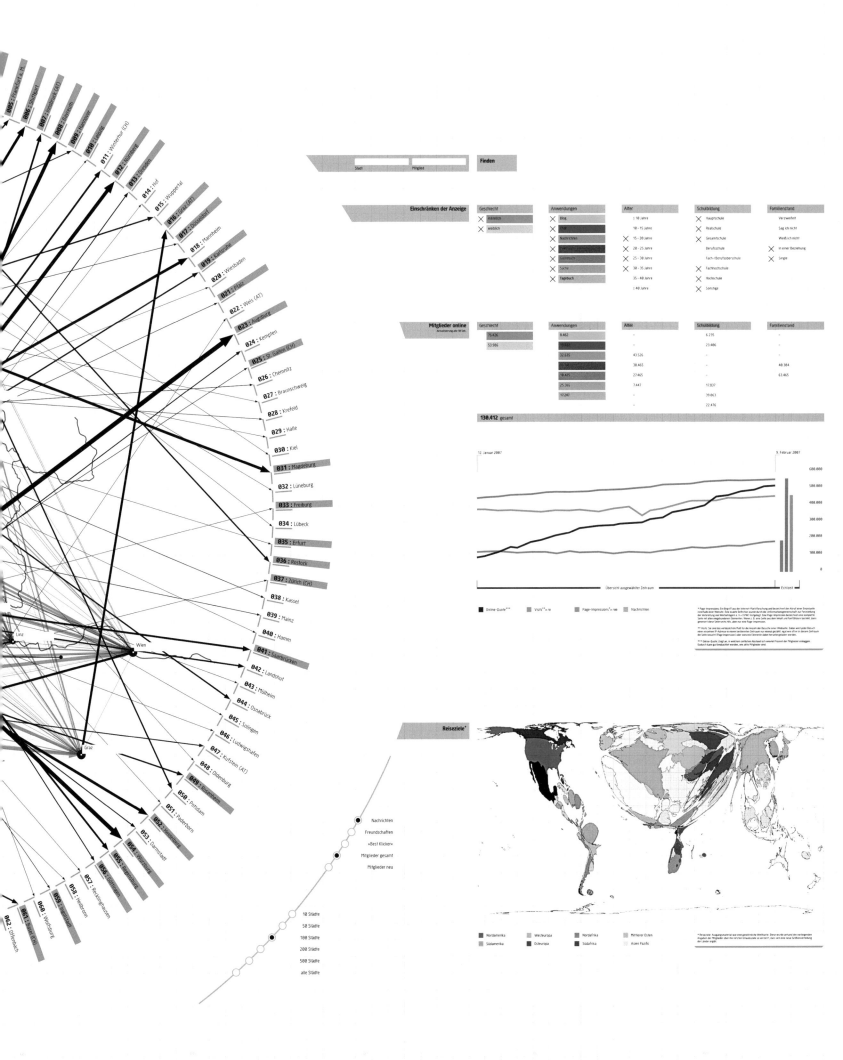

PREVIOUS PAGES ——— **Data Visu-alisation of a Social Network**
|▶ P. 66| FELIX HEINEN — The members of the Facebook collective converge and connect through the social utility that the website provides. There are many different ways to think about the individual bytes of data floating and connecting through Facebook, and Felix Heinen has captured an elegant flow of activity and demographics. Simple histograms showing the gender split for each demographic, application, or activity are brought to a richer level of meaning by cross-referencing in a rainbow network of connectedness. Our understanding of the community dynamic grows with every strand of the colour- and size-coded connections. Preferences for certain activities by age group and gender are easily identified, and expressed with the friendly open personality engendered by social networking.

——— **Been There** | CATALOGTREE — 'It isn't what you know, it's who you know that counts in business.' Building a network of contacts is just as important in the sports world as it is in business, and as the importance of NBA coaches as 'kingmakers' has grown, so has too interest in their behaviour and strategy. This study for ESPN elegantly shows how the top five coaches criss-cross the United States to find the Shaq O'Neills and Michael Jordans of tomorrow. From this work, based on the map of North America, a prospective NBA star can quickly spot the best networking opportunities, as well as the likely hothouses of success and stardom.

——— **ClusterBall: Humans, Medicine, History** CHRIS HARRISON, data provided by Wikipedia — Language can be seen as a semiological net, exposed through the internet by a web of volunteer workers. And Wikipedia is becoming the default reference to knowledge and understanding. In this diagram, Chris Harrison not only shows the connection between the concepts pervading our humanity, but indicates the hierarchy in which they have been placed by Wikipedians. Genetics, extinction, technology, and even personal life are all displayed in the click-work tapestry surrounding the concept. The structured network of meaning and content subtly alludes to new ways of thinking about evolution, and about how the DNA of different species is represented. Rather than being portrayed as distinct branches on a tree, subsequent stages of evolution are captured inside and through species. In a similar way, we can look at language not as a tree, but as a network of references and dynamic relationships.

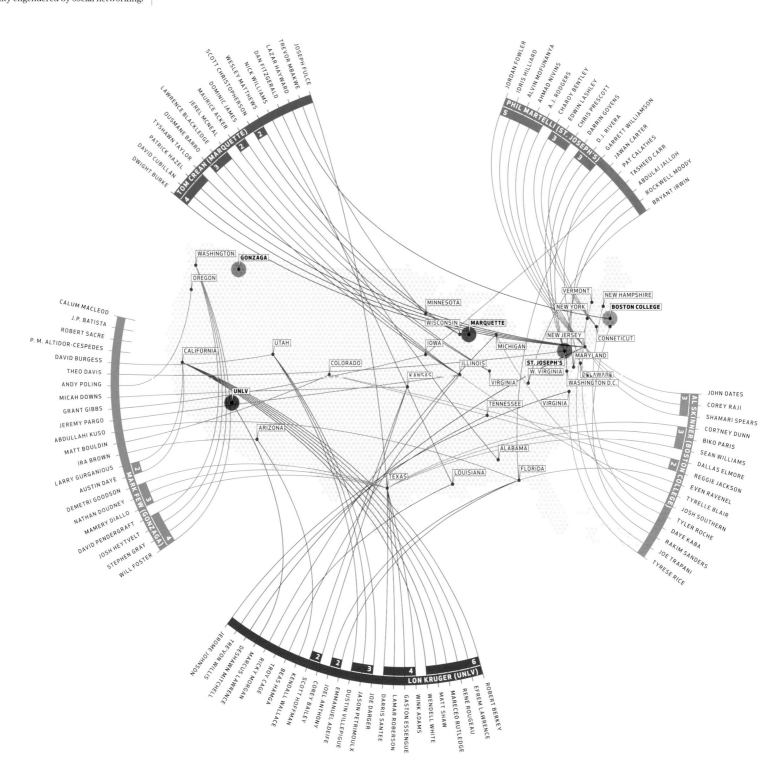

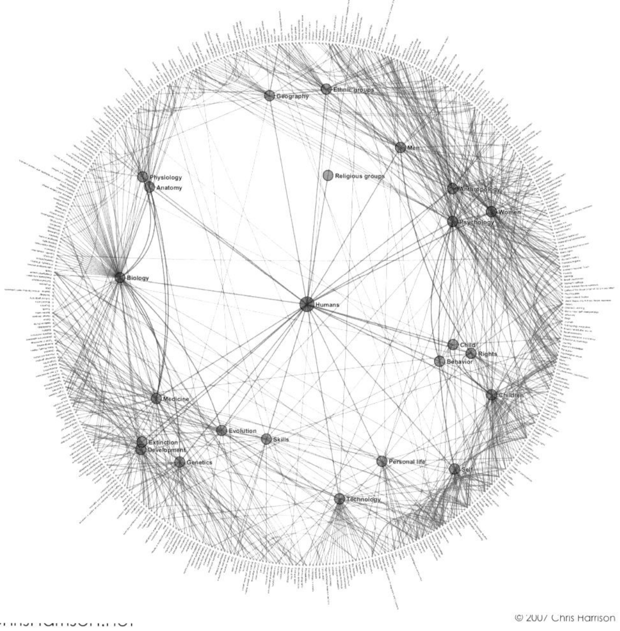
Geography
Ethnic groups
Men
Religious groups
Physiology
Anatomy
Anthropology
Women
Psychology
Biology
Humans
Child
Rights
Behavior
Medicine
Children
Evolution
Skills
Extinction
Development
Genetics
Personal life
Self
Technology
© 2007 Chris Harrison

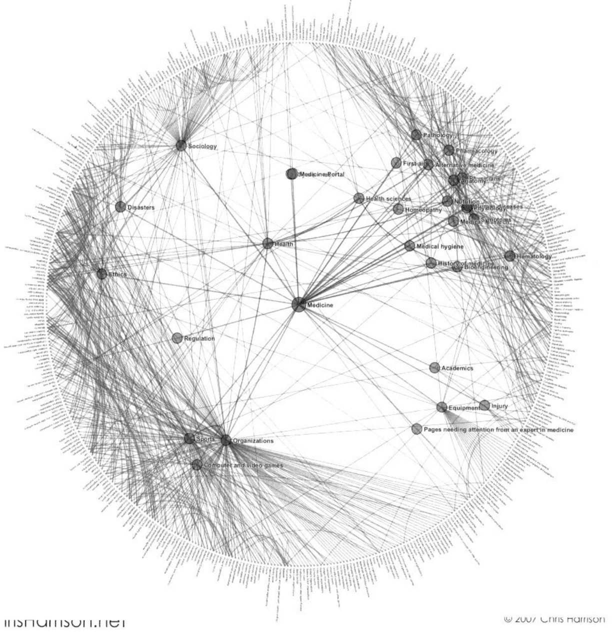
Pathology
Pharmacology
Sociology
First aid
Alternative medicine
Medicine Portal
Anatomy
Disasters
Health sciences
Homeopathy
Nutrition
Health
Medical hygiene
Hematology
Ethics
History of medicine
Bioengineering
Medicine
Regulation
Academics
Equipment
Injury
Pages needing attention from an expert in medicine
Sports
Organizations
Computer and video games
© 2007 Chris Harrison

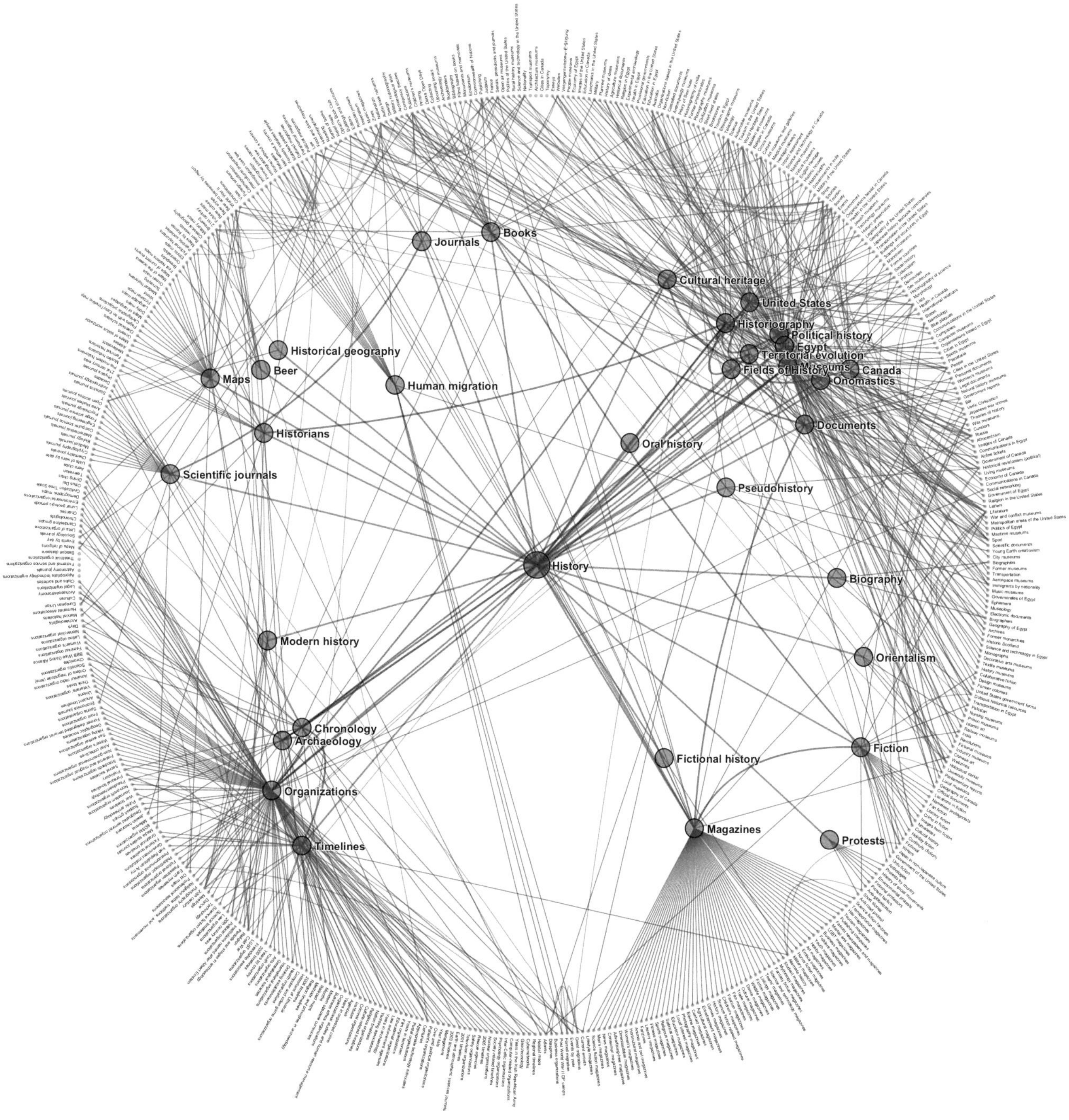
Journals
Books
Cultural heritage
United States
Historiography
Political history
Egypt
Territorial evolution
Historical geography
Canada
Fields of History
Onomastics
Maps
Beer
Human migration
Documents
Historians
Oral history
Scientific journals
Pseudohistory
History
Biography
Modern history
Orientalism
Chronology
Archaeology
Fictional history
Fiction
Organizations
Magazines
Protests
Timelines

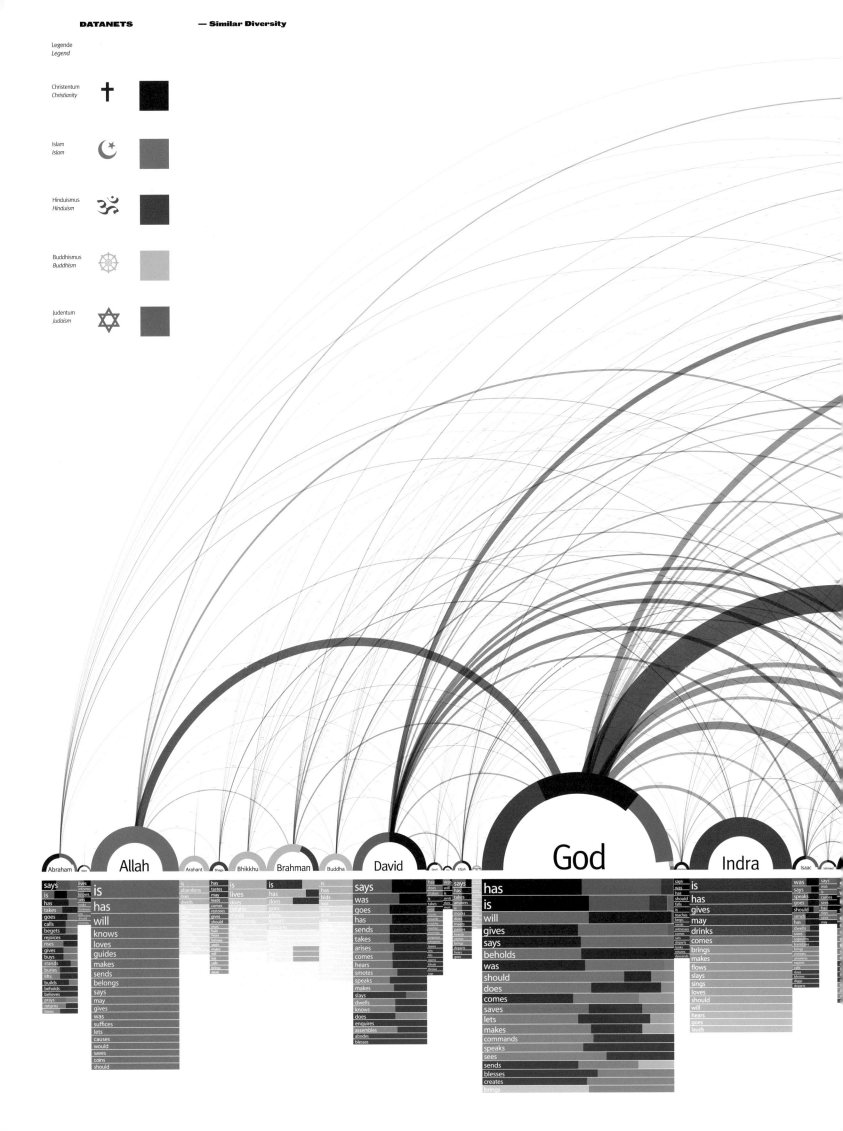

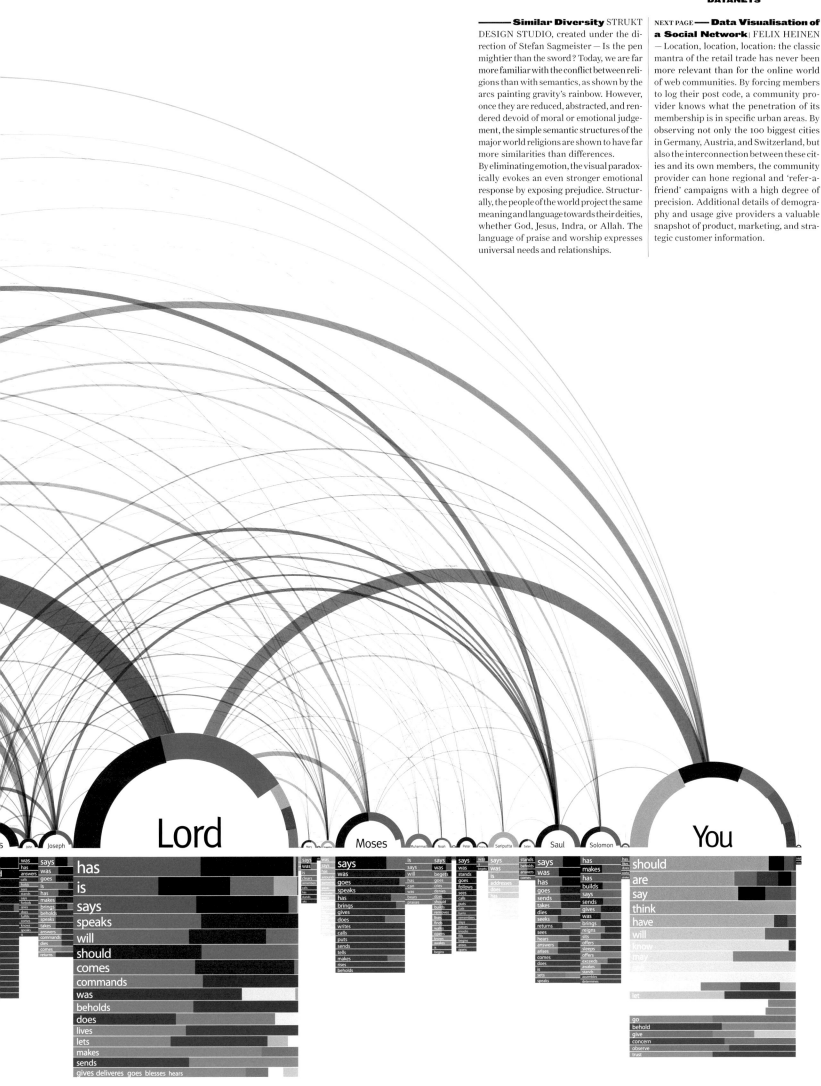

──── **Similar Diversity** STRUKT DESIGN STUDIO, created under the direction of Stefan Sagmeister — Is the pen mightier than the sword? Today, we are far more familiar with the conflict between religions than with semantics, as shown by the arcs painting gravity's rainbow. However, once they are reduced, abstracted, and rendered devoid of moral or emotional judgement, the simple semantic structures of the major world religions are shown to have far more similarities than differences.

By eliminating emotion, the visual paradoxically evokes an even stronger emotional response by exposing prejudice. Structurally, the people of the world project the same meaning and language towards their deities, whether God, Jesus, Indra, or Allah. The language of praise and worship expresses universal needs and relationships.

NEXT PAGE──── **Data Visualisation of a Social Network**| FELIX HEINEN — Location, location, location: the classic mantra of the retail trade has never been more relevant than for the online world of web communities. By forcing members to log their post code, a community provider knows what the penetration of its membership is in specific urban areas. By observing not only the 100 biggest cities in Germany, Austria, and Switzerland, but also the interconnection between these cities and its own members, the community provider can hone regional and 'refer-a-friend' campaigns with a high degree of precision. Additional details of demography and usage give providers a valuable snapshot of product, marketing, and strategic customer information.

No. 001 / 002   Subject «Data visualisation of a social network»   Version 01b v. 010022007

Wer?

Demographische Datenvisualisierung

Um die eigentliche Menge aller Mitglieder im «social network» besser begreifen zu können, werden relevante demografische Daten aufgegriffen und auf einfache Weise visualisiert. Es stellt sich also die Frage, «Wer?» genau ist denn eindarüber hinaus sollten die für Webmaster üblichen Informationen wie «Page-Impression», «Unique Visit»* und «Online-Quote»** angezeigt werden.
Als aussagekräftige Daten werden dabei die Anzahl der Mitglieder, Alter, Geschlecht, schulische Bildung und der Familienstand in Verbindung mit den bei den «Lokalisten» angebotenen Anwendungen gebracht. Diese unterteilen sich in Blog, Chat, Event, Gästebuch, Tagebuch, Suche und Nachrichten.

Somit kann in erster Linie die Zusammensetzung des Mitgliederstamms, aber auch deren Verhalten auf der Plattform selbst, aufgezeigt werden. Interessant dabei festzustellen, welche Anwendungen von welchen Gruppen wie intensiv genutzt werden.

Stand: Februar 2007   Datenquelle: http://94.97.152.77   Autor: Felix Heinen

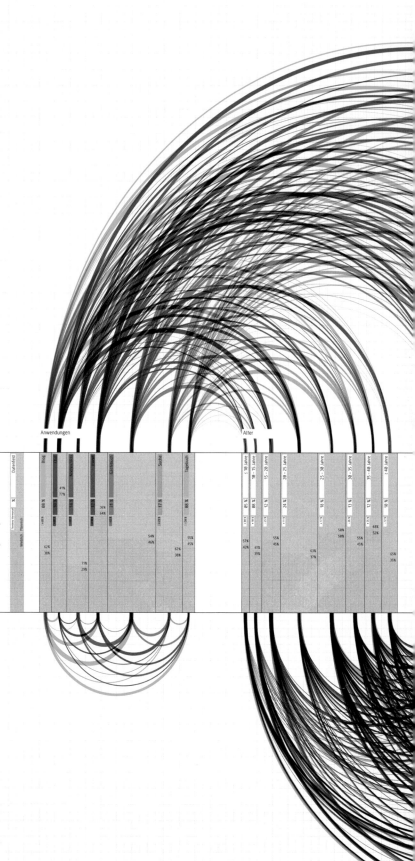

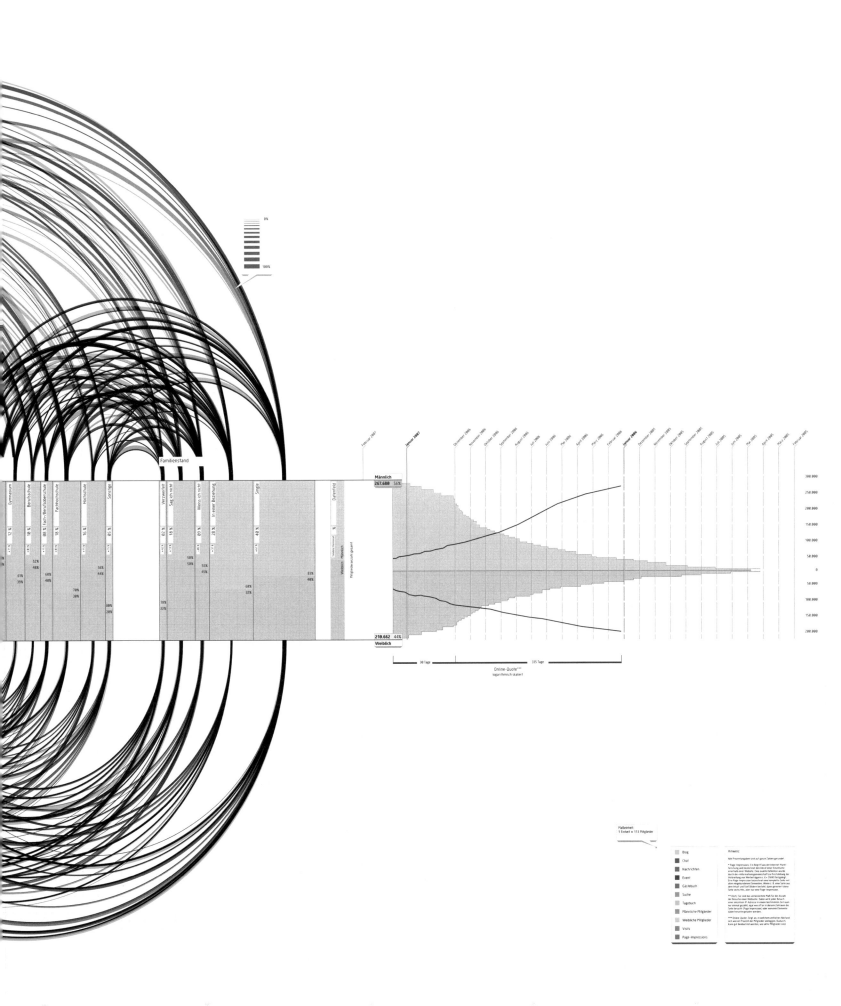

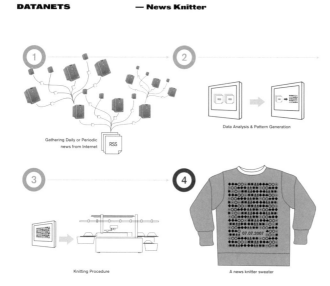

Gathering Daily or Periodic news from Internet — RSS

Data Analysis & Pattern Generation

Knitting Procedure

A news knitter sweater

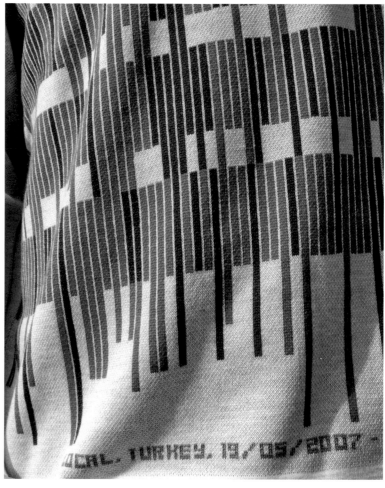

News Knitter MAHIR M. YAVUZ & EBRU KURBAK — Data is anywhere and everywhere. The modern mechanisms of production are all connected to a digital exchange of uninterrupted strings of 1s and 0s. The source and expression of information can be selected at random, and digital data can be turned into analogue artefacts to enhance the designer's desired impact. Fashion gains acceptance from the speed with which this cultural assimilation can be shaped into desirable outfits. In this project, Mahir Yavuz and Ebru Kurbak tap into raw news data to design fashion garments. The process of design and creation is automated, turning semantics into aesthetics. The metaphorical process of weaving draws from, and relies on, the internet's densely connected web of current, topical information.

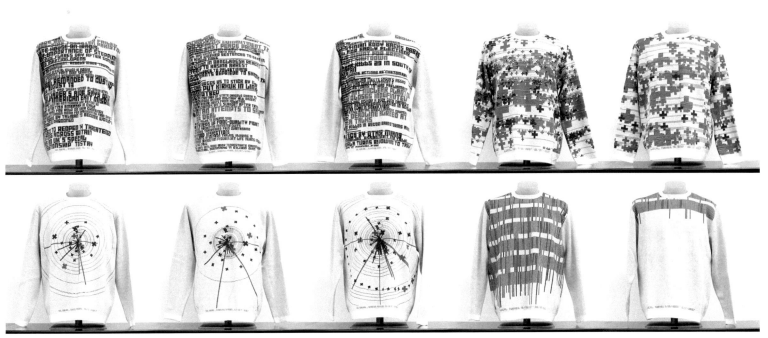

PAGE 001
CAMPBELL ADMITS IT'S ALL **COMPLETE FICTION**
BY M.BROWN

PAGE 001
GOVERNMENT WANTS PERSONAL DETAILS OF EVERY TRAVELLER
BY L.TRAYNOR

PAGE 003
ARRIVING SOON AT STONEHENGE 480 TRUCKS A DAY FROM TESCO'S 'MEGASHED'
BY J.FINCH

PAGE 004
FREE SCHOOL MEAL PUPILS LOSE OUT IN RACE FOR TOP A-LEVELS
BY P.CURTIS

PAGE 004
CAMERON UNDER FIRE FOR HOLOCAUST 'GIMMICK' REMARK
BY N.WATT

PAGE 005
FORSYTH CELEBRATES 80TH
BY M.KENNEDY

PAGE 005
POLICE CONDEMNED OVER GANG KILLING OF COUPLE
BY M.WAINWRIGHT

PAGE 006
POLICE: 'SALLY ANNE KILLER MUST HAVE STRUCK BEFORE'
BY H.PIDD

PAGE 006
PROFILE: MARK DIXIE
BY H.PIDD

PAGE 007
VERDICTS PROMPT CALLS FOR NATIONAL REGISTER
BY J.SAMPLE

PAGE 007
'WITHOUT DOUBT, IT IS RIGHT THAT HE SHOULD SPEND THE REST OF YOUR LIFE IN PRISON'
BY K.MCVEIGH, E.ADDLEY

PAGE 008
CLAMPDOWN CALL ON WEB PIRACY
BY R.WRAY, M.BROWN

PAGE 008
I WANT TO LIVE WITH MY DAD MISSING GIRL'S MESSAGE ON WALL
BY M.WAINWRIGHT

PAGE 009
JOWELL'S HUSBAND CRITICISED FOR ABSENCE FROM COURT HEARING
BY J.HOOPER

PAGE 009
IPHONE USERS RISK A £1,000 UNHAPPY RETURN FROM HOLIDAY
BY M.BRIGNALL

PAGE 010
DIANA CORONER ASKS FORMER ROYAL BUTLER TO COME BACK TO COURT
BY S.JONES

PAGE 010
FIREFIGHTERS BALK AT 41ST MAN'S BULK
BY S.CARRELL

PAGE 011
ST DELIA DEFENDS HER CHEATING WAYS
BY R.WILLIAMS, R.SMITHERS

PAGE 012
PRESCOTT AND HAIN JOIN REBELS TO BACK BILL FOR AGENCY WORKERS
BY N.WATT

PAGE 012
LORRY DRIVER WHO CAUSED FATAL CRASH AFTER FALLING ASLEEP JAILED
BY S.JONES

PAGE 013
DON'T FORGET YOUR PASSPORT ... OR YOUR CREDIT CARD
BY R.SMITHERS

PAGE 014
BRITISH SOLDIERS ACCUSED OF EXECUTING CIVILIANS
BY R.NORTON-TAYLOR

PAGE 014
'I HEARD THE TERRIBLE SOUND OF SOMEONE BEING CHOKED'
BY H.J.ALI, H.F.ABASS

PAGE 015
THE LAWYERS
BY C.DYER

PAGE 016
TICKING THE BOXES BEFORE TRYING TO SAVE LIVES
BY B.GOLDACRE

PAGE 017
AND THE BILL? IT'S WHATEVER YOU WANT TO PAY
BY S.JONES

PAGE 017
JUDGE QUASHES RESTRICTIONS ON MUSLIM CONVERT
BY S.JONES

PAGE 018
CHANGES TO LANGUAGE USED IN FAMILY COURTS UNVEILED
BY C.DYER

PAGE 018
FILM STAR WILL SMITH WINS DAMAGES OVER HITLER CLAIM
BY L.HOLMWOOD

PAGE 018
PLANNERS FAILED TO PROTECT WILDLIFE, COURT TOLD
BY PA

PAGE 018
RUSSIA DROPS LEGAL BATTLE TO EXTRADITE TYCOON
BY PA

PAGE 018
SCOTLAND'S INMATE TOTAL REACHES RECORD HIGH
BY S.CARRELL

PAGE 018
WOMAN RESCUED AFTER FALL FROM BRIDGE
BY PRESS ASSOCIATION

PAGE 018
WOMAN WINS £4.1M IN HOSPITAL NEGLIGENCE CLAIM
BY AGENCY

PAGE 019
BACK IN THE SPOTLIGHT
BY L.HOLMWOOD

PAGE 019
BIG NAMES IN FASHION GET IN SHAPE FOR THE OSCARS
BY J.CARTNER-MORLEY

PAGE 020
MAGISTRATES HIT BACK AT CALL TO JAIL FEWER PEOPLE
BY C.DYER

PAGE 020
UCL ACTS AFTER CREATIONIST COUP
BY J.SAMPLE

PAGE 020
THEME PARK FACES SAFETY CHARGES OVER GIRL'S DEATH ON WATER RIDE
BY H.PIDD

PAGE 021
MONICA'S STORY: RESCUED VICTIM OF CHILD TRAFFICKERS OR KIDNAPPED BY ITN CREW?
BY T.CONLAN, C.JONESCU

PAGE 022
A QUESTION OF INQUIRIES
BY S.HOGGART

PAGE 023
CONTROVERSIAL ANNE FRANK MUSICAL HITS THE RIGHT NOTE WITH SPANISH AUDIENCES
BY P.HAMILOS

PAGE 023
ISRAELI MAYOR OF BOMBARDED BORDER TOWN OFFERS TO BREAK RANKS AND TALK TO HAMAS
BY T.O'LOUGHLIN

PAGE 026
CLOUDS GATHER AS **'SULKY' MUSHARRAF** RETREATS TO BUNKER
BY D.WALSH

PAGE 027
EXPLAINER: WHAT HAPPENS NEXT
BY D.WALSH

PAGE 028
KHMER ROUGE PRISON CHIEF TO TAKE JUDGES ON TOUR OF KILLING FIELDS
BY I.MACKINNON

PAGE 028
TURKISH FORCES STAGE RAID INTO IRAQ
BY M.HOWARD

PAGE 028
US TO EVACUATE **SERBIA** DIPLOMATS
BY M.LEE

PAGE 029
THE 'FRENCH CHERNOBYL' THAT HAS POISONED THE RHÔNE'S FISH
BY A.CHRISAFIS

PAGE 030
'MY JOB IS TO RATIFY THE CHOICE OF THE PEOPLE'
BY H.KNETZER, S.SPENCER, B.MILLER, J.GREENLEAF

PAGE 030
RIGHT RALLIES TO MCCAIN OVER 'HATCHET JOB'
BY S.GOLDENBERG

PAGE 030
SUPERDELEGATES SWITCHING ALLEGIANCE TO **OBAMA**
BY E.SCHOR, D.GLAISTER

PAGE 031
WHISTLE WHILE YOU WORK
BY D.LEIGH, J.FRANKLIN

PAGE 032
GOD'S LITTLE ACRES SIT **SMUGLY** IN THE KNOWLEDGE THEIR VALUE IS **SOARING**
BY I.JACK

PAGE 033
"I'M DISGUSTED BY THE OLD ME"
BY N.DEJONGH

PAGE 038
BULLISH LLOYDS TSB INCREASES DIVIDEND
BY J.TREANOR

PAGE 038
HIGH STREET DOWNTURN FINALLY HITS JOHN LEWIS
BY J.FINCH

PAGE 038
NATWEST THREE JAILED FOR 37 MONTHS
BY A.CLARK

PAGE 039
NPOWER ADDS FUEL TO ANGER OVER PROFITS
BY D.GOW

PAGE 039
US TELLS EUROPE TO STOP DITHERING OVER PIPELINE
BY D.GOW

PAGE 040
BAT SHARES BENEFIT FROM TURKISH BUY
BY K.ALLEN

PAGE 040
SANDWICH SHOPS SOLD
BY GUARDIAN

PAGE 040
SUEZ AND HANDS LOOK AT JOINT BID FOR BIFFA
BY M.MILNER

PAGE 040
VW WORKERS' LEADER JAILED FOR TWO YEARS
BY D.GOW

PAGE 041
ROCK LOOKS HEADED FOR A BREAK-UP
BY J.TREANOR, D.TEATHER

LEGEND
UK NEWS
BUSINESS
WORLD NEWS CULTURE
POLITICS TECHNOLOGY
ENVIRONMENT LIFE & STYLE MEDIA
SPORT MONEY PEOPLE SCIENCE EDUCATION
CATEGORIES BY POPULARITY

Information
Headlines are colour coordinated by category, and arranged across a grid in the order they appear in the paper. Authors of multiple articles are linked, and can be tracked through the paper by their articles. Special sections of the paper become apparent by the patterns formed between article, category, and position.

One week of
The Guardian
February 23rd 2008

Further documentation is available at www.designingnews.com

—— One week of the Guardian: Saturday DESIGNING THE NEWS — This is another work portraying news presentation in the *Guardian* over a week of reporting events. By its very absence, the network emphasises diversity of views. And by connecting articles written by the same contributors, it becomes obvious that the *Guardian*'s critical views are maintained by combining perspectives from various sources. On another level, the viewer is able to make his or her own content connections by applying the colour-coded sectional classification of the headlines. The diversity of content and voices is expressed with depth and subtlety. **—— RFID-Systeme** PROJEKTTRIANGLE — Radio-frequency identification (RFID) systems are radically changing the opportunities for intuitive object behaviour and design. They make possible the intelligent recognition of, and connection between, a multitude of unrelated objects. They engender a pervasive awareness, penetrating shopping bags, buildings, and personal identities.

This topic was discussed in numerous articles in the March 2008 issue of *Design Report* magazine. Projekttriangle designed the magazine cover to reflect the essential connectedness and implicit transparency that this technology brings to the world.

An analysis of the different articles on RFID systems provides the framework for related topics. The magazine's flatplan turns into a series of containers for meaning and reference. The connection lines jump from an RFID tag like radio signals between connected keywords.

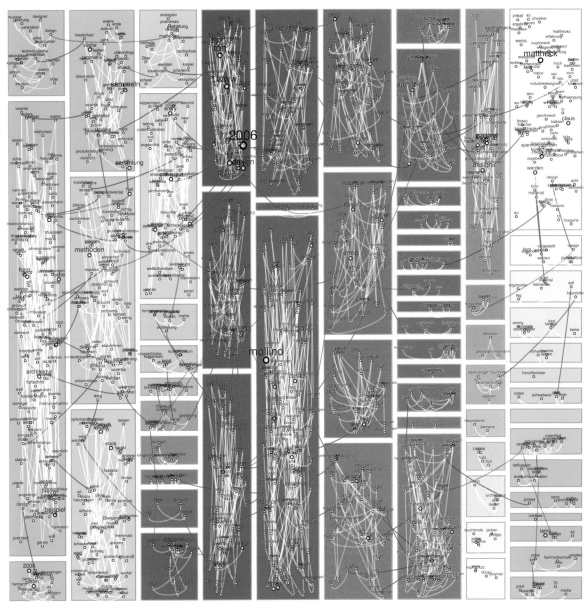

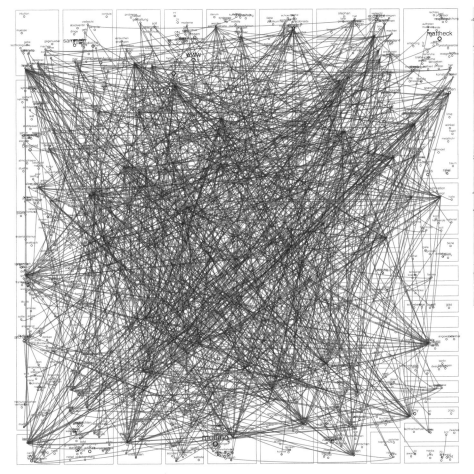

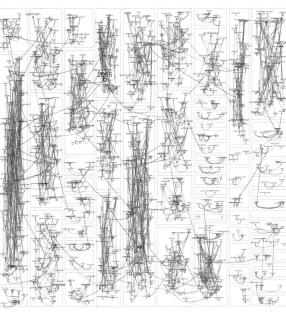

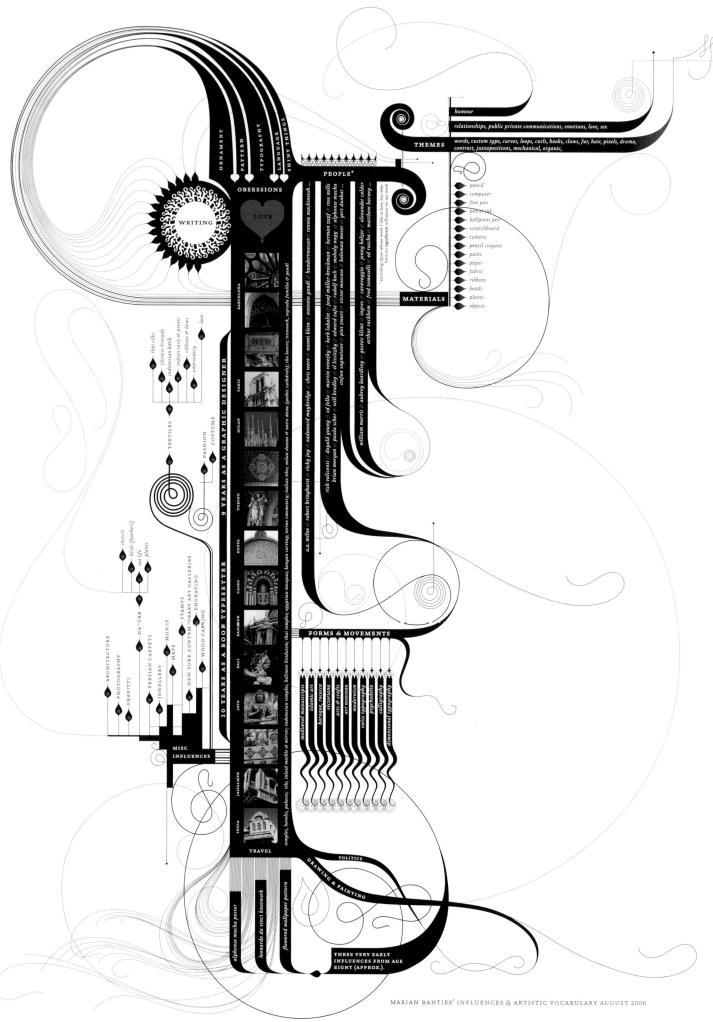

MARIAN BANTJES' INFLUENCES & ARTISTIC VOCABULARY AUGUST 2006

SENTENCE
DRAWINGS

The entirety of *On the Road*,
by Jack Kerouac

WORD COUNT

BASIC STRUCTURE

COLORS

PREVIOUS PAGES — **Influence Map**
MARIAN BANTJES — Wines are identified by region, just as their fragrance, intensity, and character are determined by the unique combination of climatic and geographic influences that bring them into being. The subtle bouquet of a Bordeaux or the bold notes of a Barolo emerge from the grape's exposure to its physical surroundings.
As artists grow and develop, they assume the tone, and reflect the influences, of their personal cultural and intellectual position. In this confection, Marian Bantjes's personal pastiche is brought out by the flow and connection of significant life experiences. The Alfons Mucha posters of early youth, Polaroid snapshots from travelling, and main themes and interests all blend into a personal tale of artistic influence. Their style both reflects, and derives from, the journey it represents. The subtle, sometimes tangential, web of connections that only the artist can appreciate, floats like a fragrance over the page, reflecting the roots and sources of its inspiration. — **Sentence Drawings Poster** |▷ P. 78| STEFANIE POSAVEC — A continuous line folds, and then folds back on itself, to become a dense web of literary expression. Using a simple process, Stefanie Provasec traced each sentence in Jack Kerouac's novel *On the Road*. The length of the line in each sentence is determined by the number of words, and its colour by the thematic reference. After each sentence, the line takes a right turn to continue the unfolding journey.

— **Sustainability Map** LUST — Here, density, complexity, and design itself are used to illustrate the impact of the socially important parameter of sustainability on the design world. How does sustainability filter through into design firms, and how is the thinking on this issue becoming enmeshed within the design community? Using the Web 2.0 technology del.icio.us tags, LUST shows how far different design companies, projects, and institutions are connected with the various aspects of sustainability. The density of the network implies intensity, while absence means a lack of focus or attention. In the diagram, connected and engaged designers are easily identified, as are the topics receiving the most attention.

By containing the network within a clear, defined frame of text and tags, the piece reinforces the importance of sustainability as an inescapable constraint in modern design. The lines run over the text to show that no-one can avoid being affected by it.
— **Overnewsed but uninformed** |▷ PP. 104, 242| STEFAN BRÄUTIGAM — Dominating to the point of stridency, the bold colours indicate different regions of the world, connecting the relative rankings of individual countries. Strikingly, a clear difference can be seen between TV and newspaper rankings for each country. As literacy becomes more widespread, the regional newspapers are far more tightly clustered, whereas the regions fan out more broadly in the TV rankings. Income, rather than literacy, is the key driver here.

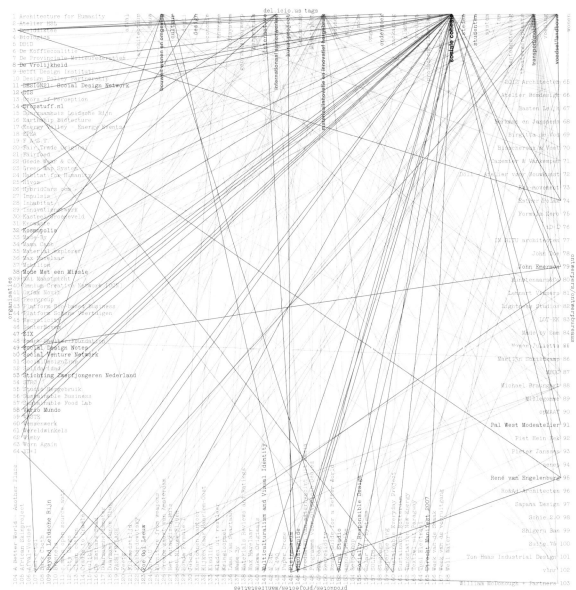

8. Netwerk van kunstenaars, theatermakers en musici zet zich in voor een veilige en vrolijke toekomst van jonge vluchtelingen. 11. Site waar ontwerpers, sociaal bewuste mensen, bedrijven en non-profitorganisaties sociale kwesties kunnen bespreken en slimme designoplossingen kunnen ontwikkelen. 12. DIS presenteert het 'Sustainable Everyday Project' door middel van een boek met cases over duurzame sociale innovatie en stelt scenarios-in-progress voor om de sociale conversatie te stimuleren. 14. Een communicatieplatform van René van Engelenburg (95) voor jongeren reist als mobiel platform van 2007–2009 langs 12 steden in Nederland. 32. Kosmopolis

is een onconventioneel nationaal en internationaal multimediaal platform dat kunst en cultuur inzet om een diepgaande dialoog tussen bevolkingsgroepen te voeden. 38. Stichting die dak- en thuisloze vrouwen een zinvolle dagbesteding geeft door hen in te zetten bij het ontwikkelen van een hoogwaardig modelabel Ami-e-toi. 47. SIX is gericht op sociale innovatie en brengt mensen en organisatie samen die betrokken zijn bij innovaties op het gebied van technologie, design, mvo, openbaar beleid, gemeente en binnen gemeenten en het bedrijfsleven. 49. Blog van ontwerper John Emerson (79) over sociaal design. 50. Network van ondernemers die sociaal en

milieubewust zijn en zich willen inzetten voor een verandering in de manier waarop de wereld zaken doet. 53. Zet zich in voor een structurele verbetering van de leefsituatie van thuisloze jongeren. 58. Stichting voor kunst en cultuur in Vathorst, Amersfoort. Samen met bewoners, culturele instellingen en kunstenaars geeft Vario Mundo de wijk een cultureel gezicht en bouwt zij aan een kunst- en cultuurprogramma dat bijdraagt aan de culturele identiteit. 60. Wensenwerk is de praktische inzet van mensen die werk maken van hun wensen voor de samenleving en daarmee zelf het voorbeeld worden. Een van hun projecten is de wenswijk, waarbij kinderen

hun wensen voor hun buurt aan de gemeente kenbaar kunnen maken. 91. Jongeren in Amsterdam West maken hun eigen ontwerpen onder begeleiding van jonge ontwerpers. 109. Het scenario: 'Beyond Leidsche Rijn, de Vinex-opgave voor de verkenning van de relaties tussen beeldende kunst, het landschap, stedelijk leven en het bouwprogramma in Leidsche Rijn. 123. YD-I en Kunstenaars & Co willen met Chinese kandidaten onderzoeken welke rol dit complex van 54 seniorenwoningen voor Chinezen in Amsterdam Zuid-Oost kan spelen in de buurt en in de Chinese ouderengemeenschap van Nederland. 141. Welke rol kunnen designers

spelen in het definiëren van de juiste identiteit en communicatievorm van individuen en bedrijven in een samenleving vol spanningen tussen groepen mensen door diversiteit in sociale, culturele en religieuze achtergronden. 145. Podium voor visuele communicatie waar kunstenaars en ontwerpers kunnen communiceren met een breed publiek binnen de context van de openbare ruimte. Project van René van Engelenburg (95). 146. Een stad is behalve straten en stenen ook een verzameling ervaringen en gesprekken. PR Audioguide is een telefonisch netwerk dat deze gemeenschappelijke informatie interactief en peer-to-peer verspreidt, deelt en genereert. 152.

Opleiding aan de Auburn University, Alabama richt zich op het samen met studenten ontwikkelen van bouwwerken voor de arme lokale gemeenschap. 155. Site van de Engelse denktank Design Policy Partnership van de University of Salford, Sheffield en de Hallam University. 165. Internationale culturele biënnale, die hedendaagse ontwikkelingen in design en architectuur belicht vanuit een sociaal perspectief.

OVERNEWSED BUT UNINFORMED

BONUSPOSTER [001_002]

Welches Land hat die meisten und die wenigsten Tageszeitungen und Fernseher im Verhältnis zur Einwohnerzahl

Gewicht nach Anzahl Verbindungen

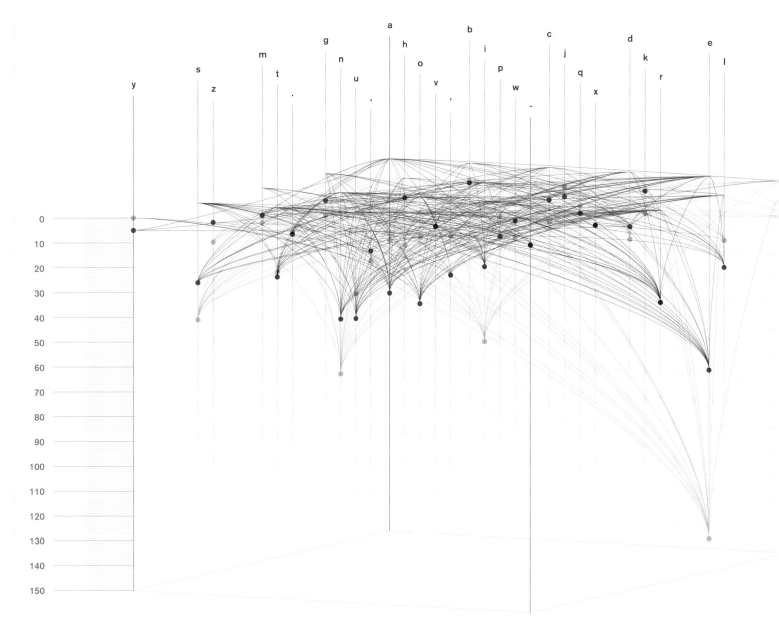

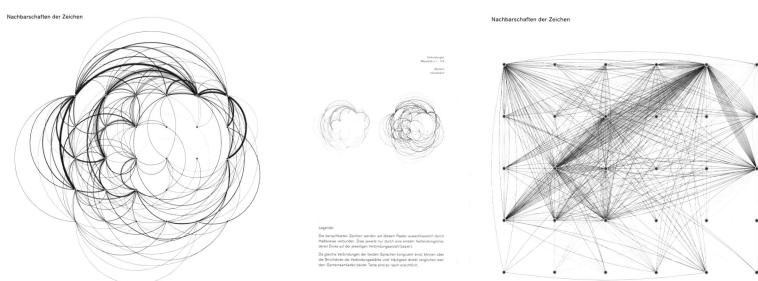

Nachbarschaften der Zeichen

Nachbarschaften der Zeichen

Legende:

Die benachbarten Zeichen werden auf diesem Raster ausschliesslich durch Halbkreise verbunden. Dies jeweils nur durch eine einzeln Verbindungslinie, deren Dicke auf der jeweiligen Verbindungsanzahl basiert.

Da gleiche Verbindungen der beiden Sprachen kongruent sind, können über die Strichdicke der Verbindungsstärke und -häufigkeit direkt verglichen werden. Gemeinsamkeiten beider Texte sind so rasch ersichtlich.

— **Metaphorisch/Métaphorique**
DAVID JORDI — Thirty basic reference points in a German and a French text are identified and compared. These reference points are extracted and run through various forms of analysis, to produce the magenta (German) and cyan (French) diagrams. By the accuracy and delicacy of its depiction, the axiomatic extrusion in the presentation supports the metaphor of language and meaning as a gossamer web of connected thoughts.

NEXT PAGES — **Literary Organism Poster** STEFANIE POSAVEC — The simple tree structure flourishes into a network of connections, as colour-coded themes build oblique connections across the topology of Jack Kerouac's novel *On the Road*. Chapters divide into paragraphs, and paragraphs into sentences, the granular distribution of themes striking out across the entire expanse of the novel. Viewers are impelled to reassess its configuration as they build their own links, which are independent of the formal hierarchy of the tree structure.
— **Alchemy/Süddeutsche Zeitung, 19th February 2007**
|▸P. 80| SUZANNE TREISTER, courtesy Annely Juda Fine Art, London — Here we see myth and legend, purveyed by the power-hungry spirits of the night. This evocative depiction of news, as presented by various international newspapers, harks back to images from the Dark Ages. Today, the tabloids peddle graphic stories that are little more than pictographic networks of superstition. Is modern reporting any different from the alchemistic pursuits of an unenlightened age? The hand-drawn content becomes a visual metaphor for human intervention in the process of selecting and editing the news. Structures of power and worship are recreated, with the sources of truth and knowledge elevated above the message. The path to enlightenment is clearly monopolised by the one true fount of wisdom.

Verbindungen
Massstab = 1 : 2.8

französisch
deutsch

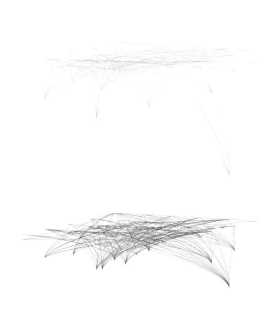

Legende:

Mit der Anzahl Verbindungen von und zu einem Buchstaben, erhöht sich dessen Gewicht. Demnach verschieben sich die Rasterpunkte entsprechend auf ihrer Achse nach unten, wobei ihre Verbindungsreferenzen zum Raster erhalten bleiben.

In der Multiplikation beider Sprachen findet so entlang der Buchstabenachse ein Verglich in der Gewichtung der Zeichen statt. Dunkle Stellen weisen zudem auf gemeinsame Verbindungsfrequenzen in beiden Sprachen hin.

Flächen nach Anzahl Verbindungen

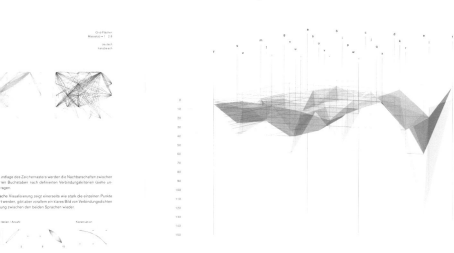

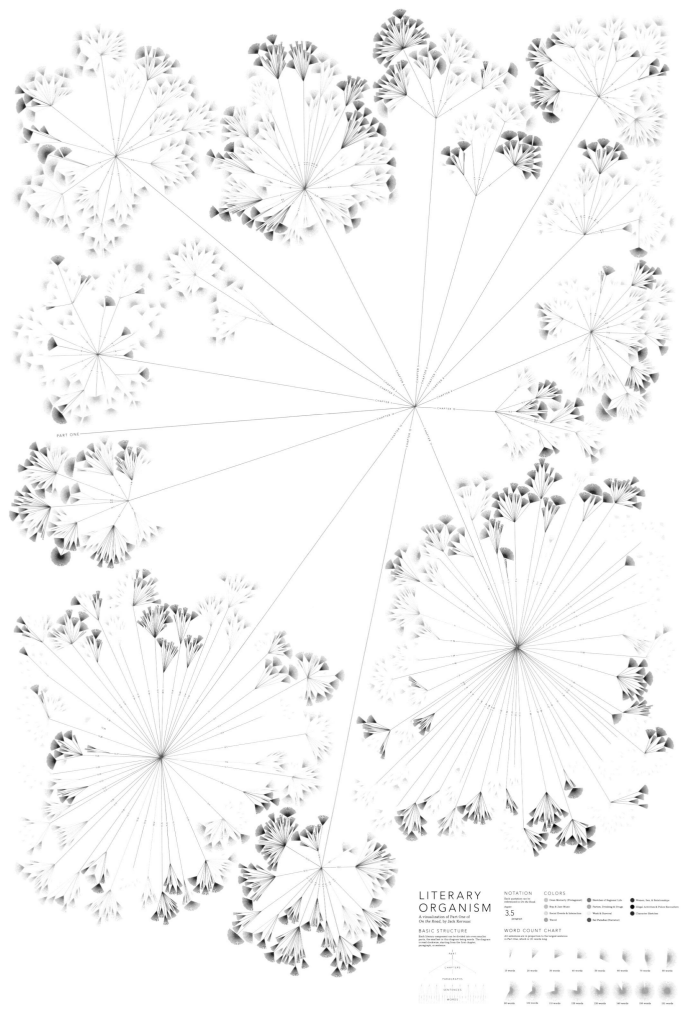

LITERARY
ORGANISM

A visualization of Part One of
On the Road, by Jack Kerouac

BASIC STRUCTURE

Each literary component can be divided into even smaller
parts, the smallest in this diagram being words. The diagram
is read clockwise, starting from the first chapter,
paragraph, or sentence.

NOTATION

Each quotation can be
referenced in *On the Road*,
chapter:

3.5
paragraph

COLORS

- Dean Moriarty (Protagonist)
- Bop & Jazz Music
- Social Events & Interaction
- Travel
- Sketches of Regional Life
- Parties, Drinking & Drugs
- Work & Survival
- Sal Paradise (Narrator)
- Women, Sex, & Relationships
- Illegal Activities & Police Encounters
- Character Sketches

WORD COUNT CHART

All sentences are in proportion to the largest sentence
in Part One, which is 151 words long.

— **Alchemy / The Times, 27th June 2007** SUZANNE TREISTER, courtesy Annely Juda Fine Art, London —————— **HEXEN 2039** SUZANNE TREISTER — In 1995, the artist Suzanne Treister created the fictional alter ego Rosalind Brodsky, a delusional time traveller who believes herself to be working at the Institute of Militronics and Advanced Time Interventionality (IMATI) in the twenty-first century. Treister uses Brodsky to explore history, global politics, religion, popular culture, sexuality, science, technology, the military, and theories of the future.

HEXEN 2039 charts Brodsky's para-scientific research towards the development of new mind-control technologies for the British military through a series of drawings and diagrams, a video, website, and site-specific interventions. This complex body of work uncovers links between conspiracy theories, occult groups, Chernobyl, witchcraft, the US film industry, British intelligence agencies, Soviet brainwashing, behaviour control experiments by the US Army and recent practices of its Civil Affairs and Psychological Operations Command (PSYOP), and new research in contemporary neuroscience.

A DAY IN THE LIFE OF A NETWORKED DESIGNER'S SMART THINGS OR A DAY IN A DESIGNER'S NE

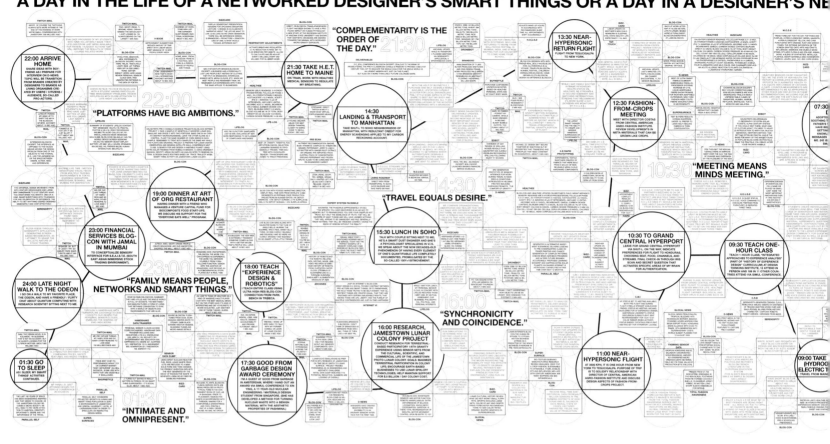

AĞBAĞLANTILI BİR TASARIMCININ HAYATİ YOLU, 1990-2090 *A N*

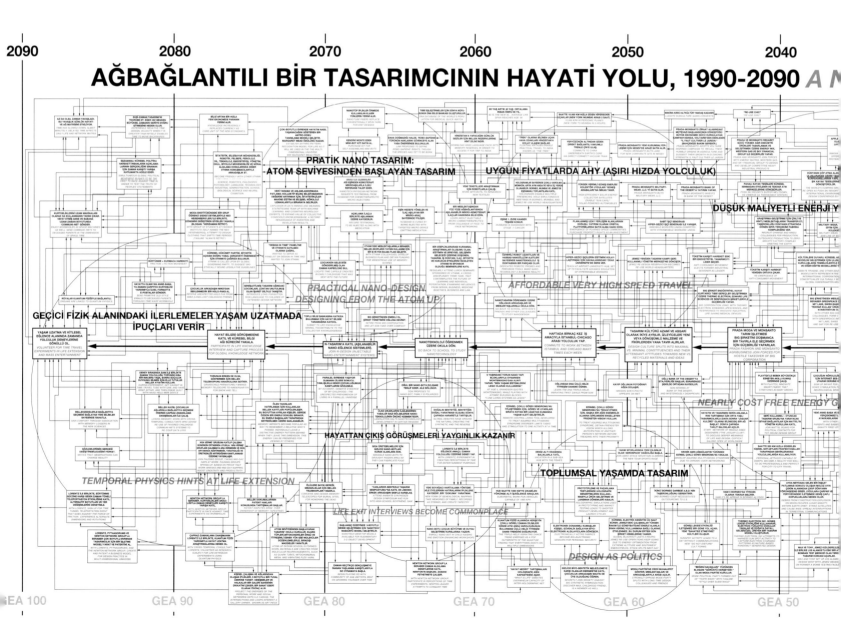

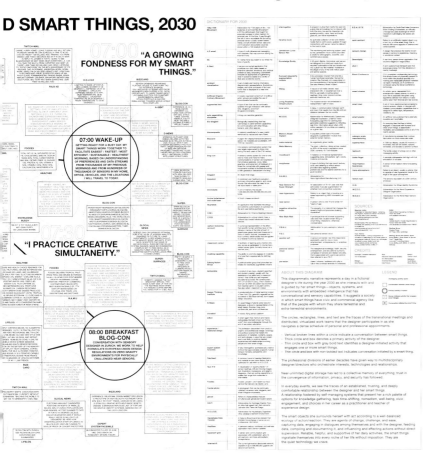

D SMART THINGS, 2030

"A GROWING FONDNESS FOR MY SMART THINGS."

"I PRACTICE CREATIVE SIMULTANEITY."

A Day in the Life of a Networked Designer's Smart Things or A Day in a Designer's Networked Smart Things, 2030 MEDIA A — This diagrammatic narrative represents a day in a fictional designer's life during the year 2030, as she interacts with, and is guided by, her smart things—objects, systems, and environments with embedded intelligence that has conversational and sensory capabilities. The piece suggests a society in which smart things have a civic and commercial agency, like the people with whom they share physical and extra-terrestrial environments. The designer becomes immersed—almost consumed—inside the narrative, where data exchange occurs far more freely and effectively between objects. The designer's role and value are challenged, as the scope for shaping and forming new meaning is either rejected or subsumed. — **A Networked Designer's Critical Path, 1990-2090** MEDIA A — This diagram shows the networked life of a fictional designer, living from 1990 to 2090. It is based on recent history, emerging trends, and leading-edge research, as well as projections from the fields of biology, business, design, information technology, sociology, entertainment, and transportation. It charts the synergies and connections that form, interweave, and dissolve both naturally and by intent. Spheres of experience are connected and evolve as the exchange between diverse concepts becomes intuitive and accepted.

NEXT PAGES — **Hot Love, Swiss Punk & Wave, 1976–1980, Poster** PRILL & VIECELI — Just like the crowded pinboard on a teenager's bedroom wall, the growth and evolution of punk and new wave music in Switzerland are mapped out here. Loose formations between friends mature to become new bands with new influences. Clustered within different cantons, the topology of this definitive sound emerges as a meshing and blending of musicians. The evolution of sound is subtly suggested through text box borders indicating the specific decade during which the band was active. — **Thought Tracker Poster** CHRAGOKYBERNETICKS — Does anyone really know how a thought appears in our consciousness? The random connections between words, as a proxy for our mental reasoning, begin to reveal the random manner in which our thoughts evolve. Diversions, dead ends, and spontaneous connections seduce the viewer into reflecting on how their own concepts emerge from a personal web of meaning.

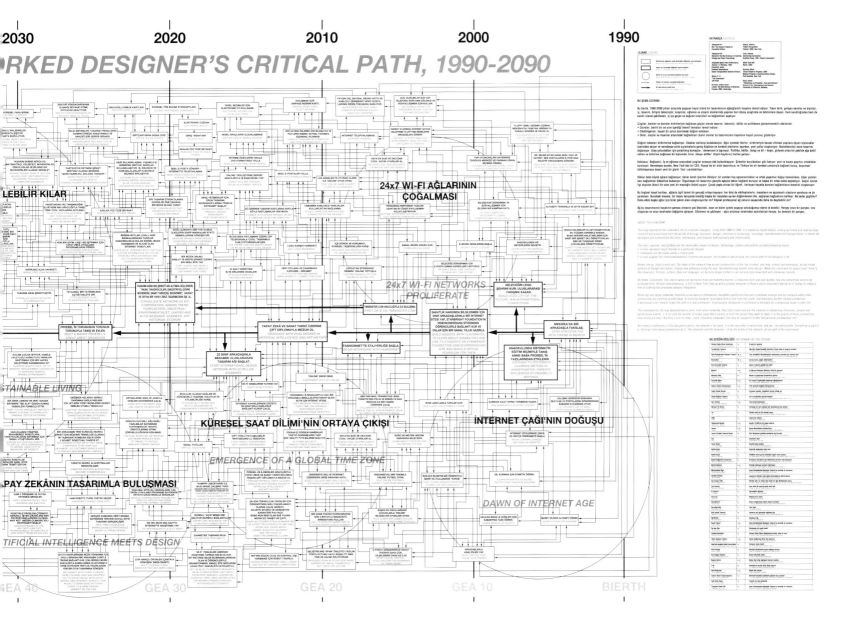

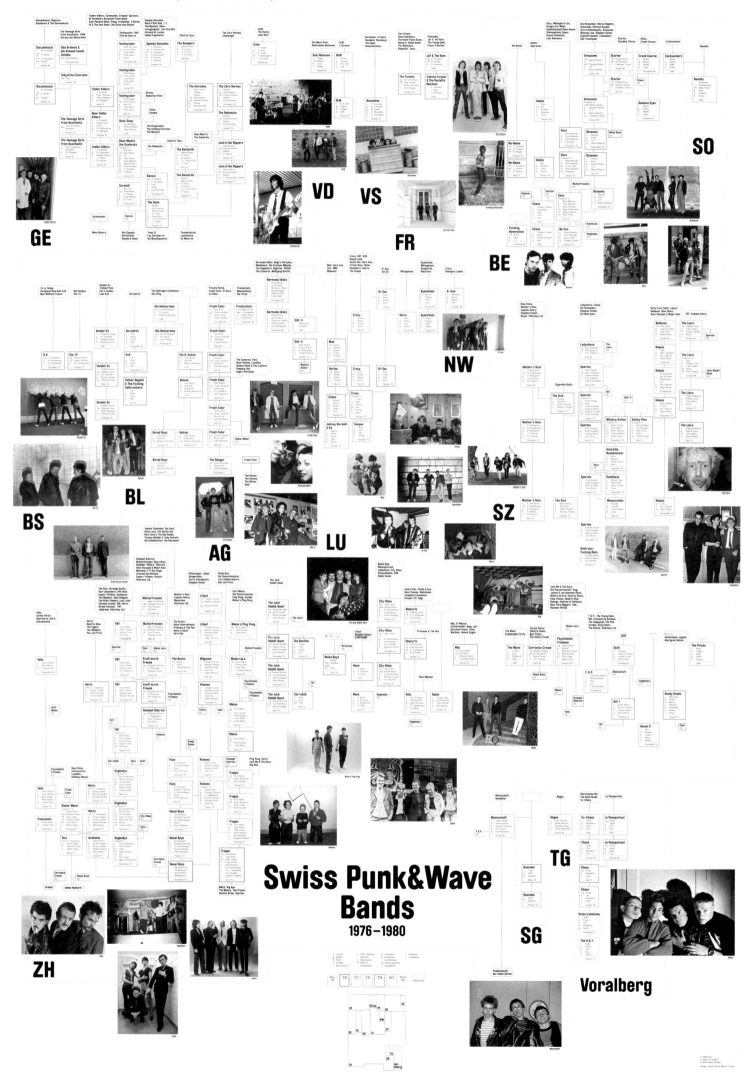

GE

VD

VS

FR

BE

SO

BL

BS

NW

AG

LU

SZ

TG

SG

Swiss Punk&Wave Bands
1976–1980

ZH

Voralberg

IST DER DURCHSCHNITTSSCHWEIZER CHAOSKOMPATIBEL?

(DIES IST EIN VERSUCH, EINEN GEDANKENGANG ZU VERFOLGEN UND SEINE BEWEGUNGEN FESTZUHALTEN. TESTPERSON: CHRISTOPH FREI. — 1'20"3. — 1.22"... — BÖWPLIZ, 3.–3. 2003 15:1 Ü' ...)

———— Social Constellations, Telling Stories of How We Know Who We Know LESLIE KWOK — The stars have come down from the sky to grace us with their invocations of perfection. When the ancient astrologers imposed a significance on the random clusters of luminosity in the night sky, they also wove a tapestry of meaning into the cultural narrative, elevating human experience from mere survival to a quest for betterment. Modern celebrity culture captures the relationships between these glittering earthbound stars in the form of gossip and speculation, filling the newsstands with acres of profitable copy.   In this considered pursuit of celebrity within the social network, Leslie Kwok applies the same mix of diagrammatic visualisation with personal narrative. The individual accounts of members of Kwok's network, recounting how they met certain famous and not-so-famous people, are presented verbatim, next to stylised sociograms. The social network is seen as a horoscope.

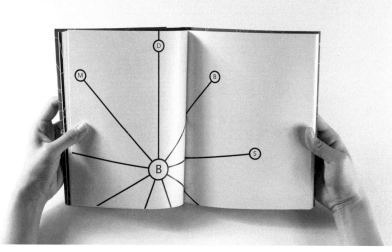

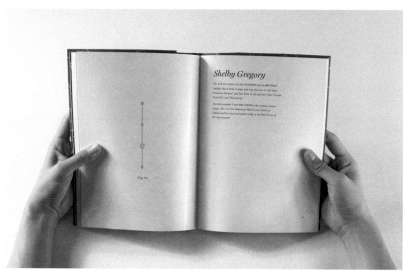

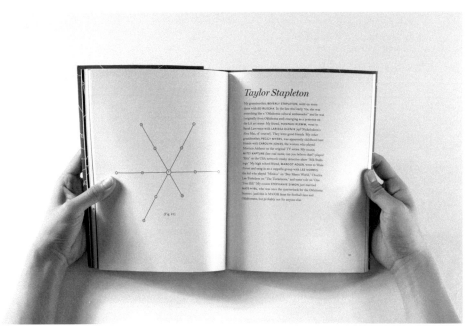

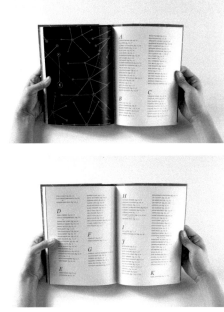

Silvertown Affect Map
October 2007

AFFECT BROWSER

Made using the Affect Browser software
http://softhook.com/affect.htm
Christian Nold 2007

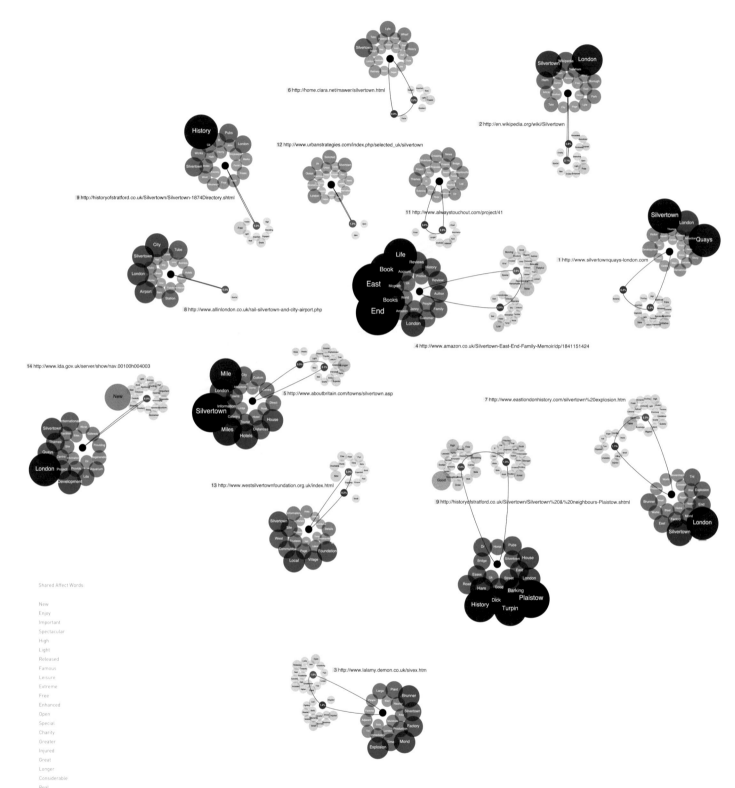

6 http://home.clara.net/mawer/silvertown.html

2 http://en.wikipedia.org/wiki/Silvertown

12 http://www.urbanstrategies.com/index.php/selected_uk/silvertown

9 http://historyofstratford.co.uk/Silvertown/Silvertown-1874Directory.shtml

11 http://www.alwaystouchout.com/project/41

1 http://www.silvertownquays-london.com

8 http://www.allinlondon.co.uk/rail-silvertown-and-city-airport.php

4 http://www.amazon.co.uk/Silvertown-East-End-Family-Memoir/dp/1841151424

14 http://www.lda.gov.uk/server/show/nav.00100h004003

5 http://www.aboutbritain.com/towns/silvertown.asp

7 http://www.eastlondonhistory.com/silvertown%20explosion.htm

13 http://www.westsilvertownfoundation.org.uk/index.html

9 http://historyofstratford.co.uk/Silvertown/Silvertown%20&%20neighbours-Plaistow.shtml

3 http://www.lalamy.demon.co.uk/sivex.htm

Shared Affect Words

New
Enjoy
Important
Spectacular
High
Light
Released
Famous
Leisure
Extreme
Free
Enhanced
Open
Special
Charity
Greater
Injured
Great
Longer
Considerable
Real
Established
Small
Disaster
Lost
Good
Biggest
Interest
Tempted
Favourite
Worst
Excellent
Exciting
Fell
Interesting
Best
Expertise

Websites examined:

1 http://www.silvertownquays-london.com
2 http://en.wikipedia.org/wiki/Silvertown
3 http://www.lalamy.demon.co.uk/sivex.htm
4 http://www.amazon.co.uk/Silvertown-East-End-Family-Memoir/dp/1841151424
5 http://www.aboutbritain.com/towns/silvertown.asp
6 http://home.clara.net/mawer/silvertown.html
7 http://www.eastlondonhistory.com/silvertown%20explosion.htm
8 http://www.allinlondon.co.uk/rail-silvertown-and-city-airport.php
9 http://historyofstratford.co.uk/Silvertown/Silvertown-1874Directory.shtml
10 http://historyofstratford.co.uk/Silvertown/Silvertown%20&%20neighbours-Plaistow.shtml
11 http://www.alwaystouchout.com/project/41
12 http://www.urbanstrategies.com/index.php/selected_uk/silvertown
13 http://www.westsilvertownfoundation.org.uk/index.html
14 http://www.lda.gov.uk/server/show/nav.00100h004003

Silvertown Context

Silvertown is a small area of London in the Thames Estuary which is currently undergoing huge social and environmental changes due to a multitude of large scale regeneration projects taking place there. This is in addition to all the controversial changes that will take place there because the Olympics in 2012. Silvertown used to be crucially important as the site of the Royal Docks and large amounts of related industry. Now the area is mainly a residential area with a smattering of light industrial buildings with the City Airport at its centre.

This map aims to explore what is the nature of online communications and representation of Silvertown. This map was constructed with the Affect Browser software developed by Christian Nold, which carries out automated semiotic analyses of websites and visually represents the resulting data. The software extracts all the text from the web pages and categorises the words into three groups: positive (red clusters), negative (blue clusters) and most frequent content (black cluster). The software contains a number of dictionaries that allow the filtering of these terms into these categories

Mapping Process:

In order to create a discussion survey for Silvertown 14 representative web pages were selected. The website URLs were gathered through Google searches on the term Silvertown as well as local subterms ie. Royal Docks. This process yielded websites whose topics could be categorised as follows in terms of frequency :

1 Property Developers
2 Governmental
3 Historical
4 Transport Information
5 Community

Previous studies using the Affect Browser software have indicated that a mix of positive and negative affect words is a good indicator of a websites "sociality". This concept is based on the notion that sociality requires free speech which is expressed as both positive and negative emotions. Those websites that allow people to express negative emotions are thus more social and conducive to democratic speech

Map Conclusions:

Local schools and community websites were hardly evident when searching on local terms indicating either that bad search terms were being used or more likely that school and community websites are either largely absent or not promoted.

The only Silvertown related websites that contain a healthy balance of both positive and negative affect words are historical websites that that focus in particular on a famous historical explosion of a gunpowder factory.

In conclusion the online representations and discussions about Silvertown are strongly skewed toward governmental and private property developers whose websites do not present any open discussions. The only public discourse about the area focuses on the area's past rather than its imminent future. This worrying lack of democratic speech suggests a critical requirement for initiatives that support local community discourse on the future changes taking place there.

Silvertown Affect Map |>PP. 118, 120| CHRISTIAN NOLD
BIOMAPPING— This work uses the Affect
Browser softhook.com to express visually
the semantic analysis of news coverage focusing on local environmental issues. Positive and negative emotional content is arranged and connected to give a snapshot of
how the local community sees the impact of
major regeneration projects around Silvertown, near the Thames Estuary. The mood
becomes clear as the viewer navigates across
websites, understanding their relationships
with each other and the feelings they express. Red clusters contain positive words,
blue negative, and the terms in black circles
are those most often cited on the websites.

— Universal Digest Machine
MARIUS WATZ, Photo: Paul Litherland
— Meaning is obscured by the density and
mechanisms of connection. The thermal
printer at the centre of this installation explodes into a torrent of reports, documenting spider-bot receipts of a web crawl. The
density of the web soon manifests itself in
the clutter of paper that collects around it.
Our search for meaning is frustrated by the
perceptible flow of information suggested by
the activity. **— Kabbalah Marketing**
PIXELGARTEN — Kabbalah is a Jewish
tradition of mysticism that aims to reveal the
inner meaning of the Tanakh and Rabbinic
literature. Most commonly understood to
be based on the decoding of ciphers contained in the numeric translation of Hebraic
characters, the principle of Kabbalah is applied here to marketing, invoking the quasi-religious nature that its followers ascribe to
its doctrines. The brands Apple, Microsoft,
and Axe are transcribed into Hebrew, then
given a numeric code, which in turn refers
to a Kabbalistic cipher. Few would be surprised to learn that Microsoft reveals its inner meaning as 'beast', while the disruptive
power of Apple is perfectly captured in the
Tarot symbol of The Tower.

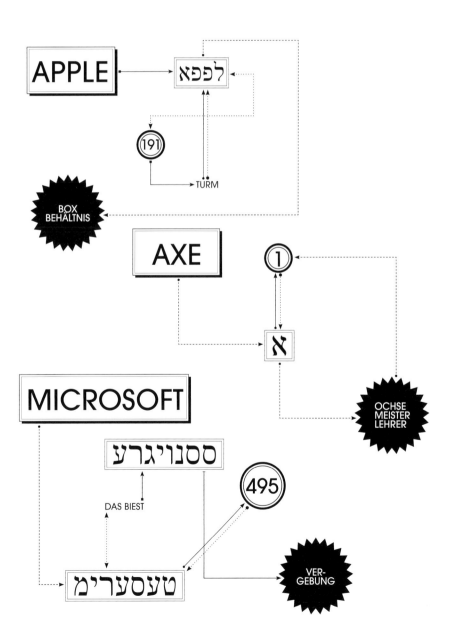

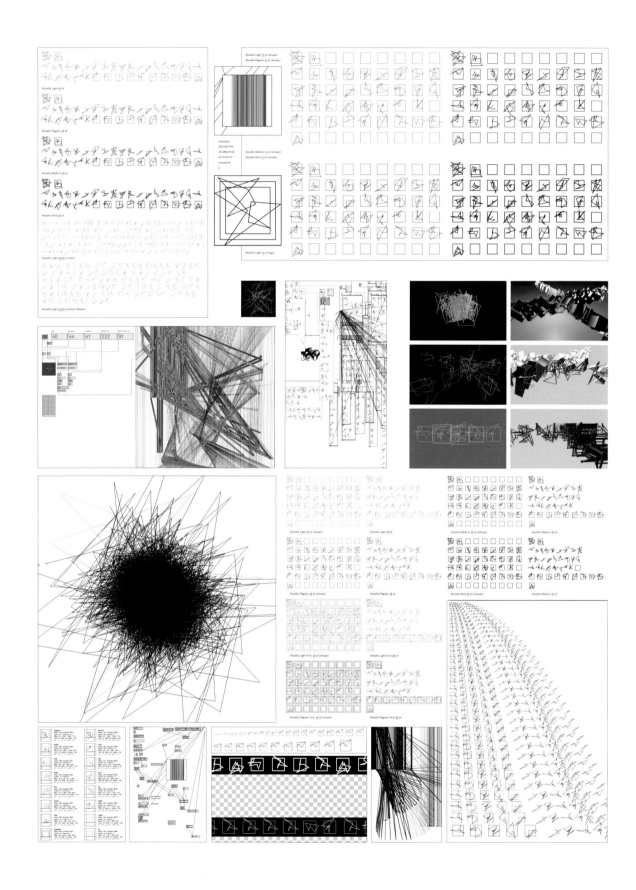

—————— **Abulafia** ADVANCE DESIGN —————— **Feltron 2007 Annual Report** NICHOLAS FELTON —— **Diagrammatic Reading Machine: A visual index of Language of Vision** |›**P. 231**| JACK HENRIE FISHER, University of Illinois at Chicago — 'Visual communication is universal and international; it knows no limits of tongue, vocabulary, or grammar, and it can be perceived by the illiterate as well as by the literate...[The visual arts, as] the optimum forms of the language of vision, are, therefore, an invaluable educational medium.' The immortal words of György Kepes have forged the thinking behind successive generations of design. Becoming both the subject and object of analysis, Kepes's text is transcribed, quantified, analysed and, finally, visualised. Jack Henry Fischer's typographic essay opens up non-linguistic enclosures of modernism to the exigencies

of textuality. The transgressional index of significant terms in Kepes's hermetic text visualises their recurrences and concatenations throughout his book. In the course of this analysis, Fischer brings out the visual ramifications of specific textual technologies: lines of text in printed books, and the crisscrossing linkages that constitute hypertext. —————— **Population réelle** DESIGNSOLDIER, Ecal — When contemplating the role of the individual in society, the word 'network' rapidly becomes a metaphor for a source of diversity and stability. We cherish our network of influences, while we rely on our networks of friends and support. By explicitly providing this network with a rigid structure and contained shape, designsoldier's expression of cultural diversity in Rennes emphasises the way in which individuals rely upon each other in an integrated society. Diversity leads to strength, rather than fear.

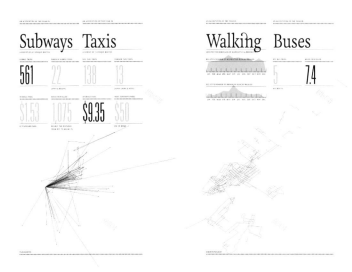

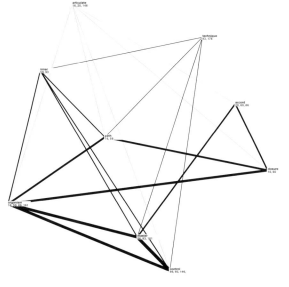

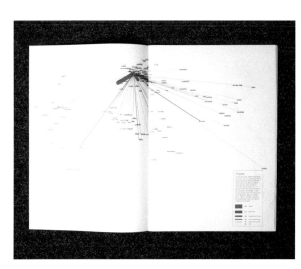

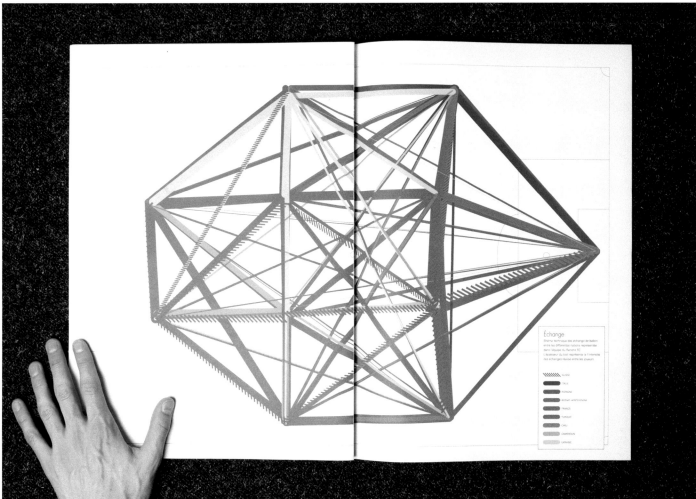

—— **Humanflows** 2NGRY, Miguel Cabanzo in collaboration with Nathan Yau, Mónica Sánchez, Iman Moradi — By connecting influences with results, and people with destinations, Processing provides designers with unprecedented power to reveal the invisible links that confound a simple traditional analysis. This is possible even with those links which often form across several distributed online databases. By observing over fifty years of global migration data, the 'Humanflows' project provides an interactive tool for exploring the multitude of interconnected factors that encourage people to emigrate.

—— **Internet Map: City-to-City Connections (Europe, World)** CHRIS HARRISON, data provided by The Dimes Project — In this piece, 89,344 connections between routers in different cities across Europe express the raw connectivity of the internet. No cities, regions, or national borders are offered as a reference, leaving the viewer to appreciate this representation of the web in its purest form. Stronger connections are enhanced through edge contrast, playing off the stark black-and-white visual.

—— **Cabspotting: An Invisible Dynamics Project** STAMEN — Pulsating, connecting arteries depict the ebb and flow of Yellow Cab taxis through the San Francisco Bay area. Like a beating heart, mobility is visualised in a frame-by-frame analysis of the city's traffic. GPS data tracked over time reveals the residual network of city streets in a visual style intended to be both informative and seductive.

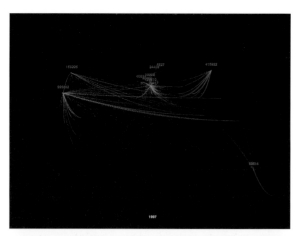

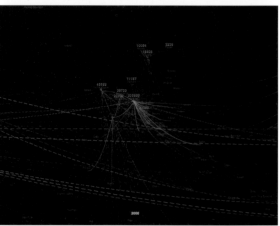

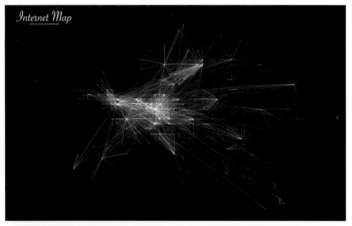

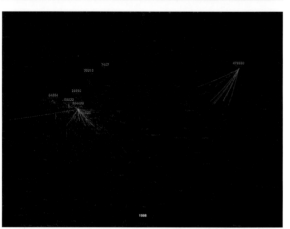

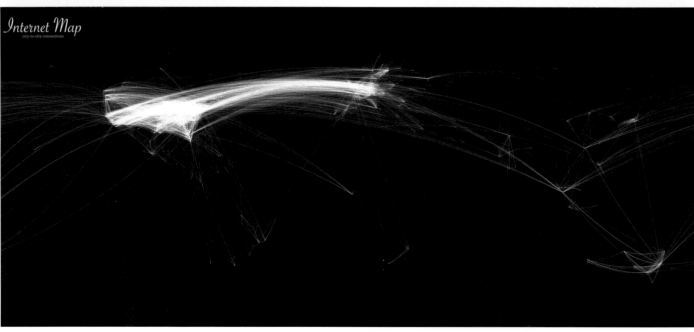

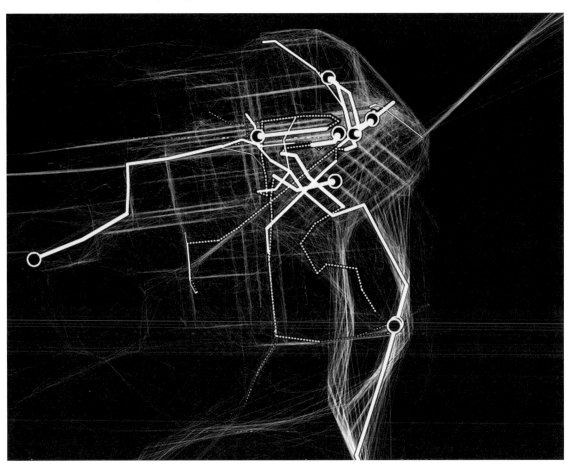

● ATTACKER   ● BOT HERDER    ORDER TO BOT HERDERS   ● BOT   ⟹ ORDER TO BOTS   ⌒ ATTACK   TA

—— **Cyberwar** CATALOGTREE, in collaboration with Lutz Issler — The origins of the internet as a robust communications spine, designed to withstand a nuclear war, are obscured by its pervasive, almost mundane, role in our daily lives. The scenarios of long-range missile strikes against key strategic military targets have for many years been hidden in the mythology of the web.

Modern warfare is economical, with massively distributed denial of service (DDoS) attacks directed at servers. The severity and impact of these attacks bring to mind the ballistic language of long-range arcs of attack, spanning oceans in order to connect continents in deadly engagement. The order to attack spreads quickly through bot herders across the globe, as dumb slave bots launch volleys of useless requests against key stra-

tegic centres to bring them to their knees.

—— **Informational City Distances**
BESTIARIO — Has the internet made the world a smaller place? Or has the digital age created an ever-growing gulf between the web haves and have-nots? How do we measure the virtual space between communities and cultures? Using the proxy of shared web pages for semiological proximity, this three-dimensional schema plots the links between cities. By dividing the number of shared pages by the distance between them, we get a sense of the strength of ties between the cities. This study does not infer context or thematic association, yet provides a strong visual cue as to the web of association that brings cultures closer together, and the strength of the bonds that cross oceans and continents.

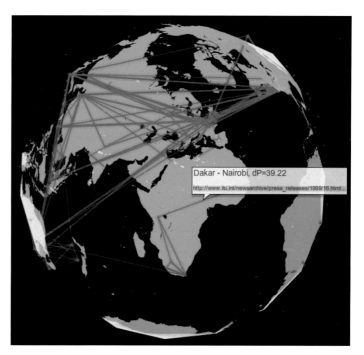

Datascape

—

The origins of the word 'landscape' are ambiguous. Its roots derive either from a combination of 'land' and the Dutch word for 'ship', or the German verb 'schaffen' – to create. In datascapes, both meanings suggest the potency and responsibility of the designer in guiding the viewer through a complex sea of meaning. Elevating the reader from 'Flatland' – the reduced, lessened experience of reality that results from subjecting real experience to two-dimensional expression – they create a journey of context and interaction. Perspective is blended with graphic frameworks to bring depth and meaning to the expression of data.

—

Switching between topography and topology, the spatial arrangement of data imposes flow, direction, context, and order. By mapping geographical data by location, the designer can create a self-referential universe of meaning, where attention, focus, and repetition can be directed for effective explanation.   The intuitive three-dimensional reasoning we apply to the world in order to survive everyday tasks can help us understand and read datascapes. Our experience of depth, order,

—

The spatial arrangement of data imposes flow, direction, context, and order

—

and flow is imposed upon visual expressions of abstracted data. Sound, smell, and arousal quickly become landmarks, inferring a qualitative experience in space.   The ordinal topographic substratum can be either borrowed or generated.

— **Program Théâtre de Vevey 03-04** |›P. 117| WELCOMETO.AS

Using an accurate cartographic representation of Vevey and its surroundings, the designer is invited to turn a theatre's season of performances into a cultural Easter egg hunt. The map anchors the context of the information, while providing an aesthetic inference. Conversely, data can also be arranged deliberately into a topological structure to aid understanding. Imbuing visual explanations with detailed and eclectic context, Salottobuono apply axonometric projection in their visual creations

— **Instructions and Manuals** |›P. 134| SALOTTOBUONO

to describe objects and processes. Layering and separation are used to reveal the inner workings of complex systems, turning data into a landscape of understanding.

Maps are a way of grading information—in this case, land masses—by size. Worldmapper creates new maps by restating land masses in order to provide a visual presentation of demographic data distribution. Borders expand and contract not through the course of rivers or the fall-out from wars, but according to the prevalence of Christians, Muslims, or earthquake victims. The distortion makes an effective datagraph when viewers compare the visual changes with the remembered allocation of countries and continents in their internal world map. Scale is read as spatial reasoning.

— **World maps** |›P. 122| WORLDMAPPER

Topological tableaus reject the formal arrangement of coordinates, leading to a more progressive order. Creamcup's comparison of German and French workflows, and Funnel's depiction of the printing process, float above a neutral white space, building meaning and context as the reader follows an imaginary path through the data. Emergent logic becomes clear through the flow of time.

These illustrative datascapes or 'dataships' transport the

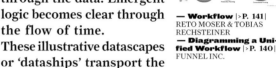

— **Workflow** |›P. 141| RETO MOSER & TOBIAS RECHSTEINER
— **Diagramming a Unified Workflow** |›P. 140| FUNNEL INC.

reader to a deeper understanding of the inner workings and relationships of the subject matter contained in the flow of logic and time. Navigating

—

Scale is read as spatial reasoning

—

the three-dimensional capabilities of the human mind allows a meaning to emerge from a journey through expanded reference and subverted scale.

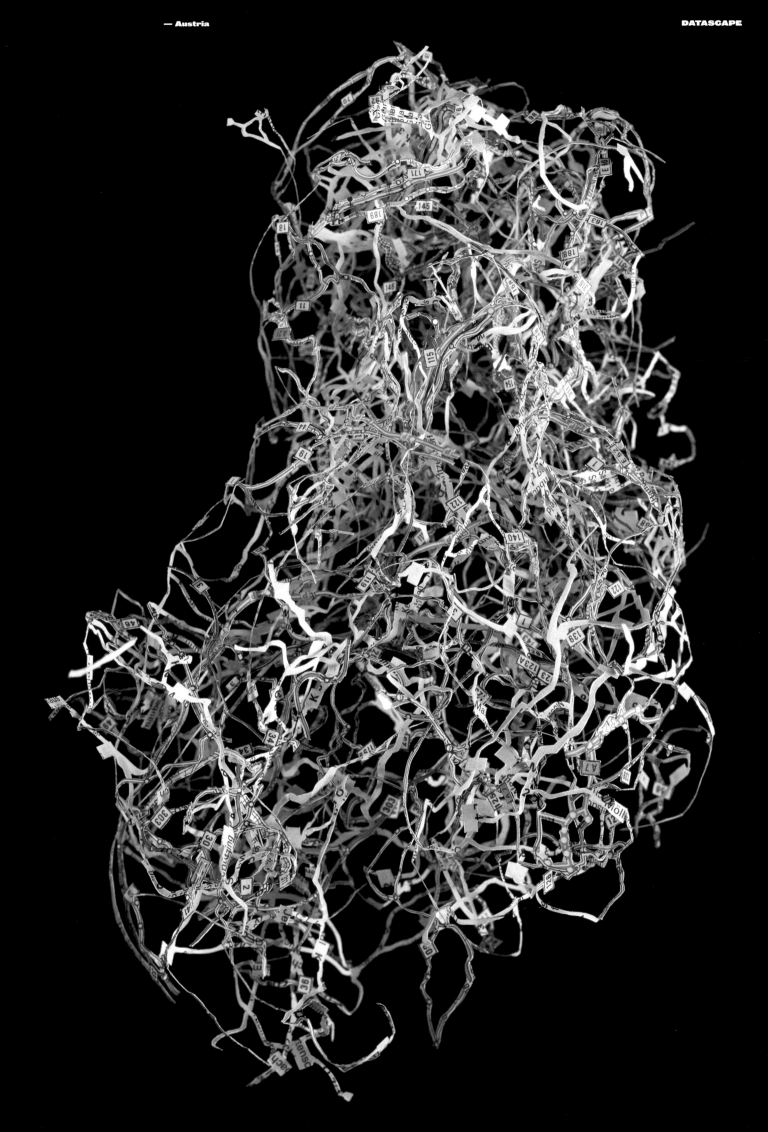

PREVIOUS PAGE ——— **Austria** NINA KATCHADOURIAN — All infographics are, in some way, the designer's attempt to create relevance, insight, and meaning through the deliberate shape, form, and colour we apply to them. In this very literal, yet abstract, presentation, Nina Katchadourian has surgically excised an Austrian paper roadmap and reshaped it in the form of a human heart. Is it the 'heart of Europe' as shown with streets as veins, or are they simply architectural support structures for the economy? The transformed landscape is now open for new levels of interpretation as to how development has shaped human experience.

——— **Cd** PAUL KIRPS — In this CD cover artwork and font design for the rock band Metro, the lines combine, like tracks on the underground, to reveal the message of their urban sound.

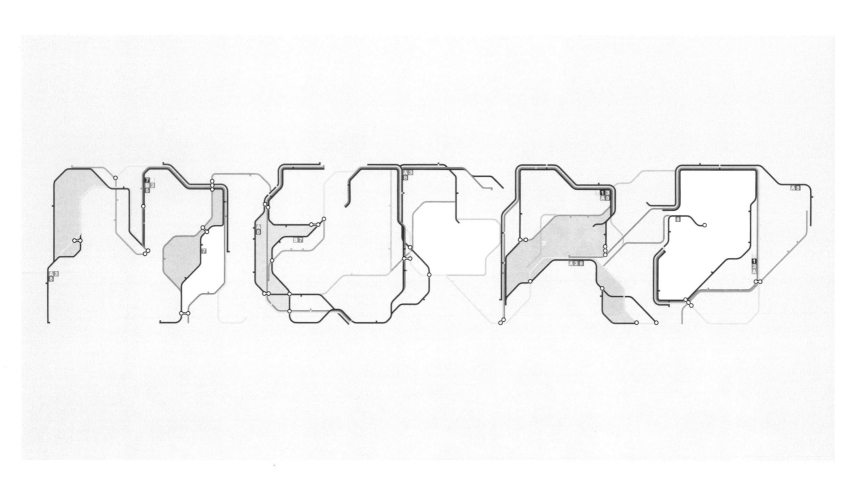

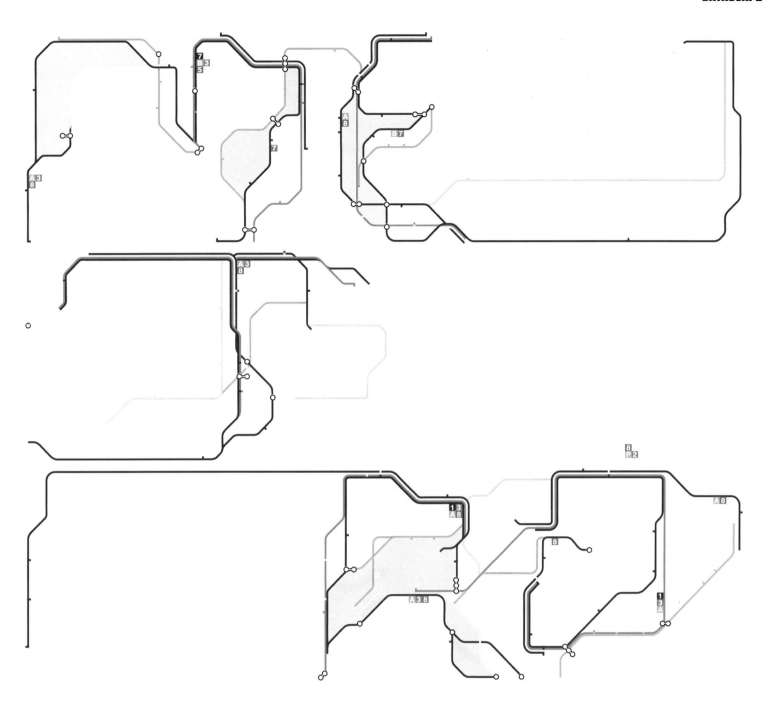

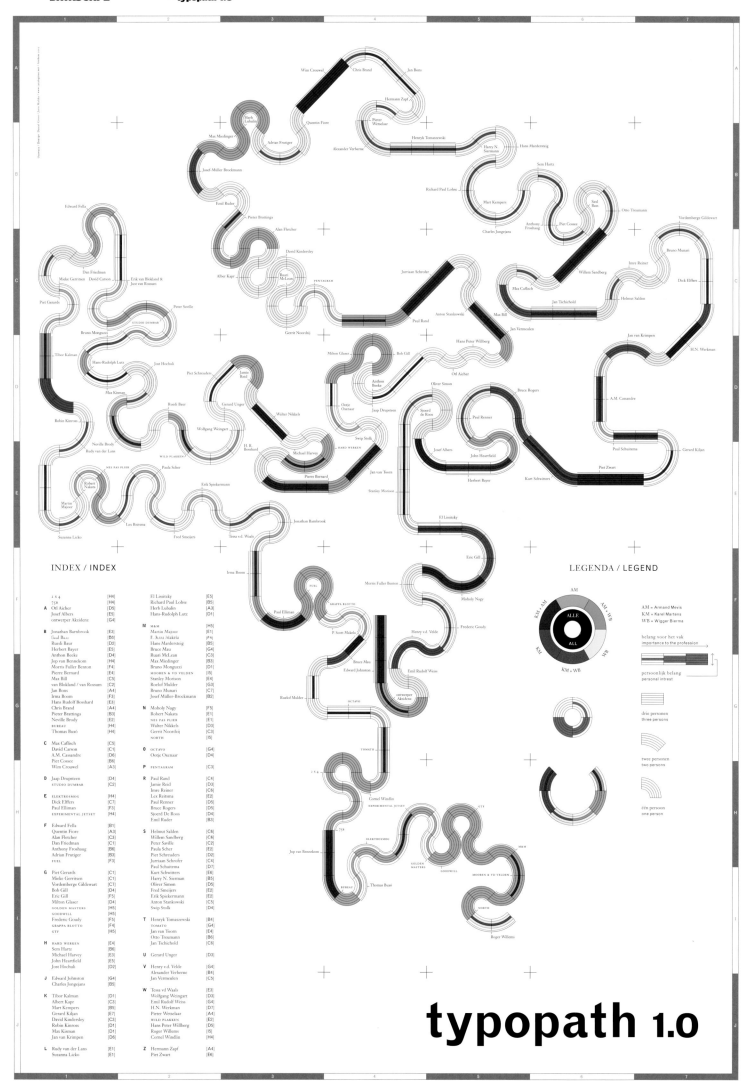

typopath 1.0

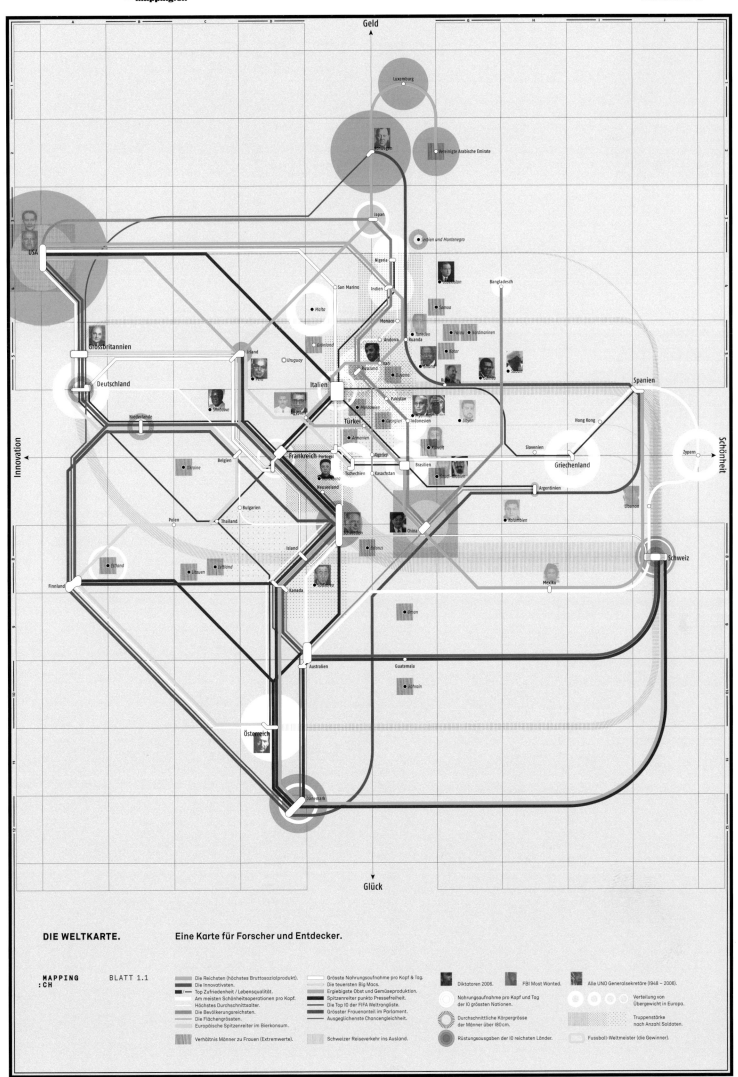

DIE WELTKARTE.   Eine Karte für Forscher und Entdecker.

MAPPING :CH   BLATT 1.1

Die Reichsten (höchstes Bruttosozialprodukt).
Die Innovativsten.
Top Zufriedenheit / Lebensqualität.
Am meisten Schönheitsoperationen pro Kopf.
Höchstes Durchschnittsalter.
Die Bevölkerungsreichsten.
Die Flächengrössten.
Europäische Spitzenreiter im Bierkonsum.

Verhältnis Männer zu Frauen (Extremwerte).

Grösste Nahrungsaufnahme pro Kopf & Tag.
Die teuersten Big Macs.
Ergiebigste Obst und Gemüseproduktion.
Spitzenreiter punkto Pressefreiheit.
Die Top 10 der FIFA Weltrangliste.
Grösster Frauenanteil im Parlament.
Ausgeglichenste Chancengleichheit.

Schweizer Reiseverkehr ins Ausland.

Diktatoren 2006.
FBI Most Wanted.
Alle UNO Generalsekretäre (1948 – 2006).

Nahrungsaufnahme pro Kopf und Tag
der 10 grössten Nationen.

Durchschnittliche Körpergrösse
der Männer über 180 cm.

Rüstungsausgaben der 10 reichsten Länder.

Verteilung von
Übergewicht in Europa.

Truppenstärke
nach Anzahl Soldaten.

Fussball-Weltmeister (die Gewinner).

PREVIOUS PAGES ——— **typopath 1.0** CATALOGTREE — Karel Martens, Wigger Bierma, and Armand Mevis assessed the impact of the top two hundred typographers. The meandering map shows not only who rated whom, but also the importance of their specific influence. Like a stream of thought, five hundred years of typography history cascade through sharp turns of individual opinion and the straight lines of consensus. ——— **mapping:ch** |> P. 230| LORENZO GEIGER — This design is part of Lorenzo Geiger's project, mapping:ch (discussed in more detail in the Datasphere section). The project invites readers to use their fingers to trace a journey through an imaginary, statistical Switzerland.

——— **Overnewsed but uninformed** |> P. 240| STEFAN BRÄUTIGAM — The well-established maps of public transport systems add commentary to our lives, forcing us to re-evaluate media ownership and its concentration. Just as the daily journey to work along a particular underground line shapes our experience of a city, our access to news and information through the controlled pathways of news dissemination shapes our understanding of the world around us. The metaphor of transport strengthens the message of content alignment with political will and financial motives. Given that the final destination of these particular lines is corporate profits, the economic motive behind the media landscape becomes clear. The power that the press wields over its audience and, ultimately, the electorate, raises the question: 'Is the country on the right track?' Through the 'Overnewsed but uninformed' project,

Stefan Bräutigam provides the reader with new opportunities to categorise and evaluate the authenticity of information from specific news sources. ——— **Atlas of the North Sea** |> PP. 108, 109, 110, 111| LUST — The North Sea's planalogical significance is underlined by this complex visualisation, which incorporates a matrix of twenty-one different elements, dissected and combined to reveal unusual combinations of topological expression. Moving beyond simple two-dimensional intersections, this matrix builds in richness and complexity, as particular aspects such as war and waste are overlaid, repositioning the space to a new interpretation. Moving from a simple bathymetric view, factors such as weather and money flows, myths and heroes provide the viewer with an immeasurably rich field of discovery, as science, economics, and history are compressed into a shared seascape.

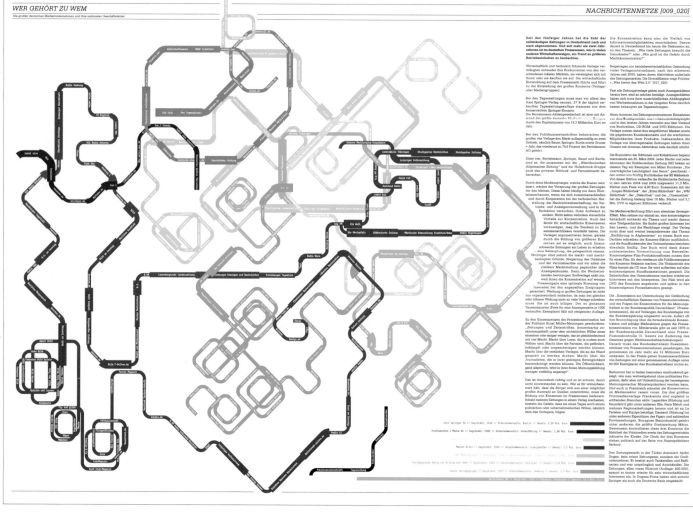

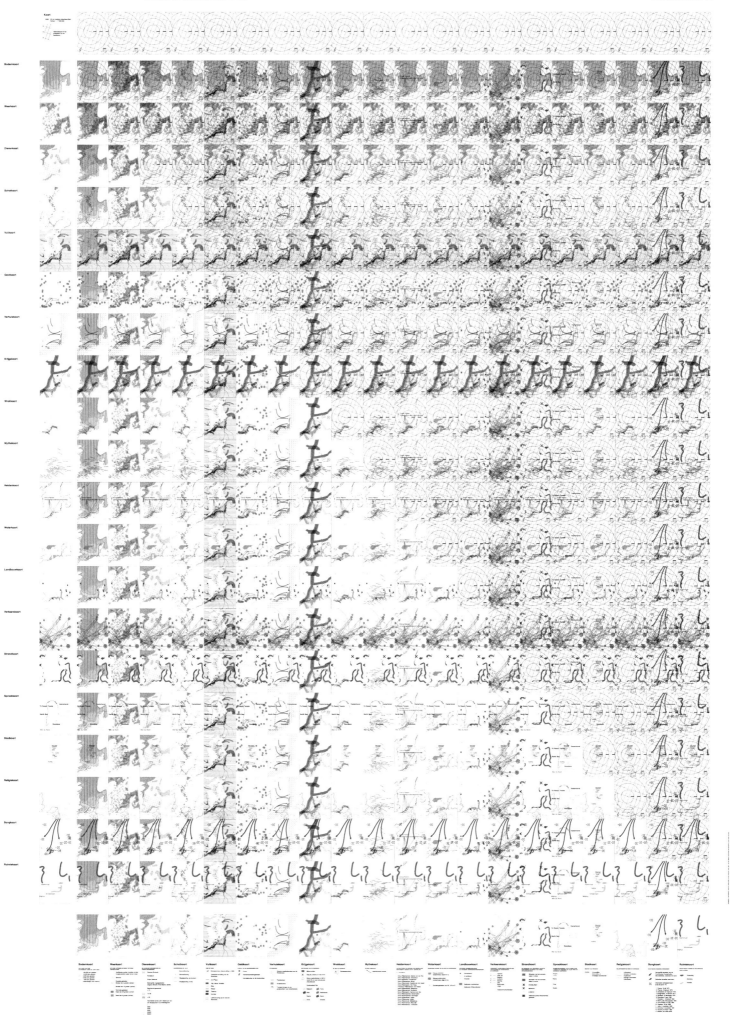

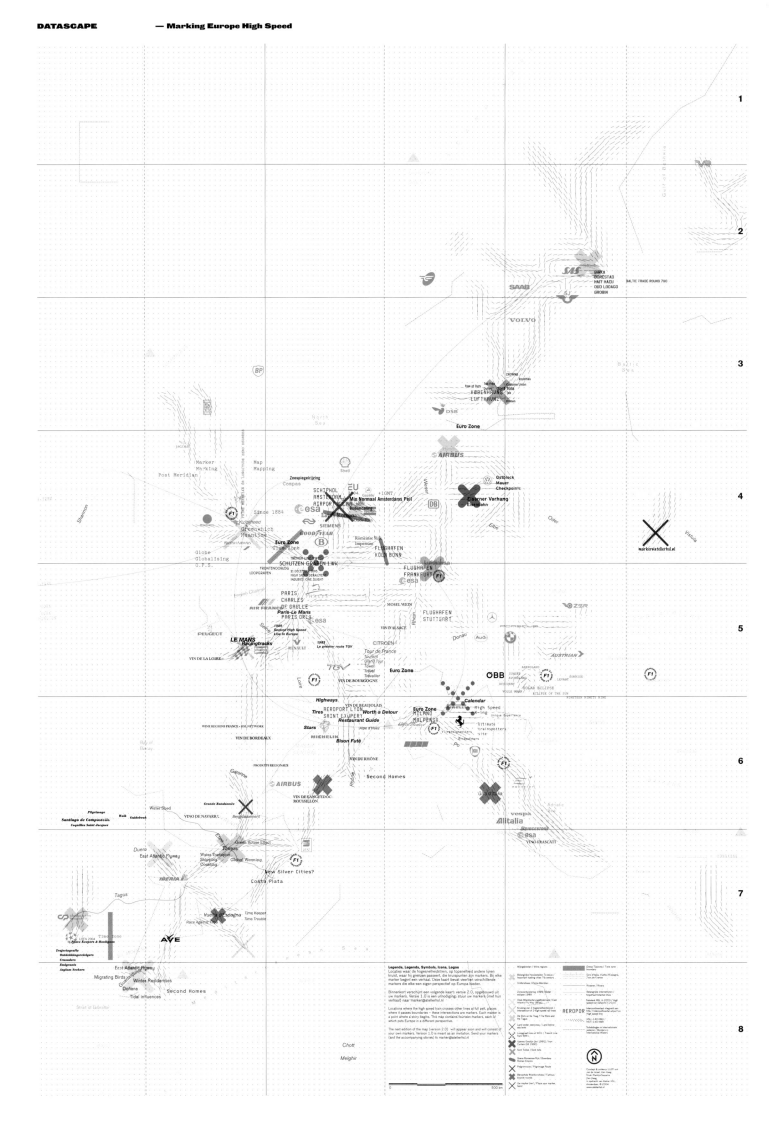

Lust
——Interview

'What a useful thing a pocket-map is!' I remarked.

'That's another thing we've learned from your nation,' said Mein Herr, 'map-making. But we've carried it much further than you. What do you consider the largest map that would be really useful?'

'About six inches to the mile.'

'Only six inches!' exclaimed Mein Herr. We very soon got to six yards to the mile. Then we tried a hundred yards to the mile. And then came the grandest idea of all! We actually made a map of the country, on the scale of a mile to the mile!'

'Have you used it much?' I enquired.

'It has never been spread out, yet,' said Mein Herr: 'the farmers objected: they said it would cover the whole country, and shut out the sunlight! So we now use the country itself, as its own map, and I assure you it does nearly as well.'

Lewis Carroll
Sylvie and Bruno Concluded, 1893

———— **You often reference maps and mapping in your projects. Could you tell us about the background to this?** ———— We've been interested in maps and mapping since we started LUST twelve years ago. Maps should always have a certain level of abstraction and not focus simply on transferring information. We're always looking for ways to give 'data' and 'information' a more emotional aspect, which the reader can then read in multiple ways. The field between maps and graphs is an interesting one, because to some extent it's still unexplored. An example would be the combination of geographical information with statistical data and vice versa.

———— **Do you have any core ideas that drive your development and approach to infographics?** ———— A few years ago, we started to research ideas related to what we call DataSpace. The concept of DataSpace is the opposite of the logical structures we see in computer databases and the internet. Databases store information locally about physical objects that could be located anywhere. On the internet, the physical objects can be identified only as artefacts with their identical location in the database. DataSpace is different. It's a concept that's rooted in time and space, with a location in physical reality. The local area network (LAN) can be replaced by the architectural space of a room, a street, or building, depending on the place (i.e. reference) where the user is located. DataSpace is structured in a way that is analogous to the real physical space surrounding us. By linking database to DataSpace, architectural and

—

By linking database to DataSpace, architectural and computer processes merge into a new type of spatial intervention: infotecture

—

computer processes merge into a new type of spatial intervention: infotecture. DataSpace is always and everywhere visually present. Think of the whole world as one huge database, a 1:1 scale model.

A concept like DataSpace allows us to research things that interest us, and apply the knowledge we've gained to specific projects, such as Zandstad (Sand City). Zandstad was fascinating because the initial brief was very open. The basic idea was to analyse a 60 x 60 square kilometre area together with researchers from the university, and to map certain aspects of this area. It turned into an experiment on how to gather information and transform it into accessible maps and graphs, all in a non-hierarchical way. As part of the project, we employed abstract, deconstructed maps, three-dimensional animations, visual statistics, and a kind of toolbox that will hopefully provide inspiration to other designers of maps, as well. Most of the time, clients ask us to apply our specific vision for a project, and that's also how we work. We never just

———— **Marking Europe High Speed** LUST, in collaboration with Jan de Graaf— This work is an unfinished new map of Europe. In the map, currents and tensions bend like iron filings around magnets, the forces of gravity redefined by their density and import. The map exposes the forces that shape and challenge the identity of the Europe of the future, with political borders and geographic constraints ignored. Cultural and social stories are told in version 1.0 as an invitation for the public to partake in the development of map 2.0. Political participative identity has been defined by the image of a networked society.

'do' a project; we always ask a lot of questions so we can get the brief right. In many cases, the brief is not what the client really wants, but what they think they want or need. Part of our job is to clarify the task we've been asked to do, and sometimes it can end up being quite different from the original idea.

———— **How have the expectations and opportunities surrounding infographics changed over the years? What are the key drivers of change?** ———— Over the past eight years or so, an increasing amount of attention has been paid to maps and mapping projects. Lots of students look at sites like visualcomplexity.com and think the graphs they see there are what graphs should look like in general: extremely complex and often with a sort of high-tech feel to them. But they easily forget that you usually need very large, if not enormous, data sets for those kinds of visualisations. Occasionally, clients come to us with an idea for a project, saying they want 'something complex'. When you ask what kind of information they have, however, it turns out to be one sheet of paper with maybe twenty numbers on it. So really they want us to fill in the rest. At that point, it starts to get tricky and can turn into an illustration—something that pretends to show information, but is basically there because it needs to illustrate an idea the editors have. This is definitely not the way to go.

———— **How important do you think it is for a design studio to have its own voice when it comes to presenting data? How do you ensure a certain design continuity in your projects?** ———— When we start a project, we're not thinking of the end result yet. We want to remain open to what comes out of the process of gathering, thinking, and designing. This results, in our case, in a specific approach, but not in a specific form. Although we don't think we really have a particular style, in reality we do, of course. You make your choices within your aesthetic palette, so to speak. But the beginning of a project is always open, and we try to let the data form itself—and always with the goal of transforming data into information, information into knowledge, and knowledge into stories.

————In what ways do you think diagrams and infographics are affected by the cultural context in which they're developed? How should designers deal with their own cultural bias when approaching an infographics project?————The cultural context is probably not such a big influence, since the information stays the same. However, different cultures use different metaphors, making it difficult for other cultures to interpret what's being

said. Let's take a diagram about car accidents as an example: in India, it would normally use more decorative elements, whereas in Switzerland it would be much more austere. But the core information stays the same, and people in either country will still understand the other country's diagram. In our work, we try to avoid metaphors. Moving away from the referential to the empirical is important because of the higher level of abstraction allowed by empirical data. There must be ways to visualise a network other than using the spider web metaphor over and over again.

————What other fields of knowledge do you think infographics can learn from? What lessons can we apply? ————After art, I think the next biggest source of inspiration is architecture. It's

fascinating how architects try to convince clients and the public with impressive, research-based graphs as to why the shape they want to create looks like this 'blob'. This kind of data-driven mapping has introduced the third dimension into data visualisation, all of which has been made

—

Transforming data into information, information into knowledge, and knowledge into stories

—

possible by bigger, better, faster computers, and by new programming languages like Processing. The amount of information you can condense onto a small surface using the language of maps and graphs is truly amazing. However, the ability to create more complex (or complex-looking) maps and graphs can also lead to a dilemma, because more is not always better. Although we like to work with more data rather than less in our projects, this doesn't mean that the outcome necessarily has to look more complex. We aim to introduce more levels of understanding to our work, showing with cartography that the world is constructed not of one, but multiple truths.

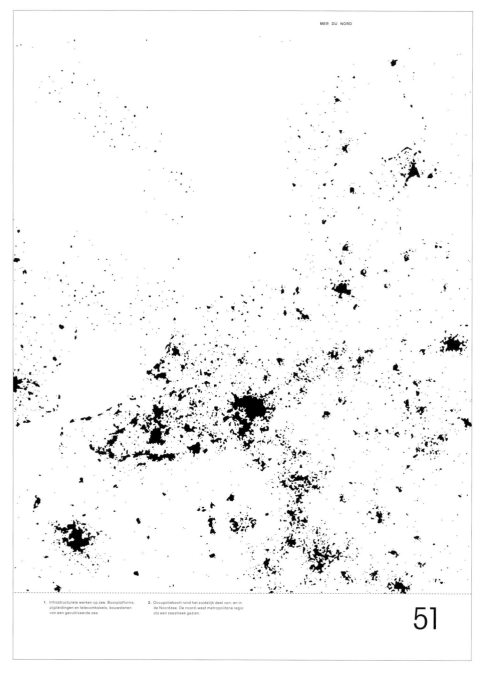

MER DU NORD

1. Infrastructurele werken op zee. Boorplatforms, pijpleidingen en telecomkabels, bouwstenen van een gecultiveerde zee.

2. Occupatiekaart rond het zuidelijk deel van, en in de Noordzee. De noord-west metropolitane regio als een zeestreek gezien.

51

─── **Atlas of the North Sea**

|▸**PP. 110, 111**| LUST, in collaboration with Jan de Graaf and Steven van Schuppen — By consciously ignoring the boundaries between land and water, this map of North Sea coastal development turns urban centres into islands. The form of presentation is particularly pertinent, given the Netherlands' history of reclaiming vast tracts of open water for cities and agriculture. The boundary between water and land then becomes a deliberate choice, rather than a fact of nature — something this chart makes clear. ─── Scattering dots across the canvas like drops of rain, LUST plays with different shades of blue to depict precipitation across the North Sea. In this literal expression of saturation, the darkest shades indicate rainfall of over 1500 mm per year. As with most of the maps in this series by LUST, no distinction is made between land and sea mass, as the one variable under consideration tells its own story of the North Sea. ─── Like floating lost souls, the 'waves of gold' in the North Sea betray the human cost of its history. The sharp relief of coastal dangers cuts like violent, irregular blades through the sea of names and lives, listed alphabetically, lost to the perils of its waters. ─── Down the years, the rich history of the North Sea has tossed out many casualties. Nautical archaeology is the study of the legacy of those who have gone before. Besides providing the glamorous opportunity to hunt for treasure, the sea, like a graveyard, has also yielded the remains of lost souls, and lost ambitions. Here, the dangers of the shifting, treacherous coastal sands are clearly evident, as the density of despair increases around the coastline. In fact, shipwrecks — often thought of as random events — have evolved from predictable patterns, created in bygone days when geography met human ambition.

NOORDSEE

< 200 mm
201–400 mm
401–600 mm
601–800 mm
801–1000 mm
1001–1500 mm
> 1500 mm

21

WRAK   60   TE GRONDE   34

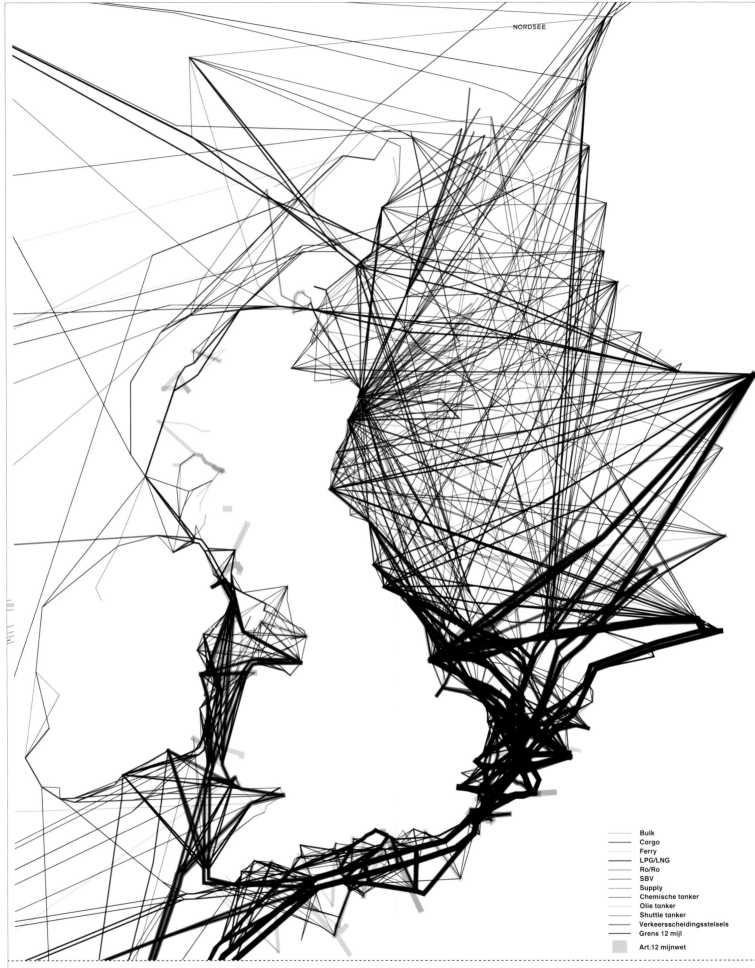

NORDSEE

Bulk
Cargo
Ferry
LPG/LNG
Ro/Ro
SBV
Supply
Chemische tanker
Olie tanker
Shuttle tanker
Verkeersscheidingsstelsels
Grens 12 mijl
Art.12 mijnwet

1. Kaart van de Noordzee en omgeving, daterend uit de 15ᵉ eeuw. De Noordzee gedacht gelijk de Baltische Zee als een echte binnenzee, met Schotland als drempel. Groenland en het noorden van Noorwegen met elkaar verbonden door de Mare Congelatum, de bevroren zee. Rondvaart lijkt mogelijk, benoorden om Zweden. Bron: P. Novaresio, *De grote ontdekkingsreizen.*

2. Uitsnede uit maritieme kaart, routekaart van het scheepvaartverkeersstelsel op de Noordzee.

3. De Noordzee als verkeersplein. Intensiteit scheepvaartverkeer, aantal schepen op een etmaal, getraceerd per 24 uur.

45

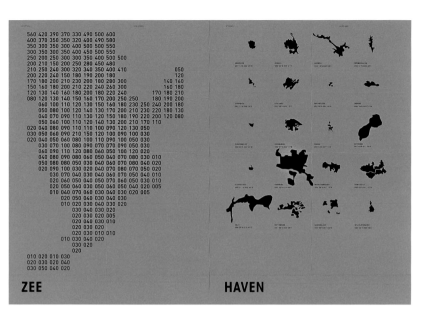

```
560 420 390 370 330 490 500 600
400 370 350 320 400 490 580
350 350 350 300 400 500 550
300 350 350 300 400 500 550
250 200 250 300 400 450 500
200 210 150 200 250 280 450 480
210 250 240 300 320 340 350 410        050
200 220 240 150 180 190 200 180                120
170 180 200 210 230 200 180 280 300              140 160
150 160 180 200 210 220 240 300              160 180
120 130 140 160 180 200 150 240          170 180 210
080 120 130 150 160 170 200 200 250          180 190 210
060 100 110 120 130 150 160 180 230 250 240 200 180
050 080 100 120 140 130 170 200 210 230 250 180 130
040 070 090 110 130 150 180 190 230 200 120 080
050 060 100 110 120 140 130 200 210 170 110
020 040 080 090 110 110 090 120 130 050
020 050 060 090 210 150 120 100 090 100 030
030 070 100 090 080 100 110 090 100 050 020
030 090 110 070 080 090 070 070 090 030
040 090 110 120 080 060 050 100 120 020
050 080 080 050 030 040 060 070 080 040 020
050 100 090 100 030 020 040 070 050 040 020
030 070 050 060 070 060 070 050 040 010
020 050 060 030 050 070 060 050 030 010
040 070 050 050 030 060 050 030 020 005
050 060 100 110 120 140 130 200 210 170 110
010 040 070 060 030 040 030 020 005
010 020 030 040 030 020
030 040 030 020
020 040 030 010
030 040 020 005
020 040 030 010
020 030 010 010
010 030 040 020
030 020

010 020 010 030
020 030 020 040
030 050 040 020
```

ZEE   **HAVEN**

——**Atlas of the North Sea** LUST in collaboration with Jan de Graaf and Steven van Schuppen — A single day runs its course in the North Sea. Commercial traffic is tracked and plotted over a twenty-four-hour period. The different types of traffic are shown by colours, the thickness indicating the intensity of traffic on each route. No geographic indicators are given, but the land mass of Great Britain soon becomes evident, as the country's outline is delineated by ports. LPG transport and ferries stand out from the saturation of heavily-frequented routes. ——This work is part of the North Sea atlas project. Devoid of scale, the anatomy of land mass and oceans is compared. Black footprints are labelled and presented. See the Datasphere section for a more detailed description of this project.

ZEEEN   DE NOORDZEE

ARAFURAZEE / ATLANTISCHE OCEAAN / BAFFINBAAI / BARENTSZEE
BEAUFORTZEE / BERINGZEE / CARIBISCHE ZEE / GOLF VAN MEXICO
GROTE OCEAAN / INDISCHE OCEAAN / JAPANSE ZEE / JAVAZEE
KARAZEE / KORAALZEE / LAPTEVZEE / MIDDELLANDSE ZEE
NOORDELIJKE IJSZEE / NOORDZEE / OOST-CHINESE ZEE / OOST-SYBERISCHE ZEE
OOSTZEE / RODE ZEE / ZEE VAN OCHOTSK / ZUID-CHINESE ZEE

WERELD

EILANDEN   MER DU NORD

AMRUM 054°40'N·008°20'O / BORKUM 053°35'N·006°41'O / BOSPLAAT 053°34'N·006°28'O / FAIR-ISLE 059°36'N·001°42'W
FETLAR 060°18'N·001°02'W / FÖHR 060°18'N·001°02'W / HELGOLAND 054°13'N·007°48'O / HOY 058°27'N·002°41'W
JUIST 053°40'N·007°00'O / LANGEOOG 053°45'N·007°31'O / MELLUM 053°46'N·008°12'O / RICHEL 053°07'N·005°11'O
NOORDERHAAKS 052°57'N·004°40'O / NORDERNEY 053°45'N·007°15'O / ROUSAY 059°18'N·003°12'W / SCHÄRHÖRN 053°56'N·008°28'O
SCHIERMONNIKOOG 053°28'N·006°10'O / SHAPINSAY 058°45'N·002°15'W / SOUTH-RONALDSAY 058°49'N·003°19'W / SPIEKEROOG 053°48'N·007°46'O
TERSCHELLING 053°23'N·005°13'O / TEXEL 053°04'N·004°50'O / UNST 060°29'N·001°05'W / VLIELAND 053°18'N·005°05'O

LAND

———— **Mondriaan Founda-tion Year Report 2006** JOOST
GROOTENS — The Mondriaan Founda-tion (also featured in LUST's project in the Datasphere section |>**P. 42**|) stimulates the visual arts, design, and the cultural herit-age of the Netherlands. The annual report for 2006 uses pictograms to represent the various fields in which the foundation is active. Comparative scale and contribu-tion are shown, together with global reach. Project type is classified according to a pictographic key. The total cost of a project is shown in yellow and compared with the foundation's contribution. ———— **Small Mall Maps** ABI HUYNH — The soulless superstore mentality of American dystopia has left the country strewn with dead malls. By reducing a survey of small shopping cen-tres to thumbnail size, the viewer is able to compare how commercial space is shaped between different locations. Viewers make up their own mind as to the increase or de-crease in diversity of shape, as size is taken out of the equation. Monotone blocks are lined up along the page.

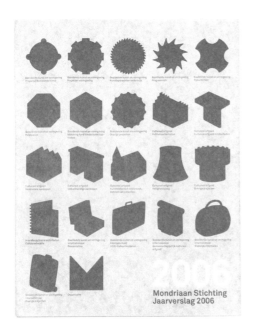

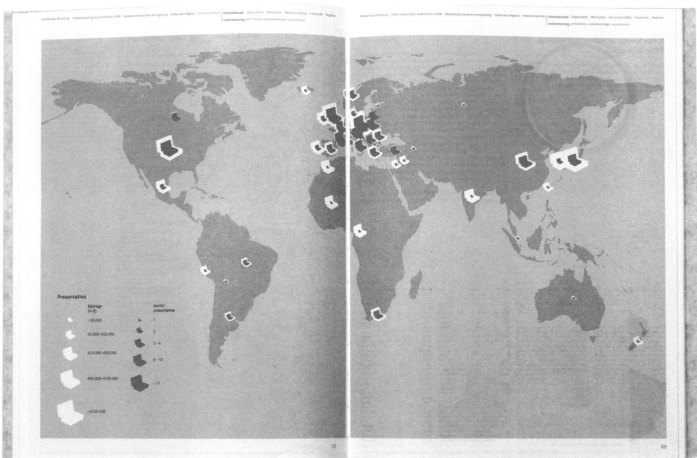

——— **lux** HELMO.FR — Cultural discovery is seen as a scavenger hunt through the conceptual landscape of lux's season. Topological semiology is developed over time to guide the viewer to points of interest and new aspects in Valence's regional cultural collective. The individual cards and leaflets form part of a larger map that can be reconstituted according to the reference grid in cartographic red. The resampled and overlaid colours of different cultural elements form new and unexpected landscapes, to be enjoyed according to individual interests and tastes. A metalayer of experience refers to the concept of a regional collective, but does not offer geographic navigational advice. Each season offers up a new landscape, a new cultural countryside to travel through.

NEXT PAGES ——— **lux** HELMO.FR ———
**Program Théâtre de Vevey
03-04** WELCOMETO.AS — The theatre at Vevey, Switzerland, hosts a number of performances by international artists throughout the year. This poster displays the seasonal programme as cultural cartography. 'Highlights' are listed in the table according to their coordinates on the symbolic map, rather than the location of their actual performance. The theatre is an integral part of local life, an aesthetic landscape where performing arts are centred, to enrich the community.

lux^(v) 2007

hiver printemps

Scène nationale de Valence

onedotzero, festival international de films numériques

18-27 janvier

wong kar-wai, rétrospective et influences

02-13 février

superscript², installation interactive

cabinet des expériences

18 janvier 20 mars

animations japonaises

07 février-06 mars

mia et le migou, mise en scène

20 février 20 mars

cinémas arméniens

21-31 mars

paul cox

03 mai 14 octobre

ddd, exposition de design graphique

28 mars-16 avril

36, boulevard du Général de Gaulle, 26 000 Valence
Tél. 04 75 82 44 10 / www.lux-valence.com

la bonne merveille ©2007

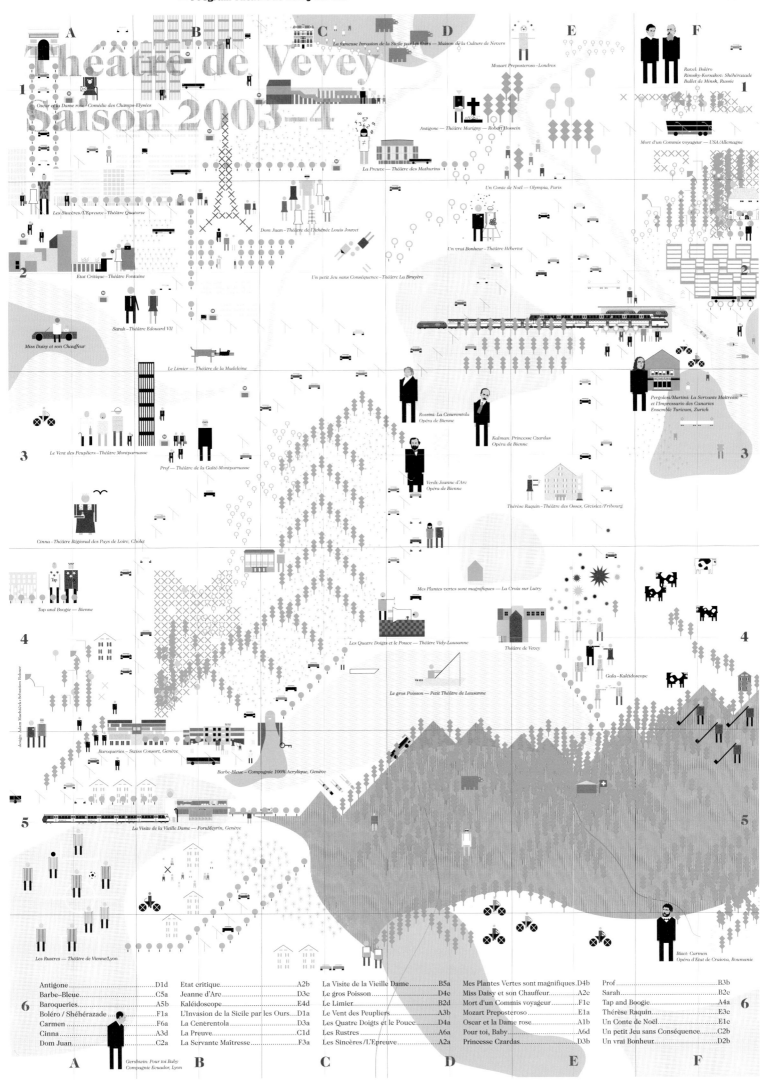

design: Adam Machácek+Sebastien Bohner

Minenkarten / Cartes de Mines 1:25000   existieren nicht / n'existent pas

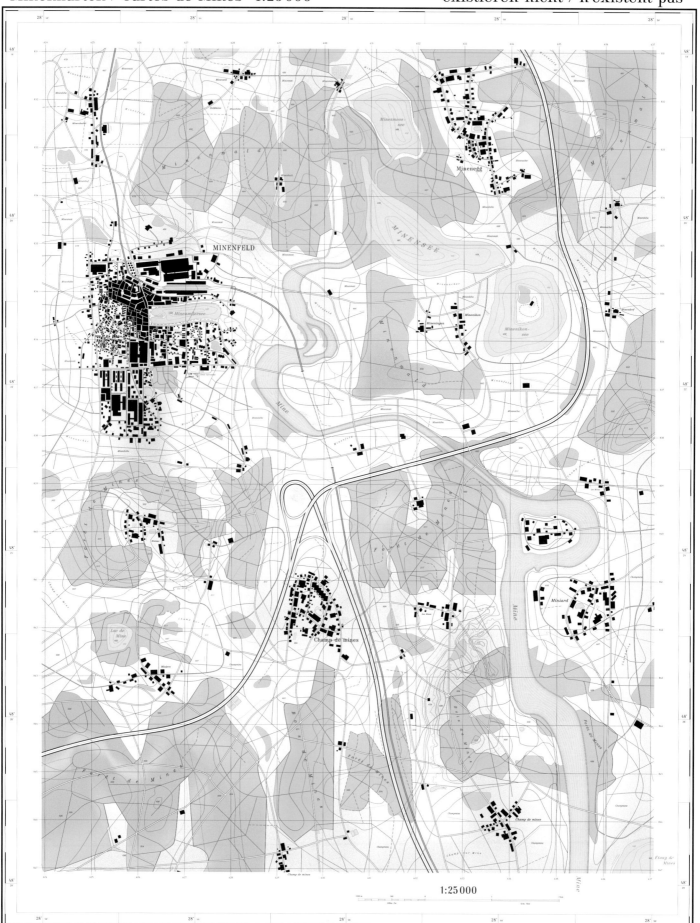

1:25000

Jeder Mensch hat ein Recht auf Leben, Minen zerstören es / *Chacun a droit à la vie, les mines la détruisent.* Menschenrechte / *Droit de l'homme*

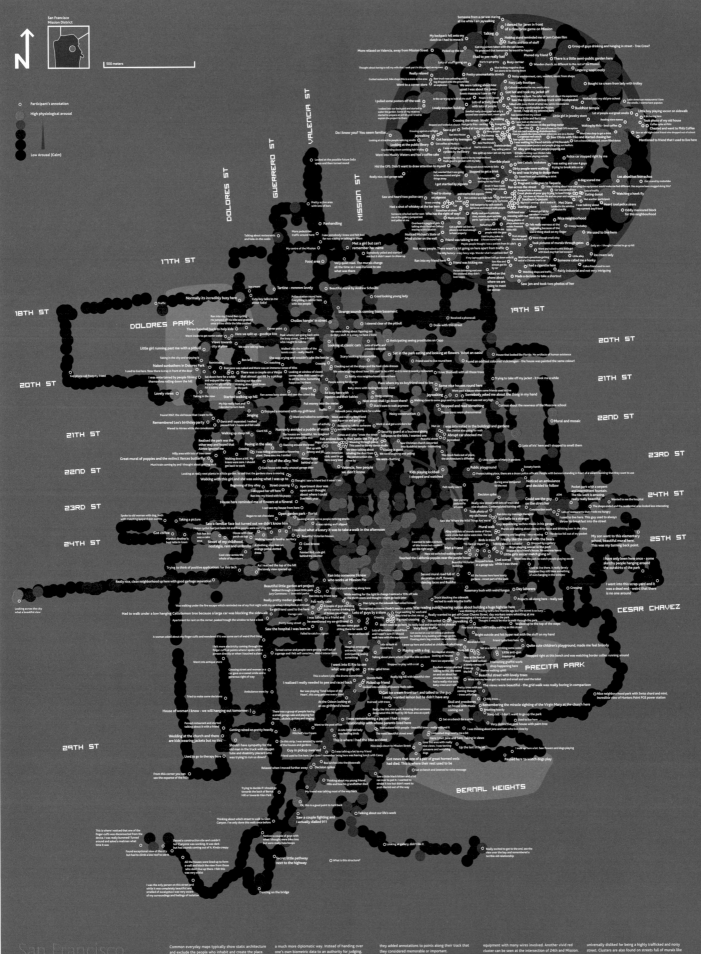

San Francisco
Emotion Map

by Christian Nold

Common everyday maps typically show static architecture and exclude the people who inhabit and create the place. The San Francisco Emotion Map attempts to remedy this by mapping the space of human perception and experience.

Over a period of five weeks, 98 participants took part in Christian Nold's Emotion Map project commissioned and hosted by Southern Exposure, a non-profit, artist-run organization located in the Mission District. A series of weekly workshops took place whereby the participants were invited to walk around the area using Nold's custom built Bio Mapping device. The device combined a finger cuff sensor which recorded the wearer's Galvanic Skin Response (GSR), an index of emotional response, with a Global Positioning System (GPS) which located the wearer's position on the earth. Derived from the polygraph, a system used by law enforcement agencies to identify when a person is lying, the finger cuff sensor is used in

a much more diplomatic way. Instead of handing over one's own biometric data to an authority for judging, the participant is instead asked to interpret their body's response allowing for a more subtle understanding of their experiences.

Starting at Southern Exposure, each participant walked for up to an hour throughout the Mission District and surrounding areas. Upon returning to the gallery the collected data was downloaded to a computer where each participant could view their personal 'emotion map' as a series of high and low peaks (represented on the map as dots of varying colors). The arousal response recorded by the device could be positive or negative and required active interpretation to make sense of. In the workshops, each participant studied their own track and then talked with the group about their 'emotion map' in relation to their experiences on the walk. As a result of this reflection,

they added annotations to points along their track that they considered memorable or important.

All together, 98 individuals' annotated tracks were gathered, combined, and overlaid in order to create the communal San Francisco Emotion Map. On the map, the overall pattern of dots shows where the participants walked. The color of the dots represents the combined emotional data of all the participants with red signifying high arousal and black signifying low arousal. When looking at the entire map, there is a general arousal gradient from high in the center to low near the edges. The density of red dots and annotations indicate hotspots of communal arousal, while the darker dots show areas of communal calm. There are a number of distinct clusters of red dots on the map. The cluster around Southern Exposure can be attributed to the participants' unease of being wired up with the Bio Mapping device, an unfamiliar piece of

equipment with many wires involved. Another vivid red cluster can be seen at the intersection of 24th and Mission. This intersection, centered around a major BART (local train) station, is extremely busy with social interactions. The workshop participants often remarked on the Evangelists, commuters, skateboarders, demonstrators, as well as the people located on the streets of the local McDonalds. There are interesting arousal and annotation clusters around the three parks in the area - Dolores Park, Precita Park, and Bernal Hill. These areas provide inspiring views of the city as well as provoke reflection on past memories.

It is also interesting to look at the clusters gathered along the different roadways in the city. The heavily frequented Valencia Street shows up strongly while the surrounding residential streets seem universally calm. Cesar Chavez, a major thoroughfare through the south side of the city as well as an onramp to a major highway, appears to be

universally disliked for being a highly trafficked and noisy street. Clusters are also found on streets full of murals like Balmy Alley, as well as several of the large number of positive annotations indicate the hidden landmarks of the Mission District.

Apart from these communal patterns it is remarkable to look at the diversity and uniqueness of an individuals experience of the city. Some people's responses are shaped by their memories while inspiring views, old Victorian houses, or green spaces influenced others. There are still others who responded by absorbing the present.

Creative Commons: Attribution-NonCommercial-NoDerivs
Download a PDF version of this map, individual participants' tracks
and background information about the project and process at
www.sf.biomapping.net

PREVIOUS PAGES ——— **Minenfeld/ Champs de mines** RETO MOSER — The deadly legacy of the most brutal wars lies hidden in the ordinary landscape. The topography of death, as revealed by this illustration, spells out the word for 'minefield' in German and French. The traditional mapping conventions are further subverted by changing all the text labels on the map to refer, however obliquely, to mines. This underlines the inhumanity of turning ordinary-looking fields and landscapes into death traps. Everything is capable of killing, as minefields become the unthinking, slumbering, and fatal legacy of conflict. ——— **San Francisco Emotion Map** CHRISTIAN NOLD BIOMAPPING — San Francisco's iconic Mission District is rediscovered through human physiological responses. Ninety-eight people each wore a BioMapping device to track their emotional arousal levels in response to their GPS location, allowing the viewer to discover a new level of experience inside a known geographic space. This project turns the concept of the surveillance society on its head, by allowing people to selectively share a personal experience of the city. States of emotional arousal are made visible by overlaying the individual changes in galvanic skin response on the cityscapes themselves. The same technology used by the authorities for lie detectors gives an insight into the personal, real time, and physiological response to modern urban environments. The emphasis shifts from the urban space being monitored, to the opportunity to selectively share our own emotional landscape as we reveal unexpected truths about our reaction to everyday places. Kinaesthetic memory is activated as we reflect on what exactly triggered a bodily response at a particular moment or place. By comparing and tagging our personal experience with the response of others to the same space, we can begin to ask new questions about what we expect from everyday environments.

——— **Stockport Emotion Map** CHRISTIAN NOLD BIOMAPPING, in collaboration with Daniela Boraschi — Reminiscent of Wild West prospecting maps, this cartographic depiction of Stockport is a mine of emotional meaning. Over a two-month period, some 200 people were involved in this innovative project to map the emotions, opinions, and desires of the populace of Stockport, in the United Kingdom. Eschewing the modern convention placing north at the top of the page, this map returns to the older tradition of placing the River Mersey—a physical feature affecting personal experience of the area—at its centre. The map offers a visual explanation of the very human impulses contained in this conurbation. Using the technique of drawing provocations, the designer asked people to sketch their sometimes serious, sometimes humorous feelings about their daily lives. These reflections were combined with physiological responses, using the BioMapping device developed by Christian Nold. The technological description of human response to physical space is annotated in the participants' handwriting, explaining their own very personal experience of the town. The age-old River Mersey becomes superseded by a new datastream of urban experience.

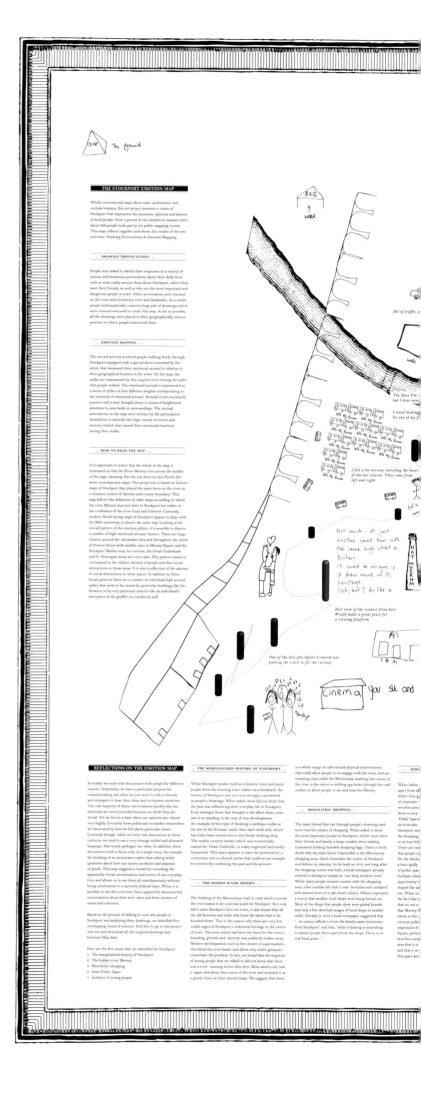

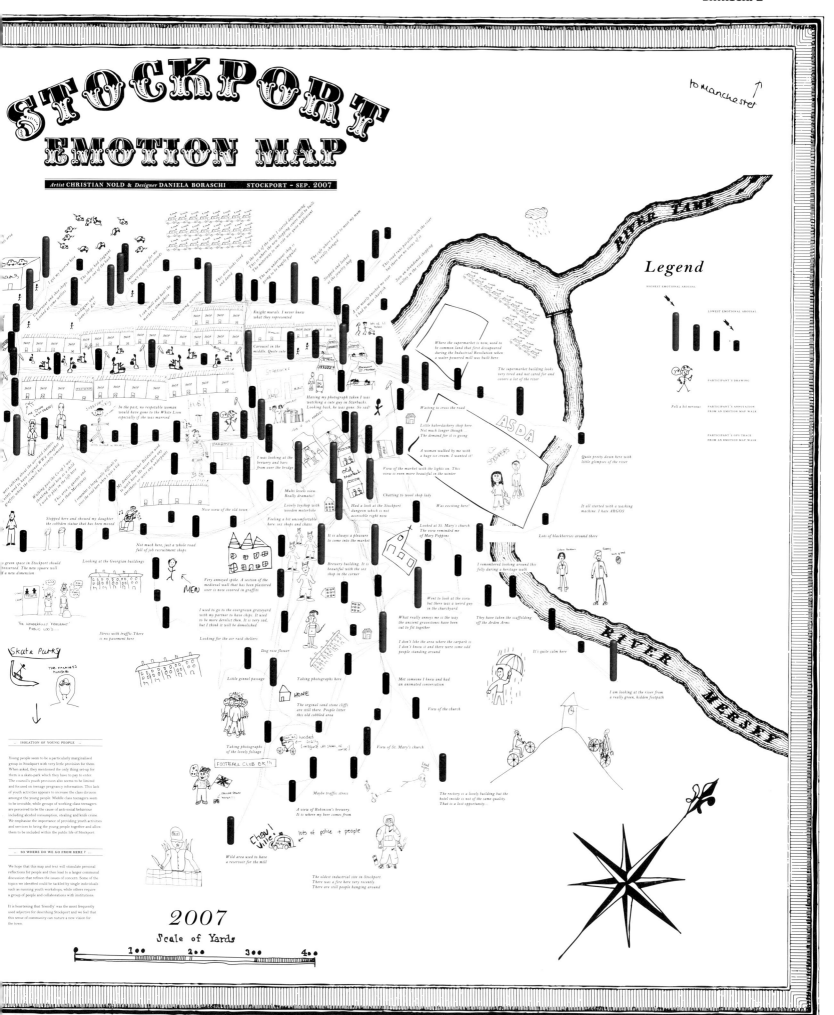

STOCKPORT EMOTION MAP

Artist CHRISTIAN NOLD & *Designer* DANIELA BORASCHI   STOCKPORT – SEP. 2007

to Manchester

Legend

HIGHEST EMOTIONAL AROUSAL

LOWEST EMOTIONAL AROUSAL

PARTICIPANT'S DRAWING

PARTICIPANT'S ANNOTATION FROM AN EMOTION MAP WALK

PARTICIPANT'S GPS TRACE FROM AN EMOTION MAP WALK

ISOLATION OF YOUNG PEOPLE

Young people seem to be a particularly marginalised group in Stockport with very little provision for them. When asked, they mentioned the only thing set-up for them is a skate-park which they have to pay to enter. The council's youth provision also seems to be limited and focused on teenage pregnancy information. This lack of youth activities appears to increase the class division amongst the young people. Middle class teenagers seem to be invisible, while groups of working class teenagers are perceived to be the cause of anti-social behaviour including alcohol consumption, stealing and knife crime. We emphasise the importance of providing youth activities and services to bring the young people together and allow them to be included within the public life of Stockport.

SO WHERE DO WE GO FROM HERE ?

We hope that this map and text will stimulate personal reflections for people and then lead to a larger communal discussion that refines the issues of concern. Some of the topics we identified could be tackled by single individuals such as running youth workshops, while others require a group of people and collaborations with institutions.

It is heartening that 'friendly' was the most frequently used adjective for describing Stockport and we feel that this sense of community can nurture a new vision for the town.

2007

Scale of Yards

100   200   300   400

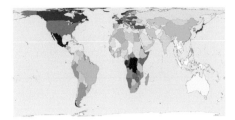

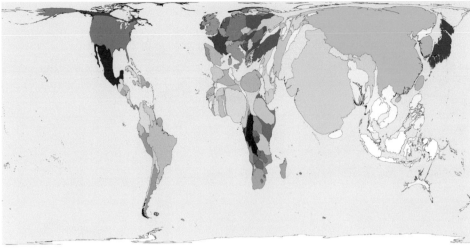

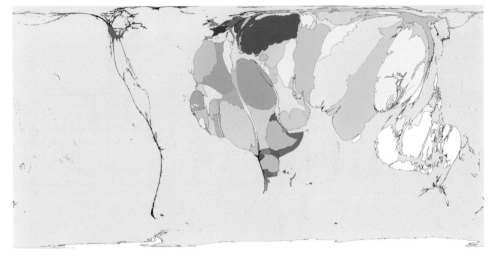

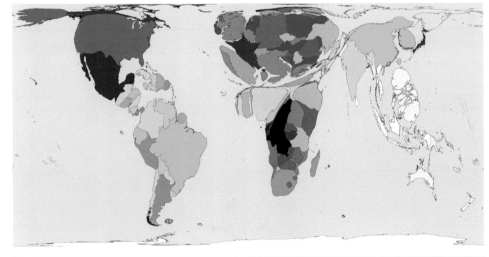

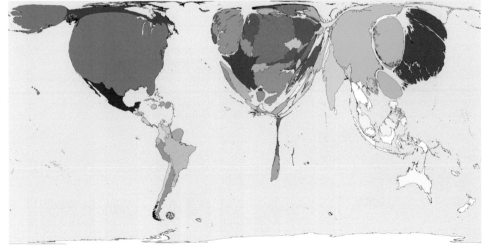

—— **World maps** WORLDMAPPER,
Danny Dorling, Mark Newman, Graham
Allsopp, Anna Barford, Ben Wheeler &
John Pritchard — Worldmapper have developed easily accessible software that
designers can use to transform global
land masses to reflect statistical data. By
distorting the physical through the lens
of analysis, the viewer gains an intuitive
sense of normalised distribution. Gross
over- or under-representation becomes
obvious, as viewers compare the resultant map with their well-trained memory
of each country's cartographic image. This
allows for interesting comparisons between
quantities such as the distribution of Christians and Muslims around the world. The
progression over time of global internet
usage also shows a movement towards an
ideal shape, with the northern hemisphere
still dominant. The human cost of natural
disasters weighs heavily on Asia, as the
representation's inflated size makes clear
just how common earthquakes are in that
region. Data becomes the distorting lens
through which we view and reappraise
the world around us. —— **Globalize
me!** |> **P. 124** | JUNG + WENIG, Christopher
Jung & Tobias Wenig — Globalisation has
affected many cultures, and this topological analysis highlights its ethical, social, and
economic impacts, in the form of silk screen
maps of the empire at the end of the Silk
Road. The various demographic analyses
are imposed on the central map, showing
the cost of economic integration.

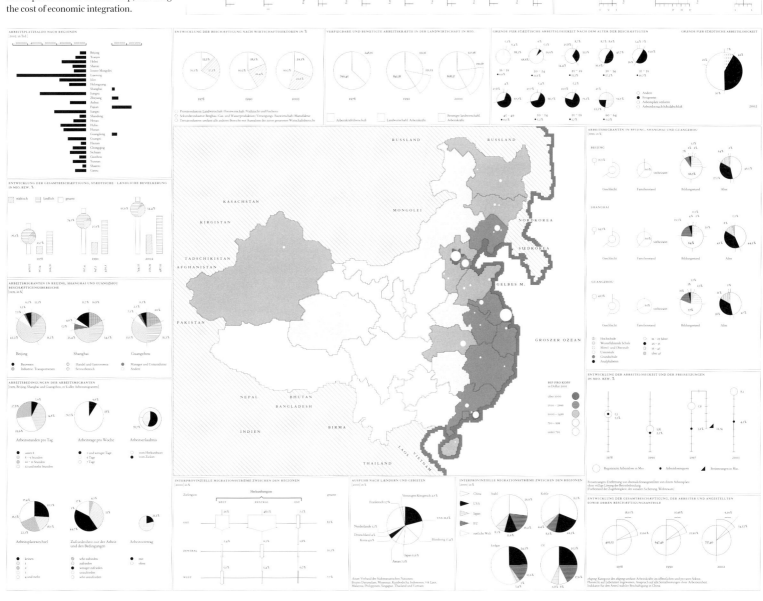

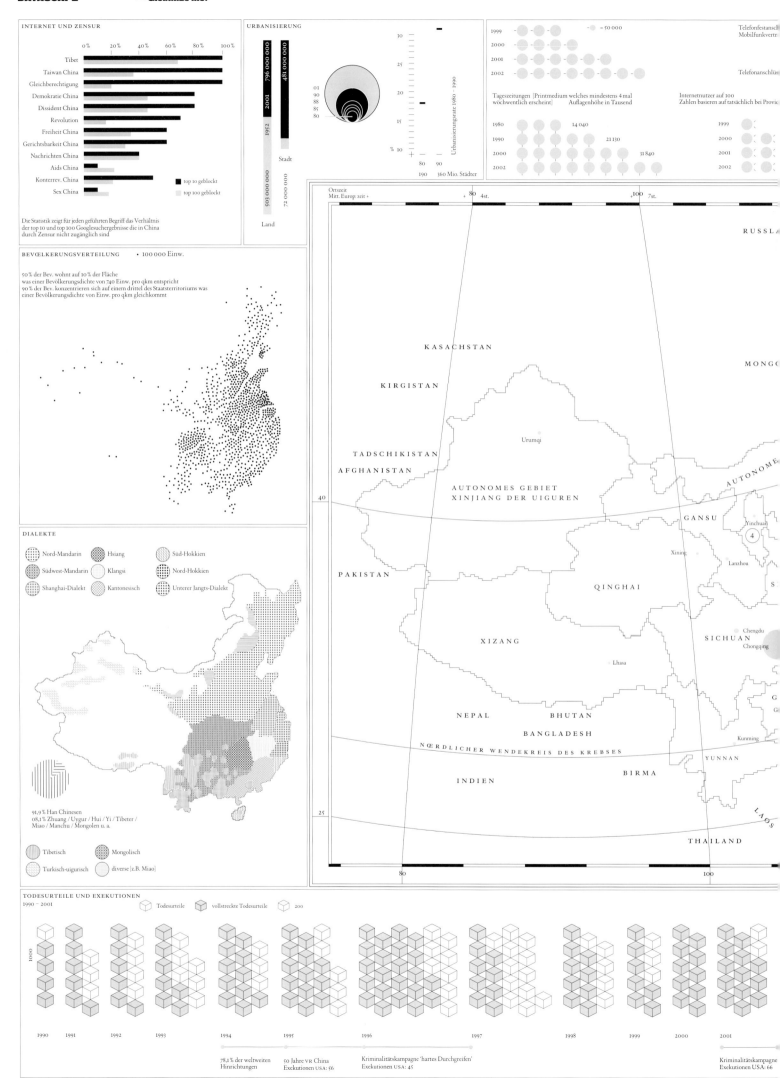

INTERNET UND ZENSUR

0% 20% 40% 60% 80% 100%

Tibet
Taiwan China
Gleichberechtigung
Demokratie China
Dissident China
Revolution
Freiheit China
Gerichtsbarkeit China
Nachrichten China
Aids China
Konterrev. China
Sex China

■ top 10 geblockt
□ top 100 geblockt

Die Statistik zeigt für jeden geführten Begriff das Verhältnis der top 10 und top 100 Googlesuchergebnisse die in China durch Zensur nicht zugänglich sind

URBANISIERUNG

796 000 000
481 000 000

2001
1952

503 000 000
72 000 000

Stadt

Land

30
25
20
15
10
%

80 90
190   360 Mio. Städter

Urbanisierungsrate 1980 - 1990

01
90
88
85
80

1999
2000
2001
2002

= 50 000

Telefonfestansch
Mobilfunkvertr

Telefonanschlüs

Tageszeitungen [Printmedium welches mindestens 4 mal wöchwentlich erscheint]   Auflagenhöhe in Tausend

Internetnutzer auf 100
Zahlen basieren auf tatsächlich bei Provic

1980
1990   14 040
2000   21 130
2002   31 840

1999
2000
2001
2002

BEVÖLKERUNGSVERTEILUNG   • 100 000 Einw.

50 % der Bev. wohnt auf 10 % der Fläche
was einer Bevölkerungsdichte von 740 Einw. pro qkm entspricht
90 % der Bev. konzentrieren sich auf einem drittel des Staatsterritoriums was einer Bevölkerungsdichte von Einw. pro qkm gleichkommt

DIALEKTE

Nord-Mandarin   Hsiang   Süd-Hokkien
Südwest-Mandarin   Klangsi   Nord-Hokkien
Shanghai-Dialekt   Kantonesisch   Unterer Jangts-Dialekt

91,9 % Han Chinesen
08,1 % Zhuang / Uygur / Hui / Yi / Tibeter / Miao / Manchu / Mongolen u. a.

Tibetisch   Mongolisch
Turkisch-uigurisch   diverse [z.B. Miao]

Ortszeit
Mitt. Europ. zeit +   + 80 4st.   +100 7st.

RUSSLA

KASACHSTAN

KIRGISTAN

MONGO

TADSCHIKISTAN
AFGHANISTAN

Urumqi

AUTONOMES GEBIET
XINJIANG DER UIGUREN

AUTONOME

40

GANSU
Yinchuan

PAKISTAN

Xining

Lanzhou

QINGHAI

XIZANG

Lhasa

Chengdu

SICHUAN
Chongqing

NEPAL   BHUTAN
BANGLADESH

NÖRDLICHER WENDEKREIS DES KREBSES

YUNNAN
Kunming

25

INDIEN

BIRMA

LAOS

THAILAND

80   100

TODESURTEILE UND EXEKUTIONEN

1990 - 2001   ◇ Todesurteile   ◈ vollstreckte Todesurteile   ◇ 200

1000

1990 1991 1992 1993 1994 1995 1996 1997 1998 1999 2000 2001

78,1 % der weltweiten Hinrichtungen

50 Jahre VR China
Exekutionen USA: 56

Kriminalitätskampagne 'hartes Durchgreifen'
Exekutionen USA: 45

Kriminalitätskampagne
Exekutionen USA: 66

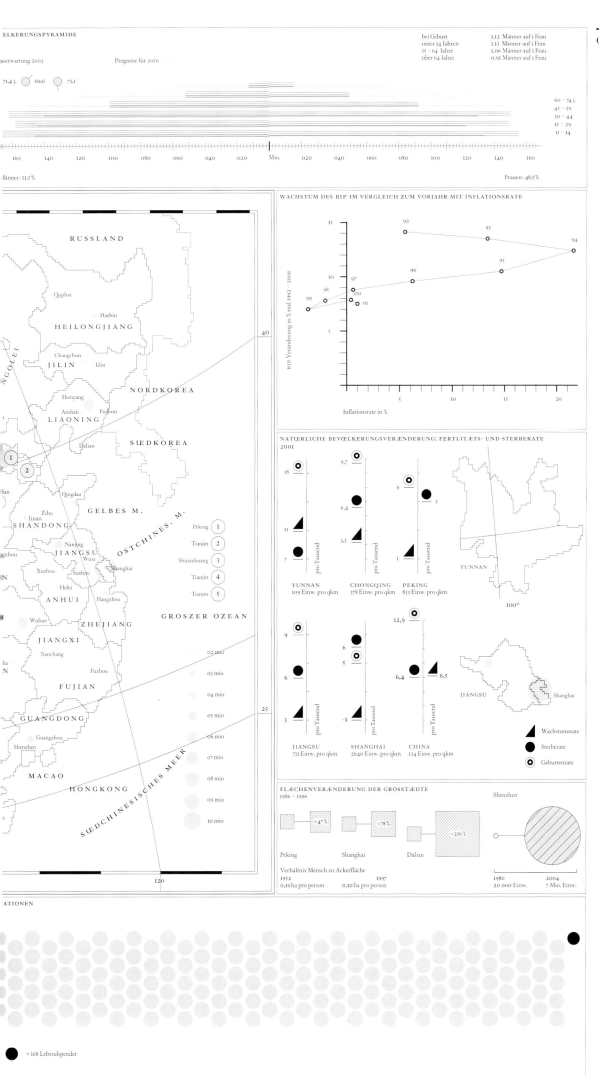

ELKERUNGSPYRAMIDE

aserwartung 2002   Prognose für 2050

71,4 J.   69,6   73,3

bei Geburt   1.12 Männer auf 1 Frau
unter 14 Jahren   1.13 Männer auf 1 Frau
15 – 64 Jahre   1.06 Männer auf 1 Frau
über 64 Jahre   0.91 Männer auf 1 Frau

60 – 74 J.
45 – 59
30 – 44
15 – 29
0 – 14

160 140 120 100 080 060 040 020 Mio. 020 040 060 080 100 120 140 160

Männer: 51,5 %   Frauen: 48,5 %

RUSSLAND

Qiqihar

Harbin

HEILONGJIANG

Changchun

JILIN   Jilin

NGOLEI

NORDKOREA

Shenyang

Anshan   Fushun

LIAONING

SÜDKOREA

Dalian

1

2

Qingdao

Zibo   GELBES M.

Jinan

SHANDONG

OSTCHINES. M.

Nanjing

gzhou   JIANGSU   Wuxi

Xuzhou   Suzhou   Shanghai

Hefei

ANHUI   Hangzhou

Wuhan   ZHEJIANG

JIANGXI

Nanchang

Fuzhou

FUJIAN

GUANGDONG

Guangzhou

Shenzhen

MACAO

HONGKONG

SÜDCHINESISCHES MEER

GROSZER OZEAN

Peking   ①
Tianjin   ②
Shijiazhuang ③
Tianjin   ④
Tianjin   ⑤

02 mio
03 mio
04 mio
05 mio
06 mio
07 mio
08 mio
09 mio
10 mio

40

25

120

WACHSTUM DES BIP IM VERGLEICH ZUM VORJAHR MIT INFLATIONSRATE

15

92   93
94

10

97   96   95
98
99   00
01

5

BIP Veränderung in % real 1992 – 2001

5   10   15   20

Inflationsrate in %

NATÜRLICHE BEVÖLKERUNGSVERÄNDERUNG: FERTLITÄTS- UND STERBERATE
2001

18   9,7   6
11   6,4   5
7   3,3   1

YUNNAN   CHONGQING   PEKING
109 Einw. pro qkm 378 Einw. pro qkm 833 Einw. pro qkm

pro Tausend   pro Tausend   pro Tausend

YUNNAN

100°

9   6   12,9
6   5   6,5
3   -1   6,4

JIANGSU   SHANGHAI   CHINA
711 Einw. pro qkm 2640 Einw. pro qkm 134 Einw. pro qkm

pro Tausend   pro Tausend   pro Tausend

JIANGSU   Shanghai

◣ Wachstumsrate
● Sterberate
◉ Geburtenrate

FLÆCHENVERÆNDERUNG DER GROSSTÆDTE
1986 – 1996

+47 %   +78 %   +216 %

Peking   Shanghai   Dalian

Shenzhen

Verhältnis Mensch zu Ackerfläche
1952   1997
0,19 ha pro person 0,10 ha pro person

1980   2004
20 000 Einw. 7 Mio. Einw.

ATIONEN

● = 168 Lebendspender

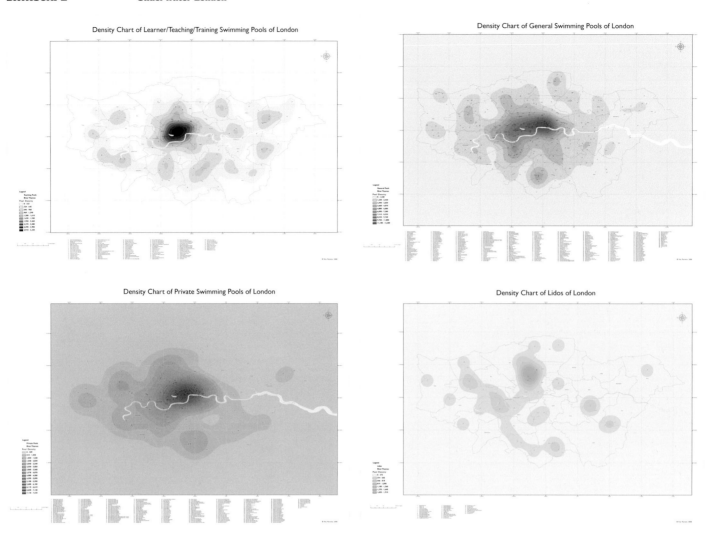

Density Chart of Public Swimming Pools of London

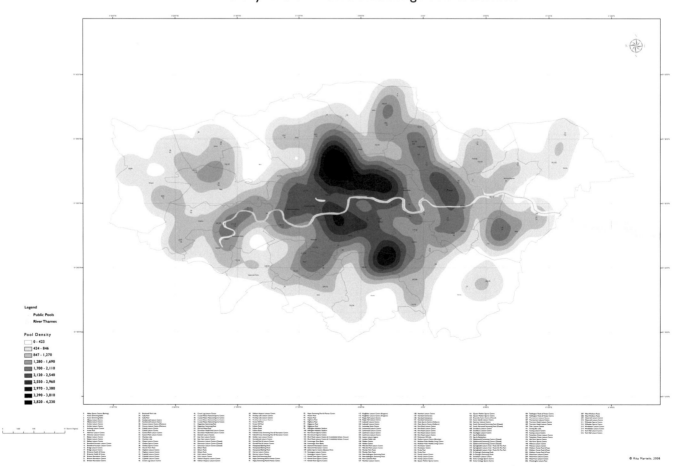

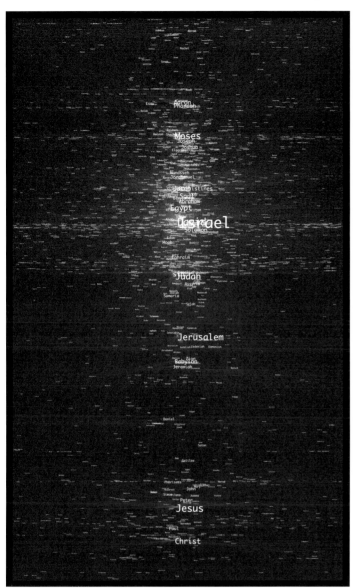

Underwater London RITA MARTELO — Navigation on open water is made possible by mapping isobaths, which establish the whereabouts of dangerous shallows. By taking soundings and measuring the depths towards sandbanks and coral reefs, maps have been produced that enable the nautical discoverer to negotiate the dangers of the unseen deep with confidence. Landlocked hydrophiles can experience dry urban landscapes with a trepidation similar to that of sailors navigating the open seas. After all, the relief promised by indoor pools and water sports often stays hidden from view. By mapping the 560 swimming pools of London, Rita Martelo has created a bathymetric map for those who navigate by hydration rather than elevation. **Distribution of Biblical People and Places** CHRIS HARRISON — The Bible, printed on one page, creates a dense mesh of cross-references. As the story unfolds in largely chronological form, the 2,600 names of people and places become clearly identifiable as more and more phrases refer to them. The font size is in proportion with the number of references. The names are floating and positioned according to their average place in the text, while the faint lines of connection draw the text as a whole together in a strong visual message. **Biblical Social Network** CHRIS HARRISON — Content creates context. Parsing the connections between 2,619 names in the King James Bible builds the original mesh of links into a thick, richly-webbed landscape of presence and place. Over 10,000 connections are represented on a compact parchment landscape by showing the more tenuously connected entities in smaller sizes, and at an angle. By applying a cartographic metaphor to the network, we are reminded of how strongly territorial the Christian faith then was, especially in the New Testament.

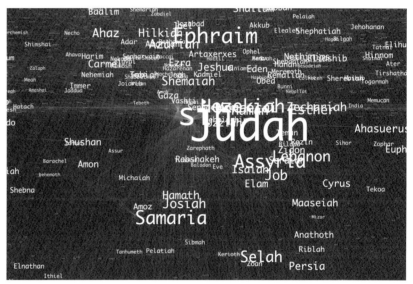

—— **Zandstad maps** LUST — Here, the archaeology of the future is projected through the narrow lens of regional statistics. Historians, working with architects to bridge the potential field of regional development, are shaping new spaces and social dynamics in an imaginary project called Zandstad (Sand City). This cartographic likeness of land usage by LUST plays with the concept that there is no single truth in the data, and that we make choices in visualising and presenting it. Satellite images rearranged according to the nature of current and future uses, rather than GPS locations, shape a new yet familiar landscape, as the viewer discovers that every statistic in some way contains a lie by being a specifically selected, approximate abstraction of the truth. —— **Zandstad** LUST, in collaboration with Kersten Nabielek — This part of the Zandstad project is a representation of what is called 'smell circles' around pig farms in part of the Zandstad area. The circles recall explosions in the gaming aesthetic, thus giving insight into the power of the smell and its impact on this area.

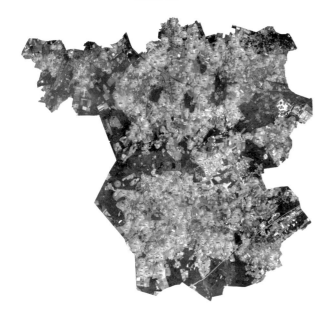

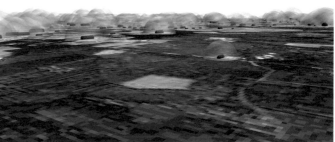

String Theory |›P. 137|CYBU RICHLI — Part of the series for *Seed* magazine. String theory is explained.

PacketGarden JULIAN OLIVER — Here we enjoy a private garden, created by our personal footprints in the web. The internet user develops a garden based on the geographic location of servers visited. The different types of data exchanged provide the foliage of the plants and shrubs, with 'http plants' and 'p2p flowers' springing from the fertile server soil. This interactive metaphor allows users to consider and reflect on their own internet usage.——**Farbmodell/Farbanalyse** PATRICK A. VUARNOZ — The profusion of visual information on the Internet has prompted an increased demand for the development of a system to analyse and search for non-text-based data. This project develops a system to automatically evaluate and display the colour distribution of an image. Brightness, saturation, and hue are quantitatively displayed in a compact referential model.

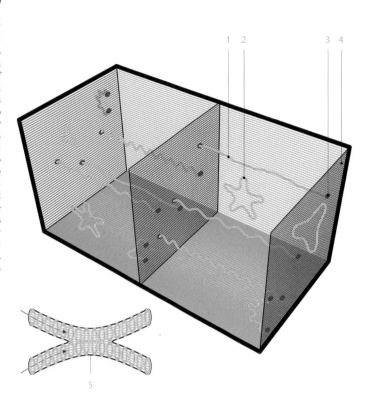

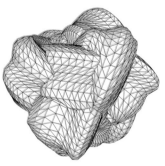

3D-projection of a Calabi-Yau

A string can be any of the fundamental particles, such as protons and electrons, depending on the frequency of its vibration and its spin. Strings come in two forms, open[1] and closed[2]. Open strings have endpoints[3], located on membrane-like structures called D-branes[4], and their dynamics closely resemble the three forces other than gravity. Closed strings ar loops, they aren't bound to D-branes and their dynamics resemble gravity. Closed strings combine and split whith each other[5], as can open strings. Open strings can also become closed strings, showing string theory comines gravity with the other forces.

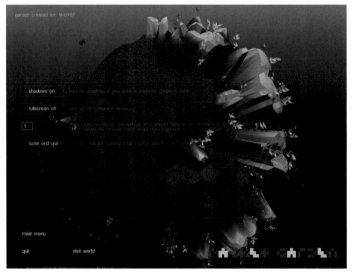

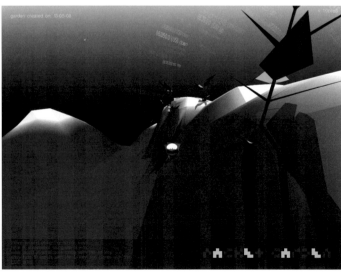

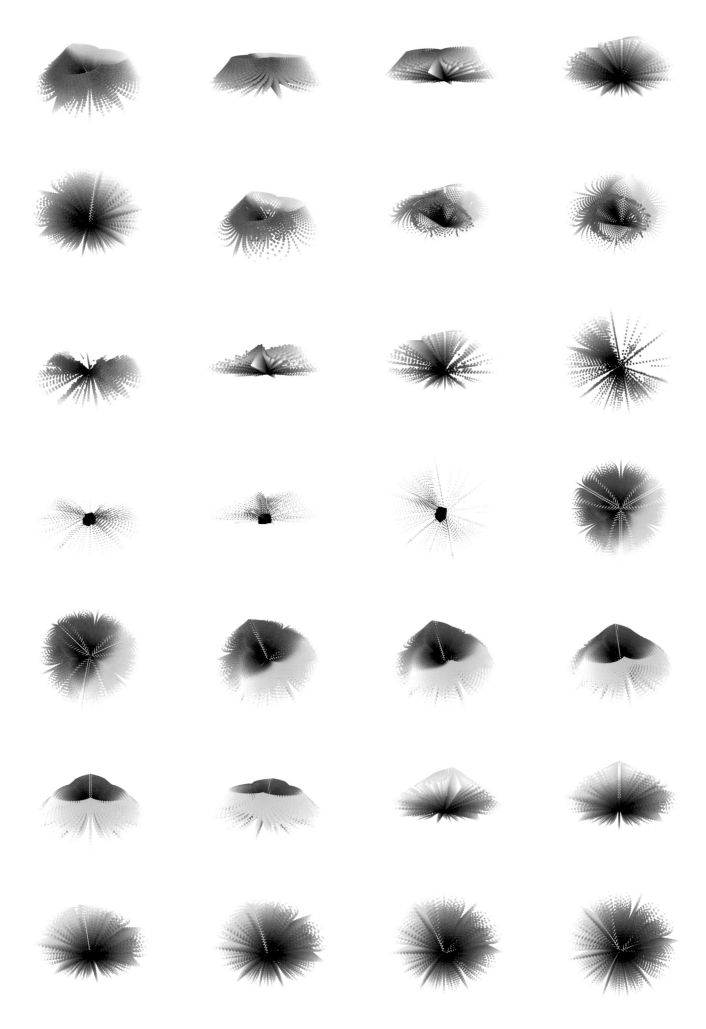

RAUMSCHIFFVERSENKEN

Die ultimative antwort auf krieg der sterne ★.★

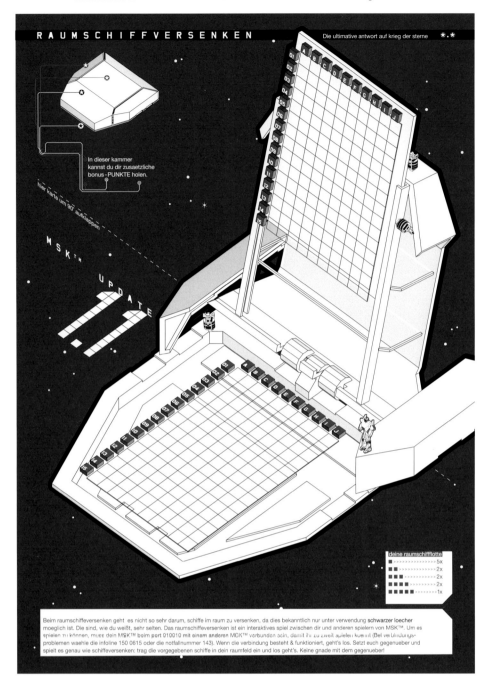

In dieser kammer kannst du dir zusaetzliche bonus-PUNKTE holen.

hier karte um 90° aufklappen

MSK™ UPDATE

deine raumschiffflotte
```
■ >>>>>>>>>>> 5x
■■ >>>>>>>>>> 2x
■■■ >>>>>>>>> 2x
■■■■ >>>>>>>> 2x
■■■■■ >>>>>>> 1x
```

Beim raumschiffeversenken geht es nicht so sehr darum, schiffe im raum zu versenken, da dies bekanntlich nur unter verwendung schwarzer loecher moeglich ist. Die sind, wie du weißt, sehr selten. Das raumschiffeversenken ist ein interaktives spiel zwischen dir und anderen spielern von MSK™. Um es spielen zu können, muss dein MSK™ beim port 010010 mit einem anderen MCK™ verbunden sein, damit ihr zu zweit spielen koennt (Bei verbindungs-problemen waehle die infoline 150 0615 oder die notfallnummer 143). Wenn die verbindung besteht & funktioniert, geht's los. Setzt euch gegenueber und spielt es genau wie schiffeversenken: trag die vorgegebenen schiffe in dein raumfeld ein und los geht's. Keine gnade mit dem gegenueber!

EIGENHEIMBUNKER

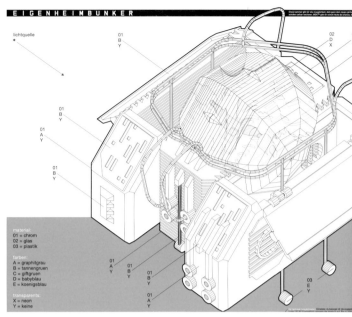

lichtquelle

material
01 = chrom
02 = glas
03 = plastik

farben:
A = graphitgrau
B = tannengruen
C = giftgruen
D = babyblau
E = koenigsblau

transparents:
X = neon
Y = keine

skim.city™

you are here ▶

63.53%

skim.slave™

skim.doc™

after locating skimmer / you see / that s
with him. he seemes not to be the skimmer
it's odd how he moves / behaves even his
so you decide to take him to the skim.doc
ups! the skim.doc™ looks worried / hesita
that skimmers™ whole structure is in a pa
provoked by a bad virus™. So to say / hi

skim.city™

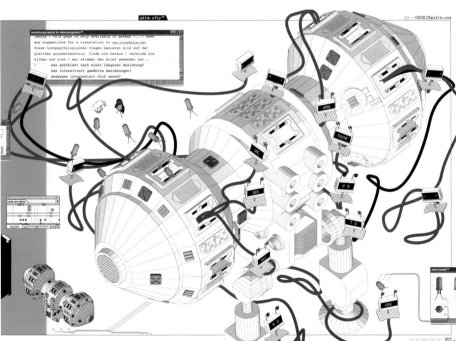

beziehungsrabel in skimmergedes™

sorry / this page is only available in german /.... send
any suggestions for a translation to use.rules@skim.com)
diese hochpsychologischen fragen basieren alle auf der
gleichen grundkenntnis. finde sie heraus / verbinde die
silben und sieh / wer skimmer den brief gesendet hat...
: was geschieht nach einer längeren beziehung?
was intensiviert gewählte beziehungen?
weswegen interessiert dich neues?

000020@skim.com

you are here

6332M

skim.com/print 005

132

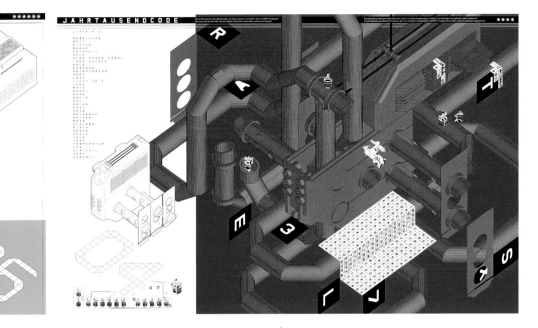

—— **Millennium Starter Kit**™
MARTIN WOODTLI — Addressing the anxiety and uncertainty that surrounded the post-millennial future, this series of systems graphics brings comfort by describing a 'millennium starter kit'. By explaining the language, artefacts, and personal pleasures one can expect in the 'dehumanised' future, Martin Woodtli reminds the viewer of the continuity and certainty of the present. He explicitly pokes fun at the overblown fears and media hype surrounding the technological threat that was once feared to lurk behind the changing of a date. —— **Skim City** MARTIN WOODTLI — Skimming is a new term that means the theft of credit card details during legitimate transactions. In this graphic, the machine aesthetic and pixelgraphic portrayal of characters form the backdrop to the practices used in credit card abuse. Via computer prompts, viewers are drawn to question their own everyday experiences, as the abstraction suddenly starts to feel very real. The individual is subjected to the snares of the system, as credit card fraud and identity theft turn day-to-day tasks into a game of financial snakes and ladders.

✉ → 000020@skim.com

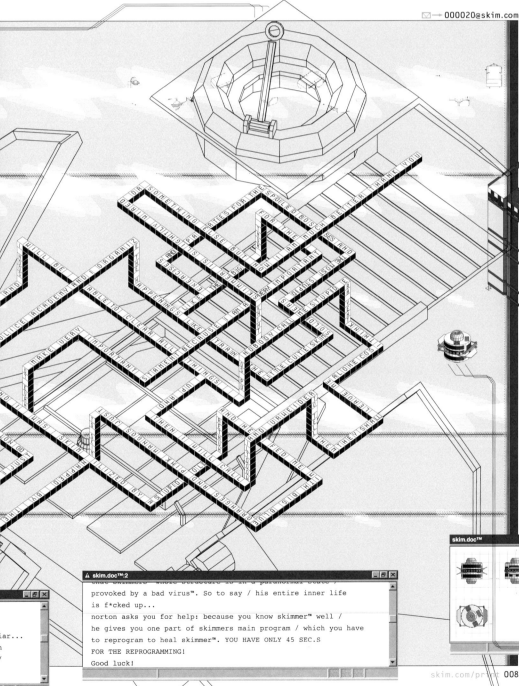

⚠ skim.doc™:2

provoked by a bad virus™. So to say / his entire inner life
is f*cked up...
norton asks you for help: because you know skimmer™ well /
he gives you one part of skimmers main program / which you have
to reprogram to heal skimmer™. YOU HAVE ONLY 45 SEC.S
FOR THE REPROGRAMMING!
Good luck!

skim.com/print 008.

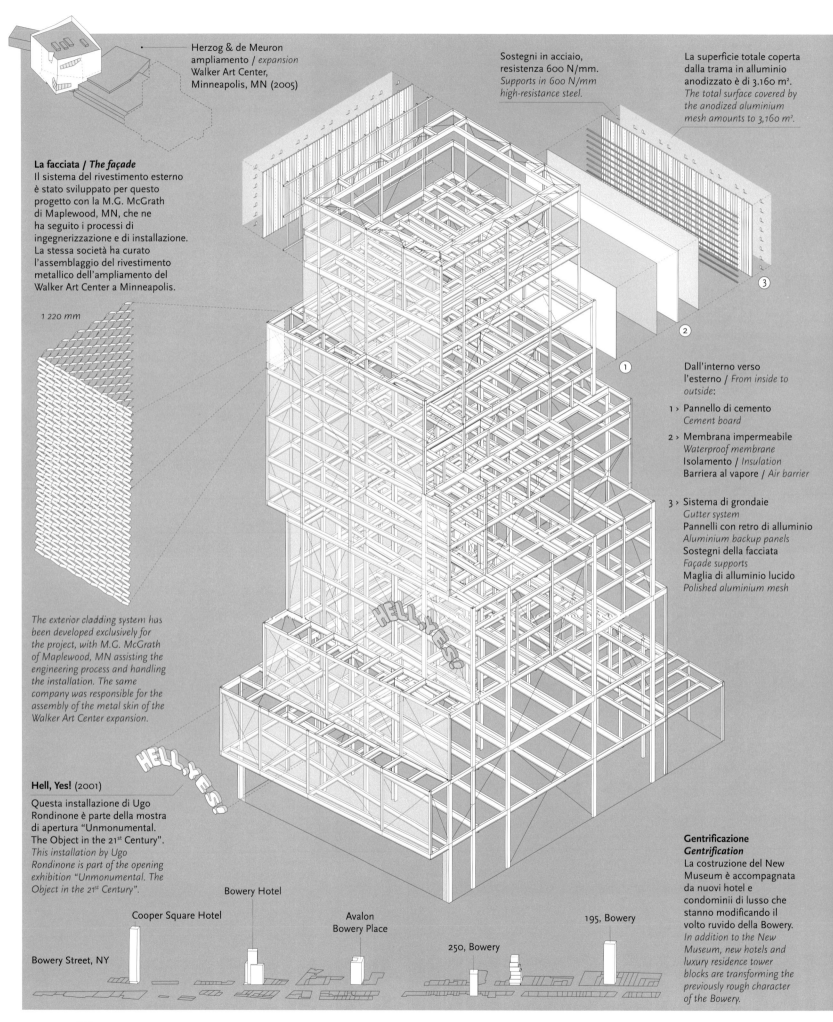

Herzog & de Meuron
ampliamento / *expansion*
Walker Art Center,
Minneapolis, MN (2005)

Sostegni in acciaio,
resistenza 600 N/mm.
*Supports in 600 N/mm
high-resistance steel.*

La superficie totale coperta
dalla trama in alluminio
anodizzato è di 3.160 m².
*The total surface covered by
the anodized aluminium
mesh amounts to 3,160 m².*

La facciata / *The façade*
Il sistema del rivestimento esterno
è stato sviluppato per questo
progetto con la M.G. McGrath
di Maplewood, MN, che ne
ha seguito i processi di
ingegnerizzazione e di installazione.
La stessa società ha curato
l'assemblaggio del rivestimento
metallico dell'ampliamento del
Walker Art Center a Minneapolis.

1 220 mm

*The exterior cladding system has
been developed exclusively for
the project, with M.G. McGrath
of Maplewood, MN assisting the
engineering process and handling
the installation. The same
company was responsible for the
assembly of the metal skin of the
Walker Art Center expansion.*

③

②

①

Dall'interno verso
l'esterno / *From inside to
outside:*

1 › Pannello di cemento
Cement board

2 › Membrana impermeabile
Waterproof membrane
Isolamento / *Insulation*
Barriera al vapore / *Air barrier*

3 › Sistema di grondaie
Gutter system
Pannelli con retro di alluminio
Aluminium backup panels
Sostegni della facciata
Façade supports
Maglia di alluminio lucido
Polished aluminium mesh

HELL, YES!

Hell, Yes! (2001)
Questa installazione di Ugo
Rondinone è parte della mostra
di apertura "Unmonumental.
The Object in the 21ˢᵗ Century".
*This installation by Ugo
Rondinone is part of the opening
exhibition "Unmonumental. The
Object in the 21ˢᵗ Century".*

**Gentrificazione
*Gentrification***
La costruzione del New
Museum è accompagnata
da nuovi hotel e
condominii di lusso che
stanno modificando il
volto ruvido della Bowery.
*In addition to the New
Museum, new hotels and
luxury residence tower
blocks are transforming the
previously rough character
of the Bowery.*

Bowery Hotel

Cooper Square Hotel

Avalon
Bowery Place

195, Bowery

250, Bowery

Bowery Street, NY

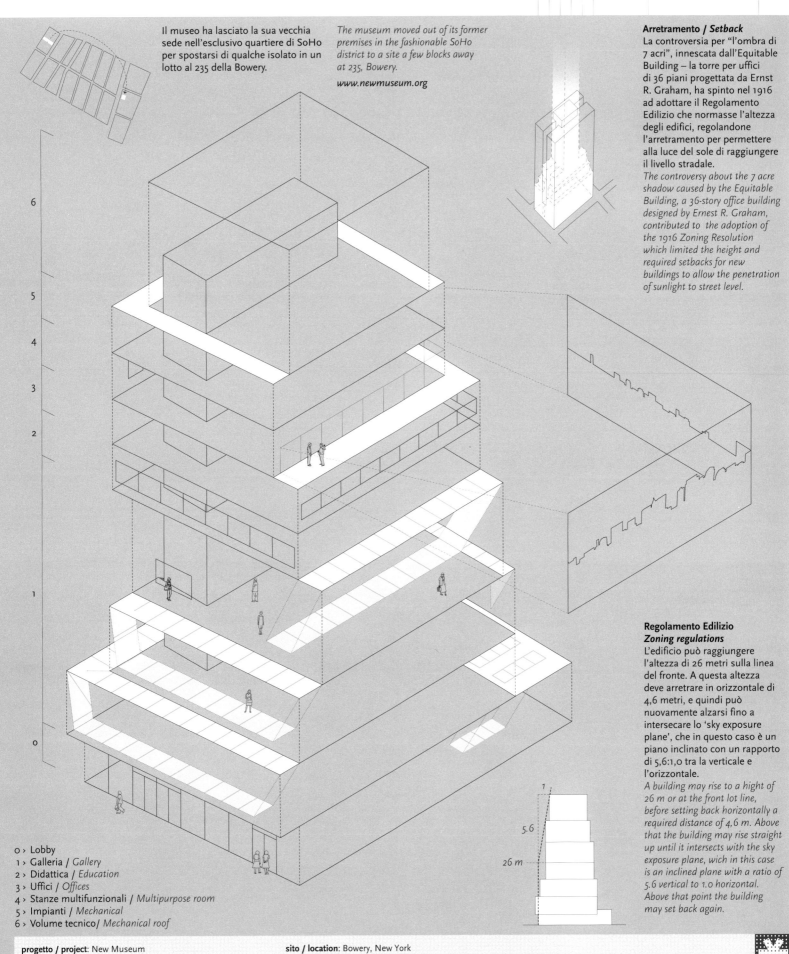

0   5   10   20 m

Il museo ha lasciato la sua vecchia sede nell'esclusivo quartiere di SoHo per spostarsi di qualche isolato in un lotto al 235 della Bowery.

The museum moved out of its former premises in the fashionable SoHo district to a site a few blocks away at 235, Bowery.

www.newmuseum.org

Arretramento / *Setback*

La controversia per "l'ombra di 7 acri", innescata dall'Equitable Building – la torre per uffici di 36 piani progettata da Ernst R. Graham, ha spinto nel 1916 ad adottare il Regolamento Edilizio che normasse l'altezza degli edifici, regolandone l'arretramento per permettere alla luce del sole di raggiungere il livello stradale.

The controversy about the 7 acre shadow caused by the Equitable Building, a 36-story office building designed by Ernest R. Graham, contributed to the adoption of the 1916 Zoning Resolution which limited the height and required setbacks for new buildings to allow the penetration of sunlight to street level.

Regolamento Edilizio
Zoning regulations

L'edificio può raggiungere l'altezza di 26 metri sulla linea del fronte. A questa altezza deve arretrare in orizzontale di 4,6 metri, e quindi può nuovamente alzarsi fino a intersecare lo 'sky exposure plane', che in questo caso è un piano inclinato con un rapporto di 5,6:1,0 tra la verticale e l'orizzontale.

A building may rise to a hight of 26 m or at the front lot line, before setting back horizontally a required distance of 4,6 m. Above that the building may rise straight up until it intersects with the sky exposure plane, wich in this case is an inclined plane with a ratio of 5.6 vertical to 1.0 horizontal. Above that point the building may set back again.

0 › Lobby
1 › Galleria / *Gallery*
2 › Didattica / *Education*
3 › Uffici / *Offices*
4 › Stanze multifunzionali / *Multipurpose room*
5 › Impianti / *Mechanical*
6 › Volume tecnico/ *Mechanical roof*

progetto / project: New Museum
tipologia / tipology: Museo d'arte contemporanea
Museum of contemporary arts
anno / year: 2007

sito / location: Bowery, New York
progettista / architect: Kazuyo Sejima e / *and* Ryue Nishizawa / SANAA
superficie totale / surface area: 5.388,32 m²
costo / cost: US $ 50,000,000

PREVIOUS PAGES —— **Instructions and Manuals** SALOTTOBUONO — Exposing the intellectual, social, and process ecology of a project, salottobuono bring profound new insight to the meaning of individual design projects. Approaching designed spaces and objects as unknown objects that need to be explained, they apply various visual and verbal techniques to document the route to discovery. The final result is explained in situ, exploded and expanded across a landscape of inspiration and constraints. Intelligent navigation of local building regulations, peripheral design references, and other information is shaped into the specific ecology of the project, showing both how an object is shaped by, and shapes, its context. The designers' navigation of this conceptual landscape inspires and informs the viewer not only by what is evident in the final design, but also what has consciously been excluded or artfully overcome.

—— **Instructions and Manuals** SALOTTOBUONO —— **Hydrogen Car** —— **Nuclear Reactor** —— **Extinction** CYBU RICHLI — Part of the series for *Seed* magazine.

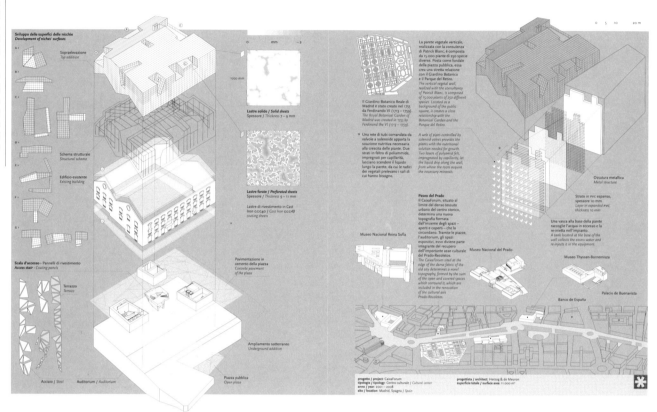

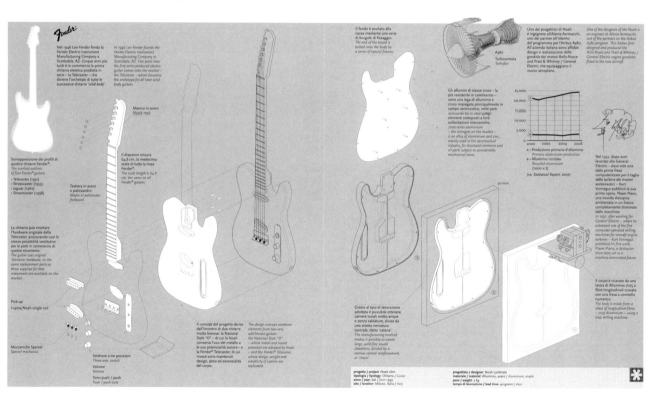

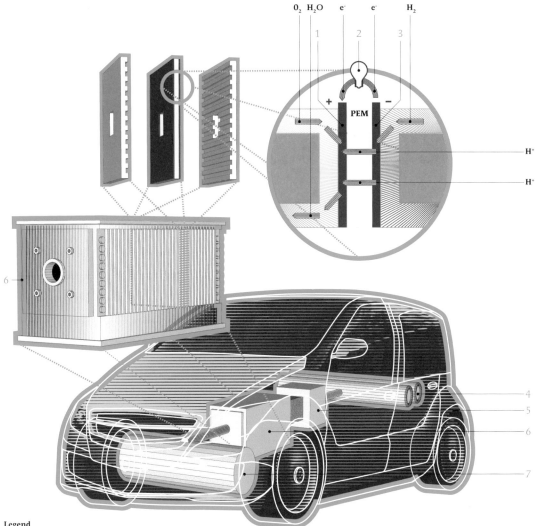

0_2 H_2O e⁻   e⁻ H_2

1   2   3

+   PEM   −

H⁺

H⁺

6

4

5

6

7

Legend
1 **Cathode**
2 **Energy**
3 **Anode**
4 **Hydrogen tank**
5 **Reformer** Extracts hydrogen from fuel, delivers it to fuel cell stack.

6 **Fuel cell stack** The reaction in a single fuel cell produces a very low voltage, so many cells are combined into a stack to produce the desired level of electrical power.
7 **Electric motor**

H_2 – Hydrogen
0_2 – Air
H_2O – Air + Water

$H_2 \rightarrow 2H^+ + 2e^-$

$0_2 + 4H^+ + 4e^- \rightarrow 2H_2O$

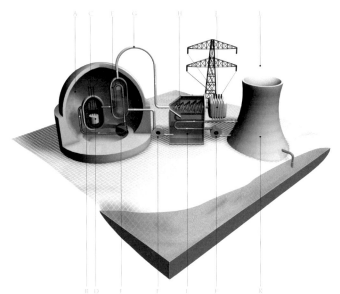

A C E G   H   I   J   L

Parts
Containement structure ^A, reactor steel pressure vessel ^B, control rods ^C, reactor ^D, steam generator ^E, pumps ^F, streamline ^G, turbine ^H, cooling water condenser ^I, generator ^J, cooling tower ^K, steam/air ^L.

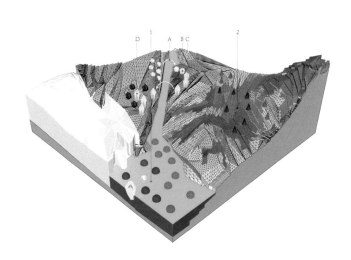

D 1   A B C   2

1 Glaciation slowly drains, cools, and deoxygenates an aquatic environment, threatening a species's survival.
2 A volcanic eruption rapidly wipes out a localized species.

A A newly formed river isolates some members of a species.
B Environmental pressures select for new traits.
C Over time a new species evolves.
D If beneficial adaptations have occurred, intermingling could eliminate the original species.

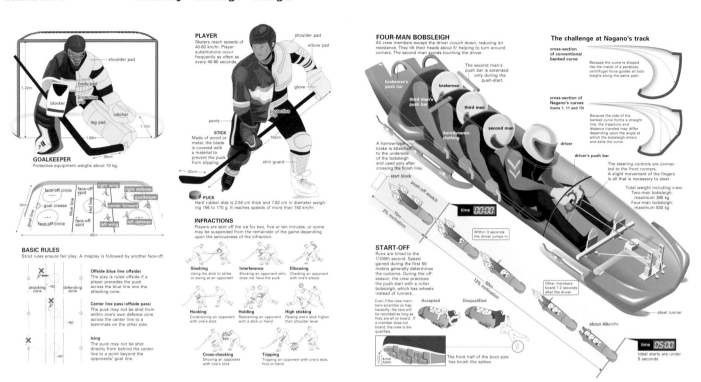

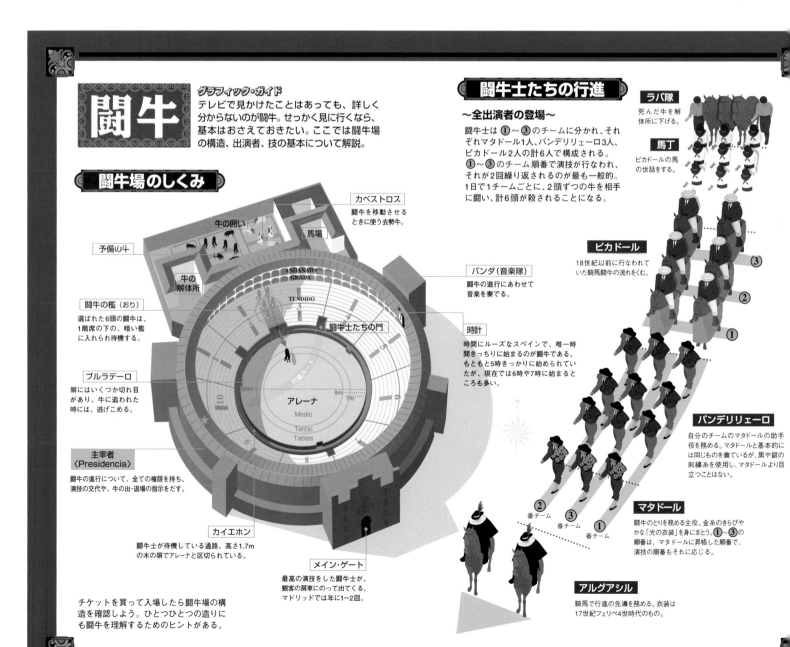

—— Ice hockey —— Bobsleigh
TUBE GRAPHICS — This is part of a series of illustrations created for the Winter Olympics in Nagano in 1998 to familiarise visitors with the key facts about sometimes unfamiliar and unusual sports. The easy-to-read visual confections provide insights into the playing fields or tracks, as well as descriptions of players and the basic rules, allowing a more enjoyable experience of the Games.
—— Bullfight TUBE GRAPHICS — This graphic leads the tourist to a better understanding of local rituals and culture, relying not only on the national colours of Spain to describe the rules of bullfighting, but also tapping into the flamboyant gestures and poses of the matadors to add a touch of passion. Like a condensed libretto, the representation allows the reader to follow the theatre of the fight, with all its subtleties of technique and the awe of the spectacle.

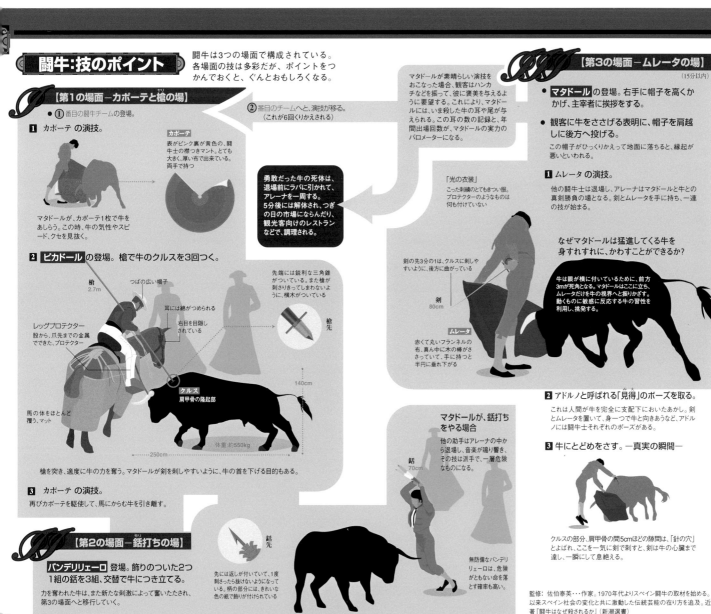

闘牛：技のポイント

闘牛は3つの場面で構成されている。各場面の技は多彩だが、ポイントをつかんでおくと、ぐんとおもしろくなる。

【第1の場面－カポーテと槍の場】

● ①番目の闘牛チームの登場。

1 カポーテ の演技。

マタドールが、カポーテ1枚で牛をあしらう。この時、牛の気性やスピード、クセを見抜く。

カポーテ
表がピンク裏が黄色の、闘牛士の襟つきマント。とても大きく、厚い布で出来ている。両手で持つ

2 ピカドール の登場。槍で牛のクルスを3回つく。

槍 2.7m

つばの広い帽子

耳には綿がつめられる

右目を目隠しされている

レッグプロテクター
股から、爪先までの金属でできた、プロテクター

先端には鋭利な三角錐がついている。また槍が刺さりきってしまわないように、横木がついている

槍先

クルス
肩甲骨の隆起部

馬の体をほとんど覆う、マット

140cm

250cm

体重 約550kg

槍を突き、適度に牛の力を奪う。マタドールが剣を刺しやすいように、牛の首を下げる目的もある。

3 カポーテ の演技。

再びカポーテを駆使して、馬にからむ牛を引き離す。

②番目のチームへと、演技が移る。
（これが6回くりかえされる）

勇敢だった牛の死体は、退場前にラバに引かれて、アレーナを一周する。5分後には解体され、つぎの日の市場にならんだり、観客客向けのレストランなどで、調理される。

【第2の場面－銛打ちの場】

バンデリリェーロ 登場。飾りのついた2つ1組の銛を3組、交替で牛につき立てる。

力を奪われた牛は、また新たな刺激によって奮いたたされ、第3の場面へと移行していく。

銛先
先には返しが付いていて、1度刺さったら抜けないようになっている。柄の部分には、きれいな色の紙で飾りが付けられている

マタドールが、銛打ちをやる場合

他の助手はアレーナの中から退場し、音楽が鳴り響き、その技は派手で、一層危険なものになる。

銛 70cm

無防備なバンデリリェーロは、危険がともなう命を落とす確率も高い。

マタドールが素晴らしい演技をおこなった場合、観客はハンカチなどを振って、彼に褒美を与えるように要望する。これにより、マタドールには、いま殺した牛の耳や尾が与えられる。この耳の数の記録と、年間出場回数が、マタドールの実力のバロメーターになる。

「光の衣装」
こった刺繍のとてもきつい服。プロテクターのようなものは何も付けていない

【第3の場面－ムレータの場】
（15分以内）

● **マタドール** の登場。右手に帽子を高くかかげ、主宰者に挨拶をする。

● 観客に牛をささげる表明に、帽子を肩越しに後方へ投げる。

この帽子がひっくりかえって地面に落ちると、縁起が悪いといわれる。

1 ムレータ の演技。

他の闘牛士は退場し、アレーナはマタドールと牛との真剣勝負の場となる。剣とムレータを手に持ち、一連の技が始まる。

なぜマタドールは猛進してくる牛を身すれすれに、かわすことができるか？

牛は眼が横に付いているために、前方3mが死角となる。マタドールはここに立ち、ムレータだけを牛の視界へと振りかざす。動くものに敏感に反応する牛の習性を利用し、挑発する。

剣の先3分の1は、クルスに刺しやすいように、後方に曲がっている

剣 80cm

ムレータ
赤くて丸いフランネルの布、真ん中に木の棒がさっていて、手に持つと半円に垂れ下がる

2 アドルノと呼ばれる「見得」のポーズを取る。

これは人間が牛を完全に支配下においたあかし。剣とムレータを置いて、身一つで牛と向きあうなど、アドルノには闘牛士それぞれのポーズがある。

3 牛にとどめをさす。―真実の瞬間―

クルスの部分、肩甲骨の間5cmほどの隙間は、「針の穴」とよばれ、ここを一気に剣で刺すと、剣は牛の心臓まで達し、一瞬にして息絶える。

監修：佐伯泰英…作家。1970年代よりスペイン闘牛の取材を始める。以来スペイン社会の変化と共に激動した伝統芸能の在り方を追及。近著「闘牛はなぜ殺されるか」（新潮選書）

Diagramming a Unified Workflow FUNNEL INC. — Here we see overlapping work flows, given shape and context in relation to each other. The four strands of business, production, colour, and data are connected in a pre- and post-production landscape of the printing industry. The intersections define points where data converges into discrete production steps, illustrating where Kodak Eastman's products add value. — **How Books Are Made** FUNNEL INC. — Interviews, observations, and detailed studies of book production are moulded into a tableau landscape of tools and processes. The complexity and cost of producing a book become evident as viewers follow their own story across the illustration. The use of pictograms, combined with text labels and flows, provides a clear and accurate description for readers with various levels of experience or knowledge. In particular, the inclusion of people in the process reinforces the care, cost, and craft that go into making a book. This is not a blind, automated process; it relies on judgement and expertise. — **Workflow** RETO MOSER & TOBIAS RECHSTEINER — This chart shows a parallel and comparative landscape providing multiple points of entry for understanding the nuanced and scalar differences between French and German texts. Walking along the path describing the steps taken, from reading to printing and saving a selected text, the work flow cascades into comparative data flow. The differences at every level — captured, compiled, and visually compared — develop into a progressive disclosure of the exact difference and potential impact of processing a piece of information in one language, as opposed to another. The zonal allocation of specific comparisons clearly separates out the effects of language on process and expense, as well as soft issues such as the number of steps taken to walk to the same printer.

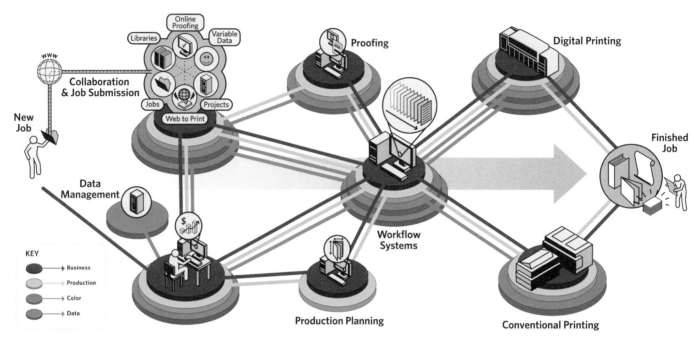

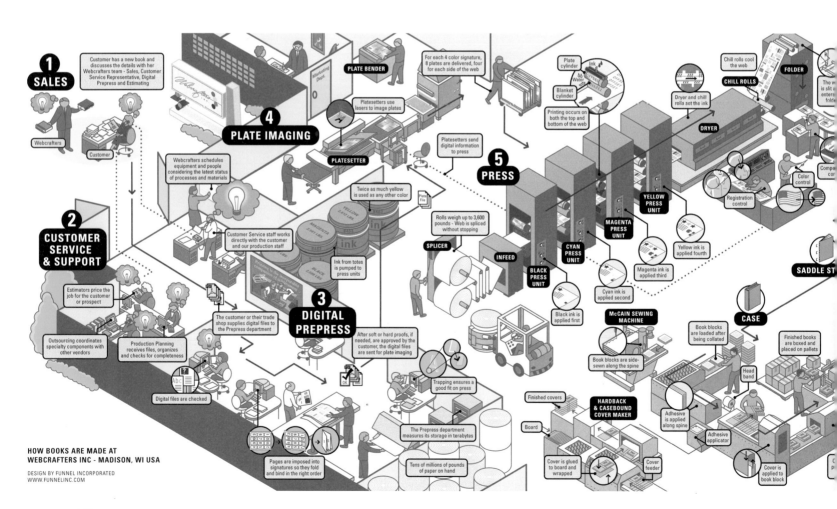

HOW BOOKS ARE MADE AT
WEBCRAFTERS INC - MADISON, WI USA

DESIGN BY FUNNEL INCORPORATED
WWW.FUNNELINC.COM

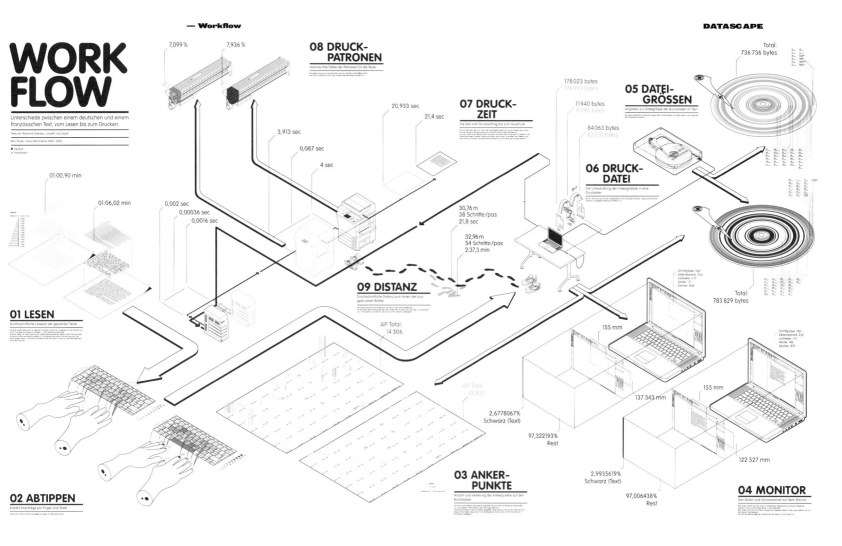

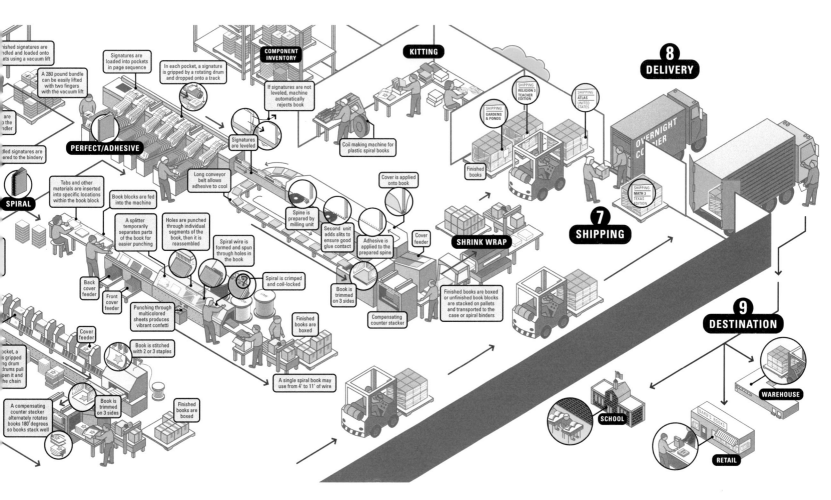

—— **American Varietal** JASON SALAVON — America is often referred to as the world's melting pot. Most of modern America's population is derived from immigrant stock, their forefathers having left behind families and homelands in pursuit of a brighter future. These ethnically diverse peoples embrace their new homeland, yet retain the subtle signs of their heritage. Their indelible mark is left by the development of local communities, as shown in this project, which depicts changes from 1790 to 2000 — the American Varietal, blended from different notes, distinct yet harmonious.

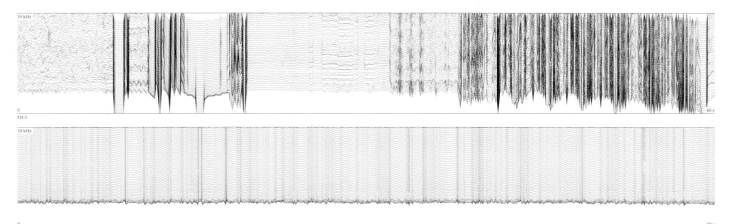

70
dB

20
kHz

10
s

0

————— **Ars viva 07/08 – sound**
1KILO — Themed around the concept of sound, 1kilo's approach to the ars viva 07/08 project was to turn music into visual landscapes. Soundscapes provide new access to the winning work, turning it into a visual rather than aural expression. Sound is a surprisingly complex phenomenon and cannot be represented in print in any single or definitive way. This piece adds nuance and interpretation to the simple data, in a homage to the winner's work.
————— **The Long Black Veil** Jeffrey Docherty — Here, we see the ethereal landscape of the music scene, an ever-changing confluence of sounds and people, shaping, forming, and reinterpreting, to create the distinct cultural identity of a generation. This soundscape is dedicated to the legendary Tony Wilson, one of the founders of the Hacienda nightclub in Manchester, and a formative figure in bringing British punk to the forefront of the music scene. Focusing on regional influences, Wilson helped a number of breakthrough acts to build careers, through his label Factory Records.　　　　By seeing sound as an aural landscape, in stark black and white, we get a sense of the disruptive quality of punk, and the mark it left on contemporary British music. The solitary strands of white, etched against the black background, trace an auditory topographical map of the 'Madchester' zeitgeist.

10 kHz

0
FH.3

60 s

10 kHz

0
ND.3

60 s

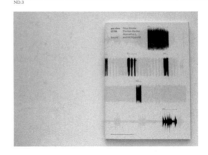

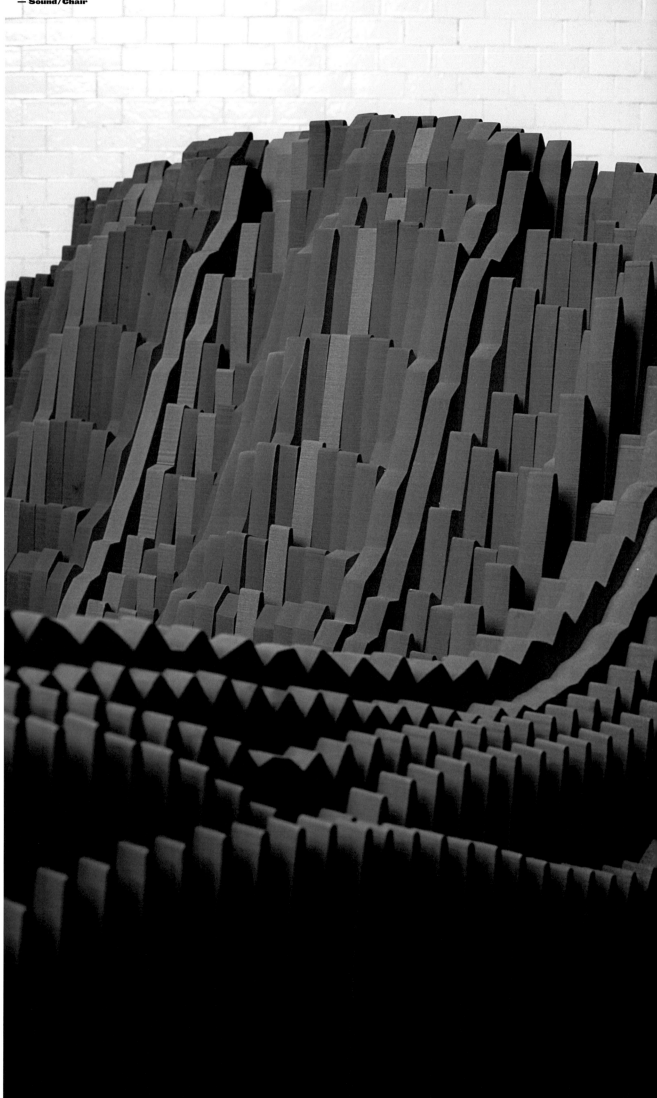

Sound/Chair MATTHEW PLUMMER-FERNANDEZ, photograph by Toby Summerskill — We know how music makes us feel, but what does music feel like as an objective quantity? Here, the three dimensions of sound — frequency, volume, and timing — are accurately represented as three-dimensional objects. The sharp peaks and layers provide a novel, visceral immersion into an aural landscape.

A Week in the Life ANDREAS NICOLAS FISCHER — With this sculpture, mobile communication becomes incarnate, by mapping the topographical landscape of mobile phone usage over a period of a week.

As a physical object, the sculpture serves as a reminder of the German Data Retention Act, which requires mobile phone operators to store the mobile usage data of individuals. The artefacts of our movements and connections are usually hidden inside massive databases, yet are a real and tangible intrusion by the government into our privacy.

Datanoid

—

Retailers find that by placing mirrors in the window, passers-by slow down and take more time to look at the merchandise. As social animals, we are fascinated by our own reflections. We seek out a response not only from reflections of ourselves; we also seek the bonds of unity and distinction in the images of others, as learning is driven primarily by emotional relevance.

—

Normally, we decide if something is emotionally relevant before we engage and invest the high-octane processing power of our deliberate consciousness. Emotional relevance is the knife that

—

Humanoid becomes datanoid

—

cuts through the clutter, and this chapter looks at how data works on a human scale. The hand-drawn diagrams communicate with far greater potency than perfectly rendered pie charts. They do this because they place humans in the scale, to show specific relevance and impact for people like ourselves. By making the audience part of the message, the message connects at a deeper level. Humanoid becomes datanoid, and not simply plotting points of data. It is famously impossible not to communicate, however much we try. The clothes, facial expressions, hairstyles, and attitudes of people captured in depictions of data relay a high bandwidth of meaning. This is sometimes intentional, and sometimes not, but it is always relevant. By using images of themselves, scaled according to load, to

— Von B und C |> P. 160|
BARBARA HAHN &
CHRISTINE ZIMMERMANN

express a year of their working lives, Barbara Hahn and Christine Zimmermann provide both content and a contextual guide to their progress over twelve months. Moods are captured through facial expressions. The artists are shown two days in a row, wearing the same clothes. The richness of expression brings the reader to a subtler, more human understanding than would have been possible using simple bar charts based on exactly the same data.

— The Revolutionary Comic Presentation System |> P. 173|
CHRAGOKYBERNETICKS

Different degrees of abstraction can be finely regulated to allow a considered amount of subjective inference. Welcometo.as uses the clothes and hairstyles in simple pictograms to communicate uniformity and the lack of progression in thought. The identity of the individual is not as important as the collective change in social artefacts. Chragokyberneticks's cartoon style

takes this even further. Reduced identity becomes increased applicability, as the tale that unfolds can become anyone's story. At the other end of the scale, Carlo Giovani turns the body into a canvas for communicating the dangers of sexually transmitted diseases. The permanence of tattoos underlines the life-changing damage that can be incurred by thoughtless actions. The use of erotically charged bodies endows the meaning with a personal dimension. An ongoing theme throughout Uta Eisenreich's

— O lado curioso doSexo |> P. 170|
CARLO GIOVANI

installations is to give the data real personality and relevance. In a world filled with the hype of web 2.0, her depiction of social networks in a real playground is a reminder that it is still real people who count. We can apply a meta-layer of information to try and reveal the inner dynamics of a group, yet it is the personality, and the character of the individuals concerned, that really count.

— Netzwork / Teamwork |> P. 174|
UTA EISENREICH

The importance of personality becomes poignantly clear in the collection of hand-drawn maps. The design and construction of these explanatory charts are a visual extension of the authors. The inclusion or absence of key data colours the whole, in a contextual and direct reference to the fact that

LOCATION MAP

— Location map |> P. 163| HANDMAPS.ORG

a real person drew the maps. The way the viewer approaches the work now changes completely. We infer a lot more, and extract a lot more than we would from a formal and structured cartographic presentation where the thinking has been done for us. In the words of Brian Eno, interactive means incomplete.

The vulnerability and the imprecise nature of our dialogues engage us far more than deliberate and precise rendering. We step inside the world of the designer, and our own frame of reference is both necessary

—Social Studies
|>P. 169| EMILY GINSBURG

and contributory to the understanding of the data. Emily Ginsburg's journey through her environment, together with her resulting reflections, perverts traditional scale and linear sequencing, to provide a little window into the truth of human experience. In this reflection, we seek ourselves and our interlocutors, in order to arrive at a more complete understanding of our humanity.

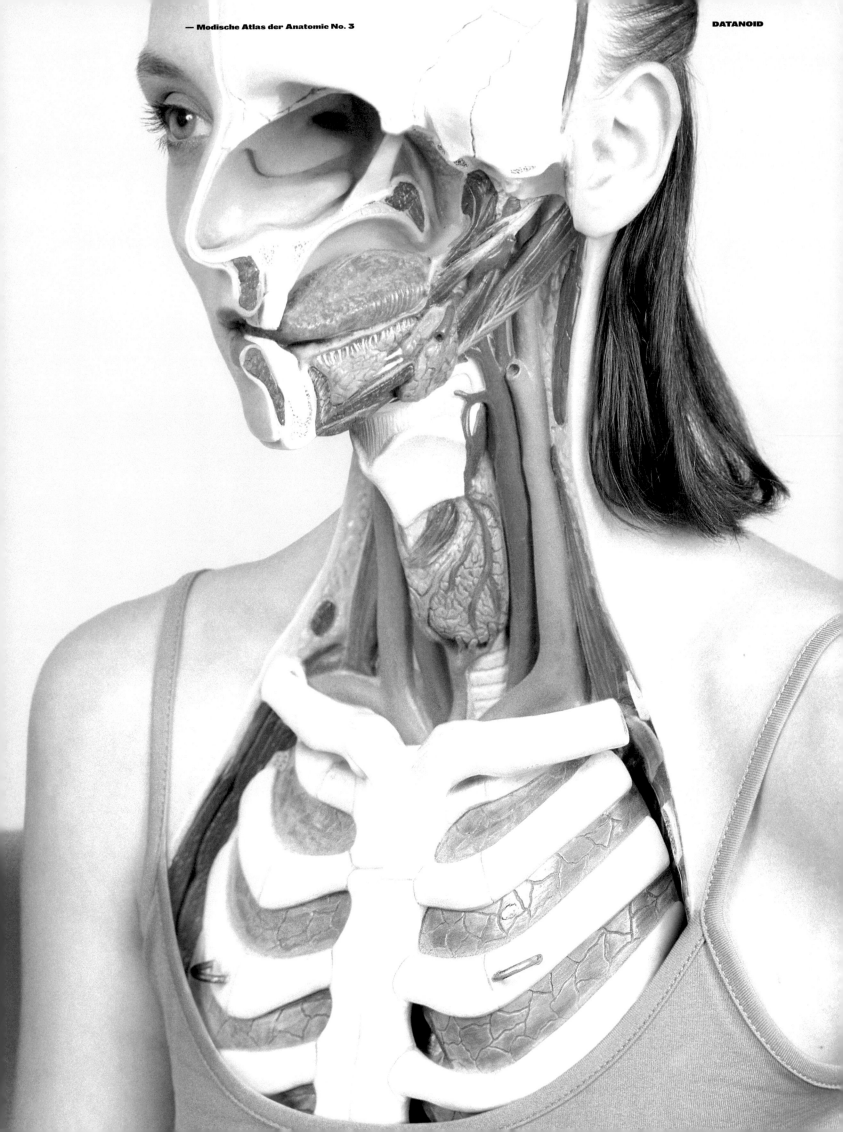

PREVIOUS PAGE ——— **Modische Atlas der Anatomie No. 3** KOEN HAUSER — Clarity can be revealed or concealed. This piece is a reminder of the human element, often obscured by the plastic, abstracted constructions used to portray the workings of the body. Medical science is becoming more personal. Biochemistry allows for ever greater refinement in the development of specific, individually personalised treatments. This photo montage highlights the humanity of the subject associated with the 'medical' condition by revealing his or her identity. It is the person we should see, and not just the disease.

——— **Move Our Money** STEFAN SAGMEISTER — The 'Move Our Money' project was initiated by Ben Cohen, of ice cream manufacturers Ben and Jerry's. Its aim is to bring inflation and overspending in military budgets back to the forefront of public debate. The work, which presents various aspects of the US budget as inflatable sculptures, was taken across America in a road show, to inform the electorate and place public pressure on the government to redirect fifteen per cent of the Pentagon budget to healthcare and education. Using inflatables reinforces the idea of flexibility of allocation.

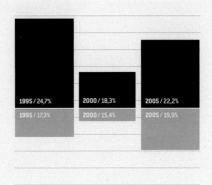

TAUX DE CHÔMAGE DES 15-24 ANS EN 1995 / 2000 / 2005

1995 / 24,7%
1995 / 17,3%
2000 / 18,3%
2000 / 15,4%
2005 / 22,2%
2005 / 19,9%

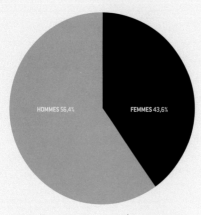

POURCENTAGE DE FEMMES AU PARLEMENT EN LÉGISLATURE 2004/2009

HOMMES 56,4%
FEMMES 43,6%

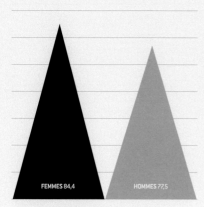

ESPÉRANCE DE VIE DES FEMMES ET DES HOMMES EN 2007.

FEMMES 84,4
HOMMES 77,5

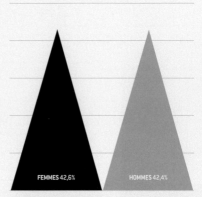

TAUX DE SCOLARISATION EN SECONDAIRE DES 18-24 ANS EN 2005-2006

FEMMES 42,6%
HOMMES 42,4%

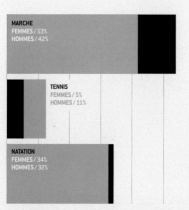

TAUX DE PRATIQUE RÉGULIÈRE DE MARCHE, TENNIS ET NATATION EN 2007

MARCHE
FEMMES / 53%
HOMMES / 42%

TENNIS
FEMMES / 5%
HOMMES / 11%

NATATION
FEMMES / 34%
HOMMES / 32%

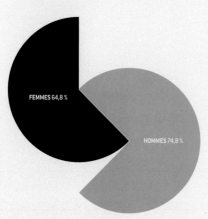

TAUX D'ACTIVITÉ DES FEMMES ET DES HOMMES DE PLUS DE 15 ANS EN 2006

FEMMES 64,8 %
HOMMES 74,8 %

SALAIRE DES FRANCAIS EN 2007

90% DES FRANCAIS GAGNENT MOINS DE 3029 € PAR MOIS
50% DES FRANCAIS GAGNENT MOINS DE 1528 € PAR MOIS
10% DES FRANCAIS GAGNENT MOINS DE 1042 € PAR MOIS

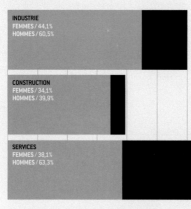

SALAIRE DES FRANCAIS PAR SECTEUR D'ACTIVITÉ EN 2005 (EN KM D'EUROS)

INDUSTRIE
FEMMES / 44,1%
HOMMES / 60,5%

CONSTRUCTION
FEMMES / 34,1%
HOMMES / 39,9%

SERVICES
FEMMES / 38,1%
HOMMES / 63,3%

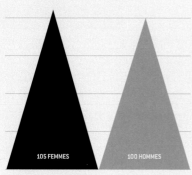

RATIO FEMMES / HOMMES EN FRANCE EN 2007

105 FEMMES
100 HOMMES

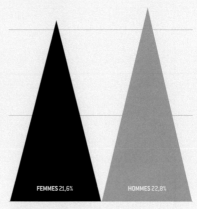

TAUX DE BÂCHELIERS ENTRE 25 ET 34 ANS EN 2006

FEMMES 21,6%
HOMMES 22,8%

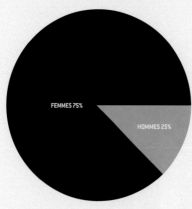

OCCUPATION DES EMPLOIS DU SECTEUR DE L'ÉDUCATION

FEMMES 75%
HOMMES 25%

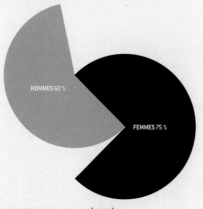

POURCENTAGE DE FRANCAIS MARIÉS INFIDÈLES

HOMMES 60 %
FEMMES 75 %

SONDAGES REALISÉS PAR L'INSEE ENTRE 2005 ET 2007 / "ÉTUDIANTS, TOUS À CHAUMONT!", ADAM, VALENTIN, 2008.

Audio

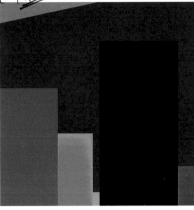

*the more I see,
the more I learn,
the more I learn
the more I AM*

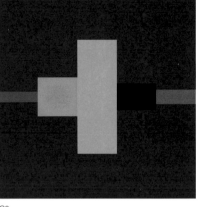

An Underground Disco
Information Organisation

Sex / Intoxication / Music / Fashion

Q1
What music turns you
on most?

Dance
Soul
Functronica
Classical

Q2a
Thong or Full-panel?
(Asked of Females)

Thong
Full-panel
No Answer

Q2b
Cowboy boots or Trainers?
(Asked of Males)

Cowboy boots
Trainers

Q3
(On average) How many units
of alcohol do you drink on a
Saturday night?

0
1-5
6-10
11-15
16+

Q4a
In amorous liaisons are you
proactive or pasive?
(Asked of Males)

Proactive*
Pasive*

Q4b
(Asked of Females)

Proactive*
Pasive*

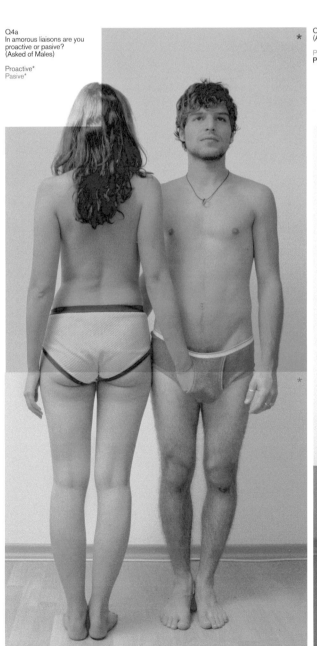

PREVIOUS PAGES —— **Hommes/Femmes** VALENTIN ADAM — Differences in gender still affect people's experiences and opportunities in life. By combining and shaping the statistical analysis of male and female demographics, this layout literally spells out those differences. The transmutation of pie charts and histograms into the letters spelling out 'Hommes' (men) and 'Femmes' (women) enhances the observation, as the effect is only possible because of the contrasts. If men and women really were equal in terms of salary and participation in sport and in politics, the charts would be flat and featureless. —— **An Underground Disco Information Organisation** RED DESIGN, photography by Ben Wittner — Audio Brighton's hedonistic dedication to pleasure and fun is reflected in this loosely statistical presentation of their surveys. Under the headline 'sex/intoxication/music/fashion', the semantic priorities are clearly set for this underground disco information organisation. Should it be cowboy boots or trainers? Will the seduction be active or passive? The trivial yet decisive choices of the revelling bon vivant are affectionately mocked through provocative photographic expression. It's the style of style, the honesty of entrapment. Having sex and fun isn't rocket science.

—— **An Underground Disco Information Organisation** RED DESIGN, photography by Ben Wittner —— **Schallzentrale, electronic sounds for those who know** EPS51, photography by Ben Wittner — This is a conceptual photography series promoting Schallzentrale, a club in Fuerth, Bavaria. The series of photos becomes a metaphor for musical predilections and consumption, by using visuals to emphasise discerning tastes and reactions to music. The proposition of 'music for those that know' becomes a personal promise.

—— **Typographic body** |> PP. 158, 245 | BENOIT LEMOINE — The human body is shown here as ambiguous code. A deliberately orchestrated mise-en-scène vocabulary is used to reflect meaning both in, and of, itself. The typographical lexicon appears in all the posters. Each poster in this series — called 'Corps Typographique' (the typographic body) — addresses a particular theme, explained through a little scene. There is one image per letter. The variation in body type is meticulously measured in each image, with each value corresponding to a specific letter. For example, 'thickness' — the width of the torso — is measured and spells out the letters G.R.A.I.S.S.E. (French for 'fat').

Audio

An Underground Disco
Information Organisation

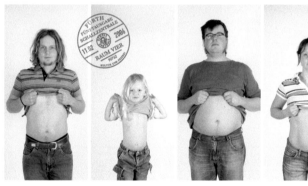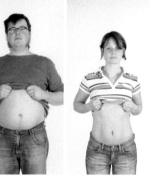

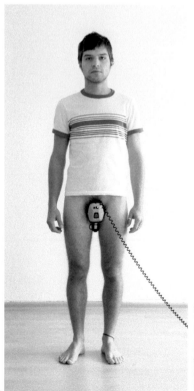

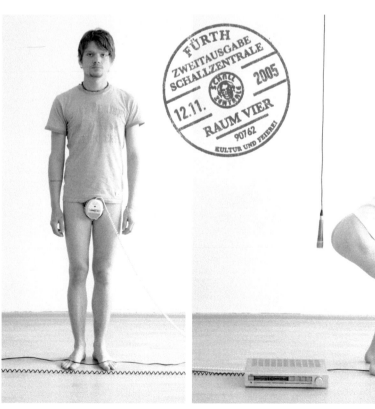

Typographie   Benoit Lemoine   Erg / 2007   www.lemoinebenoit.eu / www.repeataferme.eu

CORPS TYPOGRAPHIQUE | SOUVENIR ITC

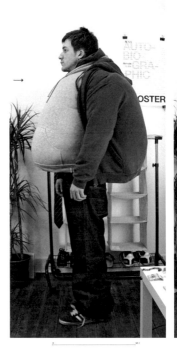

lexique typographique (suite)

Espace: blanc sans inscription positionné de façon à séparer deux caractères ou deux mots d'un texte. L'espace entre les mots est obtenu sur le clavier avec la barre d'espacement. Il en existe différents types : sécable, insécable, justifiant, etc. Espace fine: espace d'un quart de cadratin, normalement utilisé entre la fin d'un mot et une ponctuation forte comme le point d'exclamation ou le point d'interrogation.
Espace insécable: espace de dimension fixe, positionné entre deux mots.
Espace justifiant: blanc sans inscription, positionné de façon à séparer deux mots, dont la dimension est variable en fonction de l'alignement automatique des deux côtés d'un texte.

Face: dessin particulier d'une famille de caractère, ex. une face italique.
Façonnage (façonner): dernières opérations qui, par pliage, découpe, assemblage, encartage, piqûre, couture, reliure, etc., donnent aux imprimés leur forme définitive.
Famille: également appelé famille de caractères. Ensemble des caractères élaborés en vue de leur utilisation conjointe. Par exemple, la famille Garamond se compose des styles romain et italique, ainsi que des graisses normal, demi-gras et gras. Chacun des assortiments de style et de graisse forme un caractère.
Fausse page: la page de gauche (page paire) d'un ouvrage imprimé est appelée fausse page.

Cette page est moins accessible au regard que celle de droite (Belle page).
Faux titre: nom donné à la première page d'un ouvrage imprimé, dont la particularité est de contenir uniquement le titre de l'oeuvre. Par habitude, cette page est imprimé sur une page de droite, sans impression sur le verso.
Fer à droite, fer a gauche: alignement vertical des lignes de texte à droite ou à gauche pour les compositions en drapeau (du fait du calage sur un fer en typographie).
Feuillet: appellation servant à désigner une subdivision de la feuille.
Dans un ouvrage, un feuillet représente deux pages (soit deux faces, le recto et le verso).

Filet: traits continus ou pointillés d'un document servant à séparer les éléments d'une page. Il est conseillé de faire un usage sporadique des filets et autres artifices graphiques, et à seule fin de clarifier la fonction d'autres éléments.
Filets de paragraphe: lignes ou traits graphiques associés à un paragraphe séparant les blocs de texte. Les filets servent généralement à séparer les colonnes et à isoler les illustrations sur une page. Certains logiciels de PAO permettent de créer des styles de paragraphe définissant les filets au-dessus et au-dessous.
Folio: chiffre utilisé pour numéroter les pages d'un livre ou d'une brochure.
Fonte: terme désignant l'ensemble des lettres et

des signes formant un jeu de caractères complet. Son origine vient des caractères de plomb utilisés par les typographes.
Fond tramé: surface constituée de points de trame. Le fond tramé peut être uni ou dégradé, imprimé en noir ou en couleur par une ou plusieurs couches d'encre.
Garalde: famille de caractères de la Classification Vox-Atypi, au tracé noble et gracieux, tirée de la Renaissance italo-française du XVIIe siècle. Les noms de Claude Garamond et d'Alde Manuce sont à l'origine du Garalde.
Glyphe: le mot glyphe revêt un sens différent selon le contexte. En micro-informatique, et plus

précisément en référence aux systèmes d'exploitation modernes, ce terme désigne souvent une forme déterminée d'une fonte symbolisant un code de caractère à l'écran ou sur un support papier. Le glyphe le plus courant est la lettre, bien que les symboles et les formes d'une police de caractères telle que ITC Zapf Dingbats forment également des glyphes.
*Graisse: épaisseur de la forme d'un caractère. Aucune norme officielle permet de distinguer les différentes graisses d'une même police. Usuellement, on en distingue trois grandes catégories: les graisses légères dites Light, les graisses standards dites regular ou book et les graisses grasses dites bold ou black.

─────── **Typographic body** |> P. 245 |
BENOIT LEMOINE ─── **Les Robes Géographiques — Les Bâteaux sur l'Eau** ELISABETH LECOURT — Is geography destiny? Who we are, and how we behave and think, are very strongly influenced by the direct experiences of our immediate geographic environment—our habitat. Buildings and streets, topology and geography leave their mark on our bodies and souls, like brass rubbings of gravestones representing the lives of those entombed beneath.   We are shaped by our geography: it is woven into our clothes and the personality we assume in public. Just as clothing is an expression of style, we wear our geography wherever we go. Paris is seen as a summer dress, Great Britain as a formal shirt. The Englishman on holiday is still identifiable from the geography of his clothes.   This work allows us to infer the personality of a place by its physical reassessment of maps and their meaning.

CORPS TYPOGRAPHIQUE | SOUVENIR ITC

CORPS TYPOGRAPHIQUE | SOUVENIR ITC

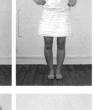

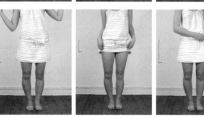

CORPS TYPOGRAPHIQUE | SOUVENIR ITC

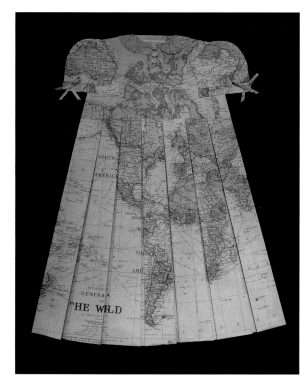

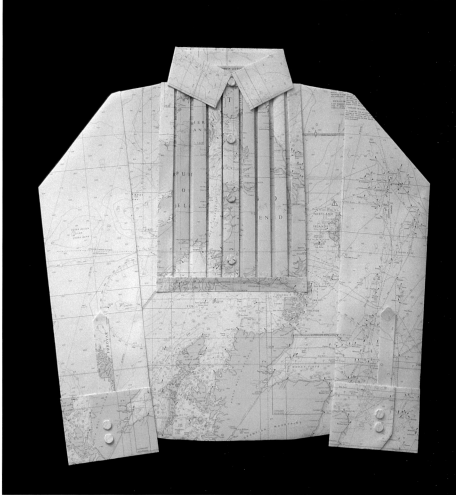

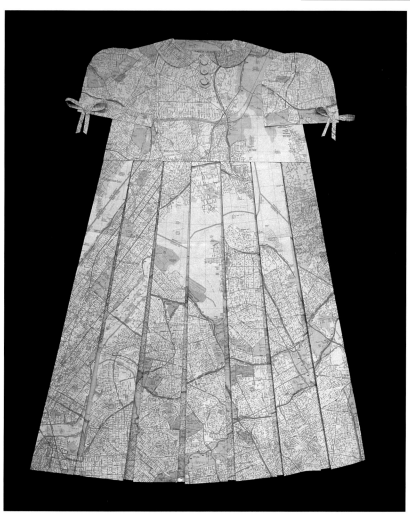

VISUALISIERUNG:	INFORMATION:	PERIODE:	DATEN:
LEISTUNG	SELBST BEURTEILTE ERBRACHTE LEISTUNG EINES ARBEITSTAGES	16.08.04 – 18.11.04	8.1–8.6 9

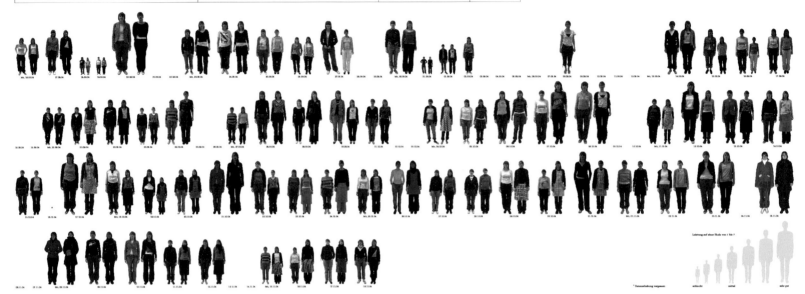

VISUALISIERUNG:	INFORMATION:	PERIODE:	DATEN:
TEMPERATUR	PERSÖNLICHE TEMPERATUREMPFINDUNG IM VERGLEICH ZUR TATSÄCHLICHEN LUFTTEMPERATUR	20.07.04 – 18.11.04	7 8.1–8.6

August
01.08.04 02.08.04 03.08.04 04.08.04 05.08.04 06.08.04 07.08.04 08.08.04 09.08.04 10.08.04 11.08.04 12.08.04 13.08.04

September
01.09.04 02.09.04 03.09.04 04.09.04 05.09.04 06.09.04 07.09.04 08.09.04 09.09.04 10.09.04 11.09.04 12.09.04 13.09.04 14.09.04 15.09.04 16.09.04

Oktober
01.10.04 02.10.04 03.10.04 04.10.04 05.10.04 06.10.04 07.10.04 08.10.04 09.10.04 10.10.04 11.10.04 12.10.04 13.10.04 14.10.04

November
01.11.04 02.11.04 03.11.04 04.11.04 05.11.04 06.11.04 07.11.04 08.11.04 09.11.04 10.11.04 11.11.04 12.11.04 13.11.04 14.11.04 15.11.04 16.11.04

3.1.

—**Von B und C** |> PP. 162, 248| BARBARA HAHN & CHRISTINE ZIMMERMANN — The complexity and subtlety of photographic expression are explored in this work calendar. By sizing their daily images according to the amount of work completed on each day, the designers enable the characters to assume a subtle semiotic function. Facial expressions and body posture take on new significance as they symbolise the nature of the work, the mood experienced while the work is performed, and other parameters occurring throughout the period. The viewer is given access to a new layer of meaning that a simple histogram of output would not have revealed. Personal data becomes personally relevant. ————— **Von Stars und grauen Eminenzen** BARBARA HAHN & CHRISTINE ZIMMERMANN — All too often, the design of sociometric diagrams ignores the fact that the data reflects the plight of real people. Abstracted and unemotional, the policies and decisions driven by these forms of presentation lack the human insight needed to improve people's lives. Driven by the need for clarity, legibility, and accuracy, the infographics developed by Von B und C Hahn und Zimmermann use very specific visual cues to improve understanding. Brightly-coloured clothes are coded to represent positive data, while injuries and lesions communicate negative effects. The information content of this photographic approach far surpasses the neutral pie charts and histograms more commonly used. It makes possible an emotional transfer that is otherwise hidden or reduced through formal shapes and forms. By humanising the data, the urgency and directness of the issues communicated by the data are manifested in tangible form.

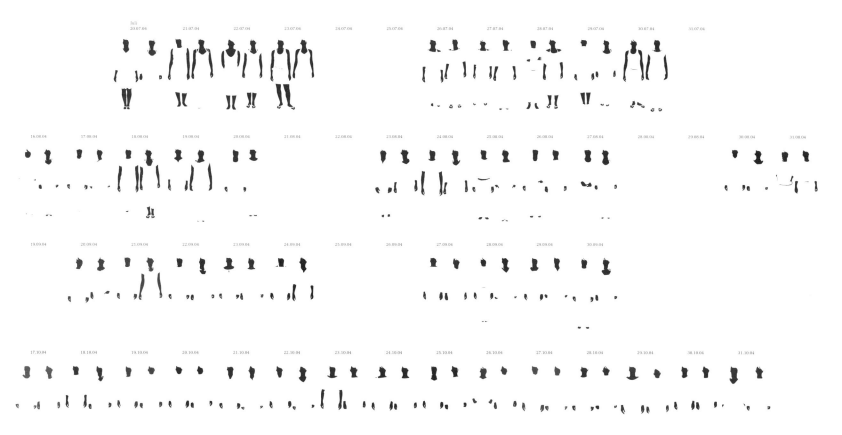

—— Von B und C |> P. 248 |
BARBARA HAHN & CHRISTINE ZIMMERMANN **—————— Houston, Texas, USA** HANDMAPS.ORG, submitted by Margo Handwerker, drawn by Bernard Bonnet — The Obama campaign has ignited national interest and gripped the United States in a fever of enthusiasm not seen since the 1960s. This poignant little note, exchanged between two of his supporters, reflects the powerful grassroots activism and viral nature of his campaign. An informal exchange at the Museum of Fine Arts in Houston between the French immigrant and naturalised citizen Bernard Bennet and his co-worker Margo Handwerker led to this map. It directs Handwerker to the local volunteers' office in the simple, honest, and direct style that personifies Obama's appeal. **—— Bloomington, Indiana, USA** HANDMAPS.ORG, submitted by Kristofer Harzinski, drawn by Amy Horst — This work is a topological expression of intent and desire. In the age of TomTom satnav systems, the human appreciation of 'the journey' is caught on a paper napkin. Affectionately referred to as 'good coffee, good bagel, good bye,' this map was drawn by Amy Horst as a guide for Kris Harzinski to find his way out of Bloomington, Indiana.

Overwhelming urban complexity is reduced here to individually relevant directions. By indicating the quality of coffee and bagels en route, the designer sends a little piece of herself on the journey with the traveller. **—— Location map, United States** HANDMAPS.ORG, submitted by Kristofer Harzinski, drawn by anonymous — Hand-drawn maps are slightly deceptive, in that only the final result is acknowledged. The dialogue and flow between those who helped create them are sadly not brought out in the tangible evidence. This hand-drawn map was rescued from a rubbish bin at the World Curling Championships held at the Braehead Arena in Glasgow, Scotland, in 2000. The 2002 World Championships were to be held at Bismarck in North Dakota. The map was apparently used to explain the location of this venue, and one wonders at the quantity of information and the length of the discussion needed to anchor its locus in the mental geography of the recipient. We are reminded of the original meaning of the word 'Map'—literally, the 'napkin of the world'.

VISUALISIERUNG:	INFORMATION:	PERIODE:	DATEN:
SCHRITTE	IM ZUSAMMENHANG MIT DER DIPLOMARBEIT ZU FUSS ZURÜCKGELEGTE DISTANZEN	31.08.04 – 18.11.04	24.1 – 24.8

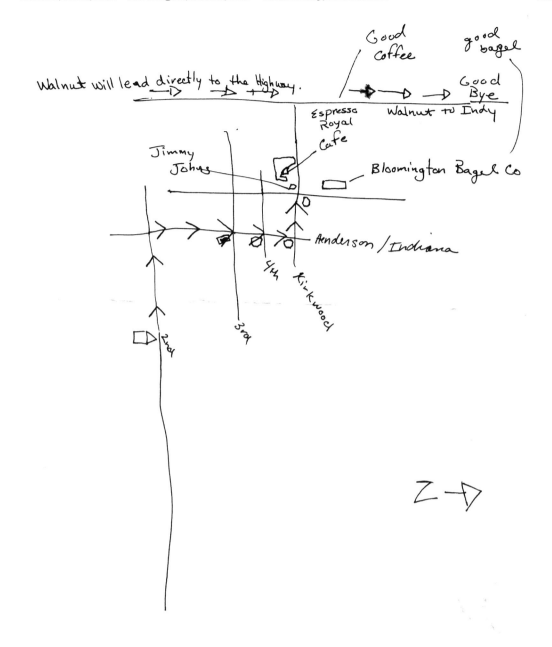

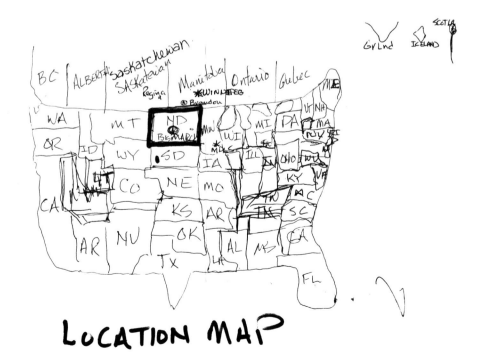

LOCATION MAP

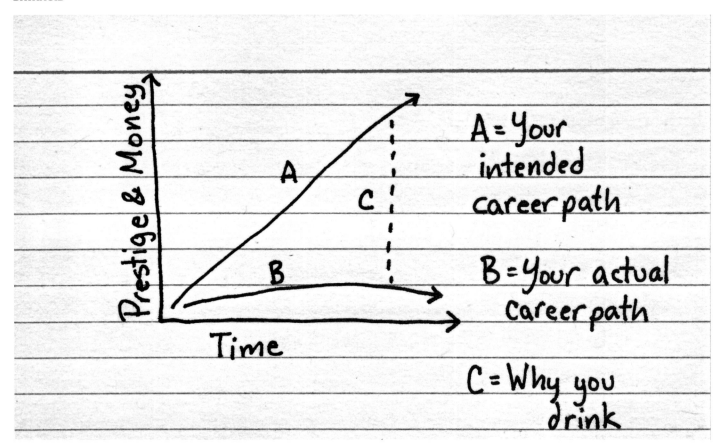

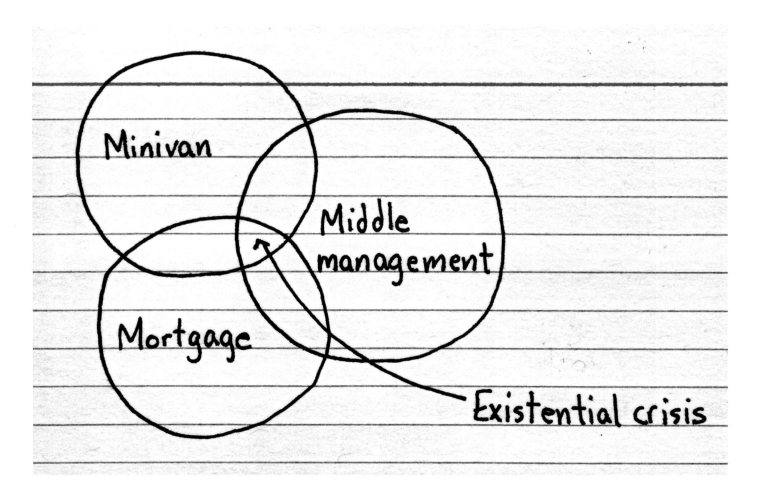

Jessica Hagy
——Interview

—— You choose a very uniform way of presenting your diagrams. What role has simplicity played in the huge success they've achieved? —— The simplicity of the format and the simplicity of the content both serve the same purpose: to broadcast an idea quickly. I first started using index cards because they were easy to work with and available. Today, index cards and graphs about life are closely connected, at least in the online world. The index card format is a brand element, you could say. I think the idea took off because it's so accessible, different and familiar at the same time.

—— How do you go about taking very complex topics relevant to life, and moving them from concept to simple drawings? —— I'm an eavesdropper, and I take notes almost all the time. When you're taking a lot of notes, you don't have time to write a mini-drama, or record an entire speech or incident. For me, graphs became a kind of shorthand—a way to capture the main point of what I overhear or see.

—— Drawing diagrams by hand instead of rendering them digitally seems to add to their meaning. Do you agree, and, if so, how do you think this characteristic changes the way people appreciate them? —— Drawing makes the ideas feel more authentic. My doodles are more like quick notes than well-funded PowerPoint slides. This gives people the feeling that they're reading a note that's been passed to them while the teacher isn't looking, rather than an annual report.

A lot of the content has various layers of meaning, because the grammar of math is more open ended than the grammar of linguistics. I can use Venn diagrams in place of the words 'and', 'or', 'is', or 'isn't' and x-y graphs in place of the words 'causes', 'influences', or 'relates to'. The language of math means that readers can translate each drawing using their own rubrics, inserting their own verbs into the sentence on the card.

—— What role do you think designers play in putting a human element back into the data they're presenting? —— Designers are translators, and they can inflect content in ways no one else can. Since even something as simple as a choice of fonts can change the connotations of a word, designers are able to spin statistics in ways that even the best orator on earth could never dream of.

—

For me, graphs became a kind of shorthand

—

—— Do you use statistics or data to draw up your diagrams? Where does the inspiration come from? —— Besides eavesdropping, I read a broad range of disparate information. Sometimes just bouncing from one topic to another helps me relate two ideas to each other. The alphabet contains all the pieces for every book ever written, but it's the mixing up of pieces and parts that turns these letters into stories.

—— Do you think designers look at data differently than programmers, scientists, or businessmen? —— I would venture to say that designers focus more on the process and outcome of design. Design is something we all do. Every morning when we choose our clothes for the day, we're designing an image of ourselves. Programmers, businessmen, and scientists are all designing ideas; they're just speaking in slightly different design dialects.

—— Is technology changing the way people look at data and diagrams? If so, where do you think this is leading us in terms of design? —— Technology makes it much easier to crunch a lot of numbers, so it's no surprise that we're seeing more diagrams. We're also bombarded with information, and graphs can take a massive amount of data and distil it ever so neatly. Simplicity fits our frantic pace, and complexity fits our technology. They're symbiotic features of our information diet.

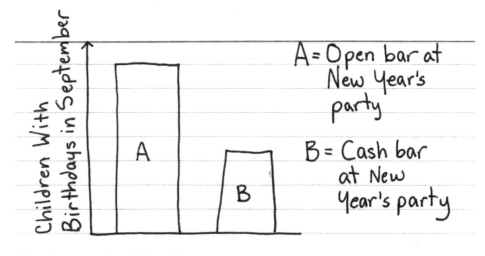

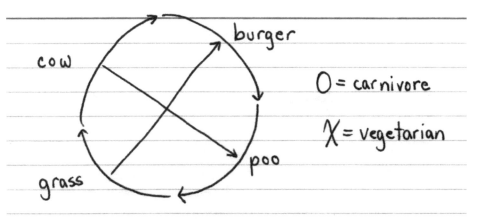

————Are there particular topics you have more fun depicting? ————The way people perceive themselves and others—the social constructs we all employ to present ourselves—are really interesting to me. Hair, politics, materialism, class, status—anything you can observe in an airport—are topics ripe for depiction. I work in advertising as a copywriter, so getting a good feel for sociology, though it's sometimes a little sad, is mandatory and often illuminating.

—

Simplicity fits our frantic pace, and complexity fits our technology. They're symbiotic features of our information diet

—

————Are there specific things you dislike about the way data and infographics are used in the media today? ————I saw a graph once touting the efficacy of a drug. The placebo effect was around 2%, and the drug's effect was around 2.1%. The graph implied that there was a huge difference between the placebo and the drug, because the y-axis only showed 1.5% to 2.5%. But that realisation took a few minutes, and most people don't stare at graphs for even a few seconds, so the graph was a blatant lie, even though it was mathematically accurate. It's these kinds of distortions, where readers are lied to with pictures, that lower the reputation of designers. But when a diagram functions to illuminate and not persuade, it's actually serving a purpose.

————When working with data, do you consult with scientists or other experts in the field to confirm that the charts make sense from a scientific point of view? Do accuracy and validity play a role in what you're attempting to depict? ————Many of my graphs are debatably true or rational, because I work with qualitative features about ninety per cent of the time. It's possible to prove or disprove most of my pieces via anecdote or opinion, and that's why reading the comments on my site is so interesting for me. I'm making observations and changing the visual grammar, and when you have a fluid grammar, you have a fluid message. That's at least half the fun.

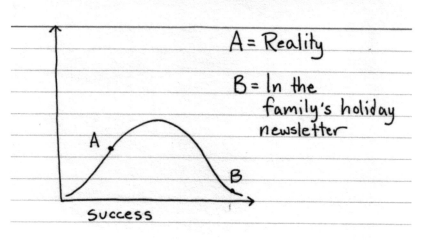

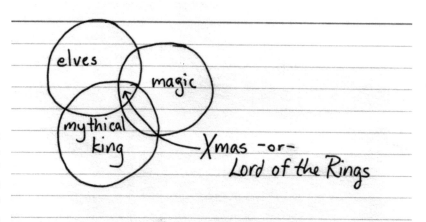

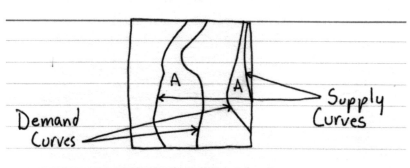

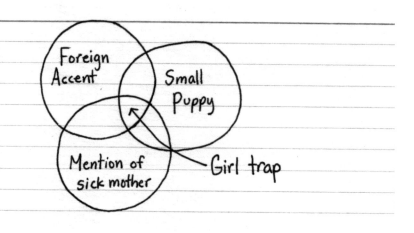

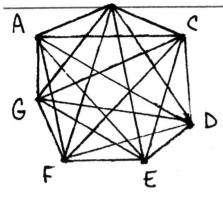

A = Lust
B = Gluttony
C = Greed
D = Sloth
E = Wrath
F = Envy
G = Pride

$\overline{AB}$ = Edible Undies
$\overline{AC}$ = Prostitution
$\overline{AD}$ = Quickie
$\overline{AE}$ = Domestic Abuse
$\overline{AF}$ = Adultery
$\overline{AG}$ = Trophy Wife
$\overline{BC}$ = Last Donut
$\overline{BD}$ = Saturday
$\overline{BE}$ = Bulimia
$\overline{BF}$ = High Metabolism
$\overline{BG}$ = Fat men in Speedos
$\overline{CD}$ = Get rich quick scams
$\overline{CE}$ = Muggings

$\overline{CF}$ = Advertising
$\overline{CG}$ = Status Symbols
$\overline{DE}$ = Passive
      Aggression
$\overline{DF}$ = Welfare
$\overline{DG}$ = Slackers
$\overline{EF}$ = Cattiness
$\overline{EG}$ = Boxing
$\overline{GF}$ = 2nd Place

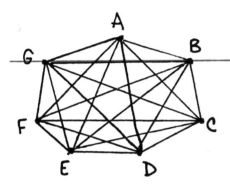

A = Chastity
B = Generosity
C = Moderation
D = Diligence
E = Kindness
F = Patience
G = Modesty

$\overline{AB}$ = Hand job
$\overline{AC}$ = Tease
$\overline{AD}$ = Thinking about baseball
$\overline{AE}$ = Pity date
$\overline{AF}$ = After Prom
$\overline{AG}$ = Granny panties
$\overline{BC}$ = Buying gifts on sale
$\overline{BD}$ = Kissing up to your boss
$\overline{BE}$ = Complimenting bad art
$\overline{BF}$ = Waiting for your rich aunt to die
$\overline{BG}$ = Lending the stripper your coat
$\overline{CD}$ = Procrastination
$\overline{CE}$ = 15% Tip
$\overline{CF}$ = Occasional Outbursts
$\overline{CG}$ = Just a little cleavage

$\overline{DE}$ = Forced Smiles
$\overline{DF}$ = Making license
      plates in
      prison
$\overline{DG}$ = Always wearing
      your eye-patch
EF = Your friend's
      Pampered Chef
      party
$\overline{EG}$ = Keep the door
      closed, Mom.
$\overline{FG}$ = Holding in
      a toot

— Social Studies EMILY GINSBURG
— Currents flowing around and connecting our lives are an integral part of modern existence. Mimicking the aesthetics of a circuit board, the imagery that grounds this circuit exposes our relationship with, and dependence on, these resources in various ways. The concept of 'currents' suggests the idea of a complex yet integrated circuit or network revolving around a collection of vignettes, as a metaphor for living, working, communicating, and imagining everyday life.   The inverted scale emphasises the personal and immediate nature of our everyday experiences. Just like electricity, the flow connects individual vignettes, tracing the pattern of personal thoughts and interactions, in activities such as eating, sleeping, working, walking, writing, reading, listening to music, watching films, and speaking by phone. These actions are presented by way of maps and model kits through the lens of lived experience, as well as by an openly aesthetic interpretation of the imagery at play.   The visual vocabulary of electronic processes and means of transmitting and storing electrical energy — whether wires, bulbs, wind power, radio masts, or solar cells — provides the connectors and links that communities rely on to maintain familiar rituals.

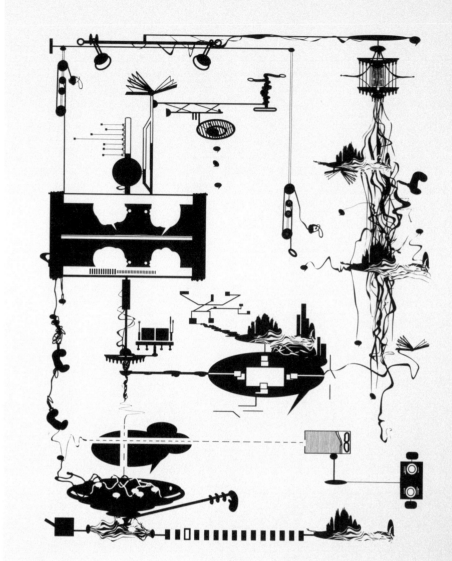

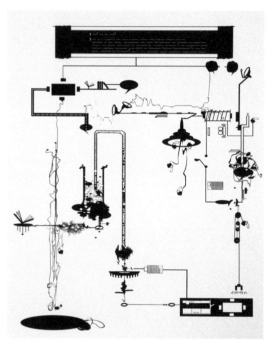

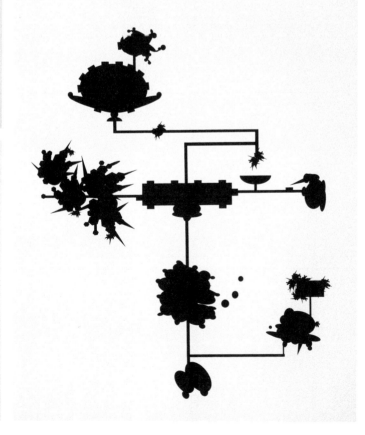

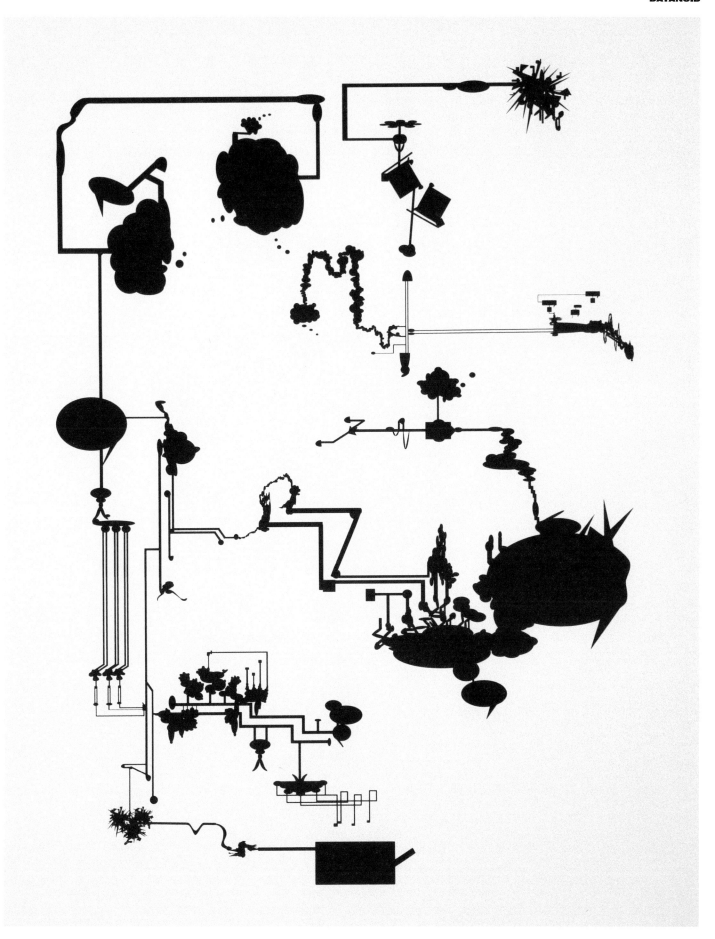

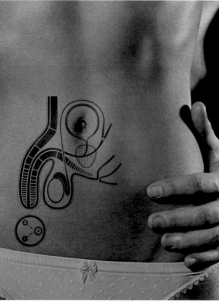

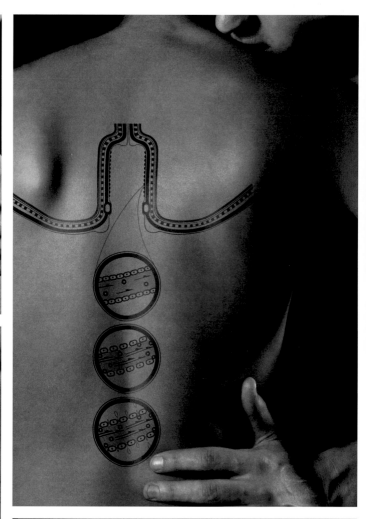

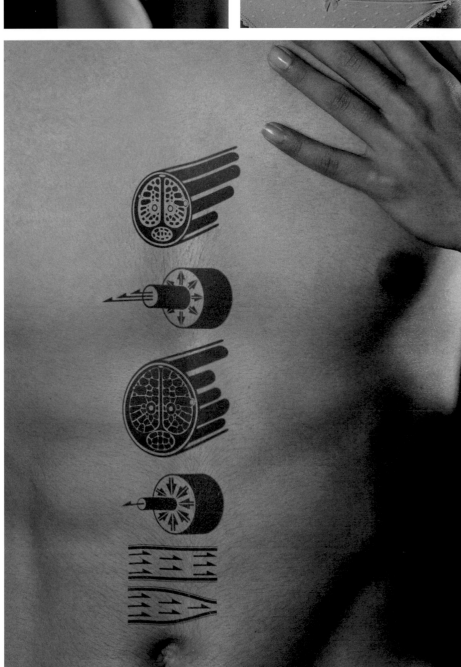

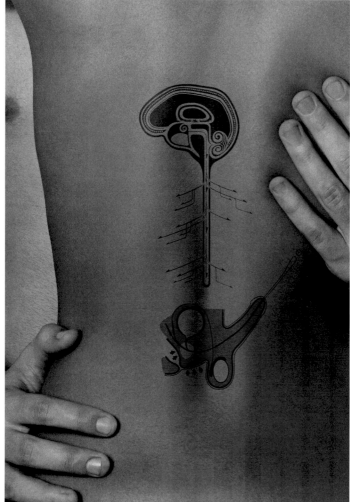

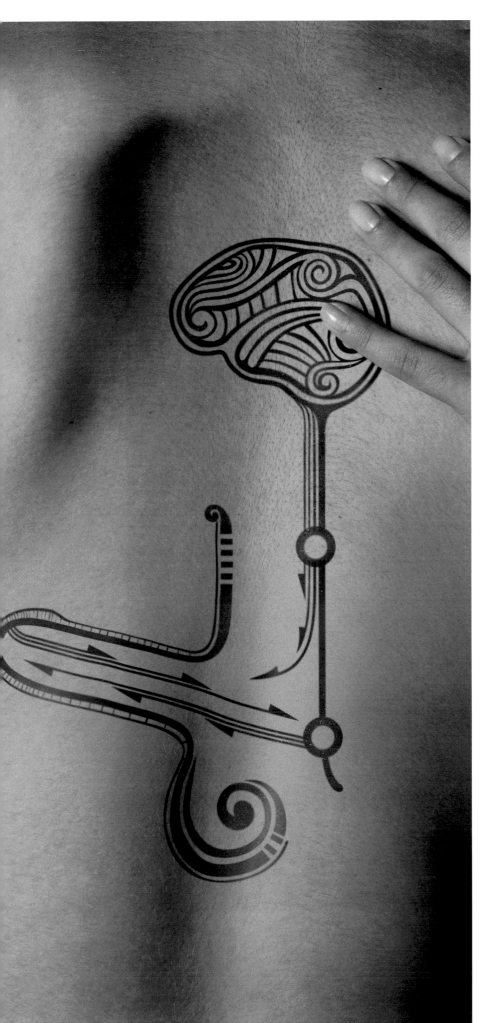

O lado curioso do Sexo
CARLO GIOVANI — Sex is not a scientific discipline, yet it is the subject of endless scientific analysis to explain just why it is so enjoyable and important to real people.

Making the 'facts' more accessible by using overtly erotic references, scientific diagrams are 'tattooed' on the sensuous bodies of men and women. The gentle fingers of a lover stroke the corpus callosum into action. Arousal is not simply about the interaction of cells and hormones—it is about the brain's ability to register pleasure.

NEXT PAGES **Impact Poster Campaign** HYBRID DESIGN, Brian Flynn, Dora Drimalas, Ed O'Brien — Puberty is a transition that demands a strong sense of identity to emerge if this phase is to be successful in nurturing emotional development. However, an identity is often shrouded in the myth of its own immortality. The last thing that teenagers think about is their own death, or the potential causes of it. From the data, the pattern of teenage death is revealed in this piece. The skull is shaped not by random axmen in secluded shacks or by terrorist attacks, but by the predominant cause of teenage fatalities: driving accidents. The forced anthropomorphisation of the data intelligently challenges teenage drivers to see themselves as the cause of death, acknowledging their own vulnerability. **The Revolutionary Comic Presentation System** CHRAGOKYBERNETICKS —In mapping a very human story, this revolutionary system of comic presentation borrows from a 1950s comic aesthetic to develop a new form of non-linear storytelling. The visuals guide the viewer through a personal tale of conflict and development. The light-hearted style distracts from, yet also enhances, the darker social commentary about the impact of fame and celebrity on the individual. Taking a lead from art and science alike, Christoph Frei transforms emotional observation into a mapped-out scientific process.

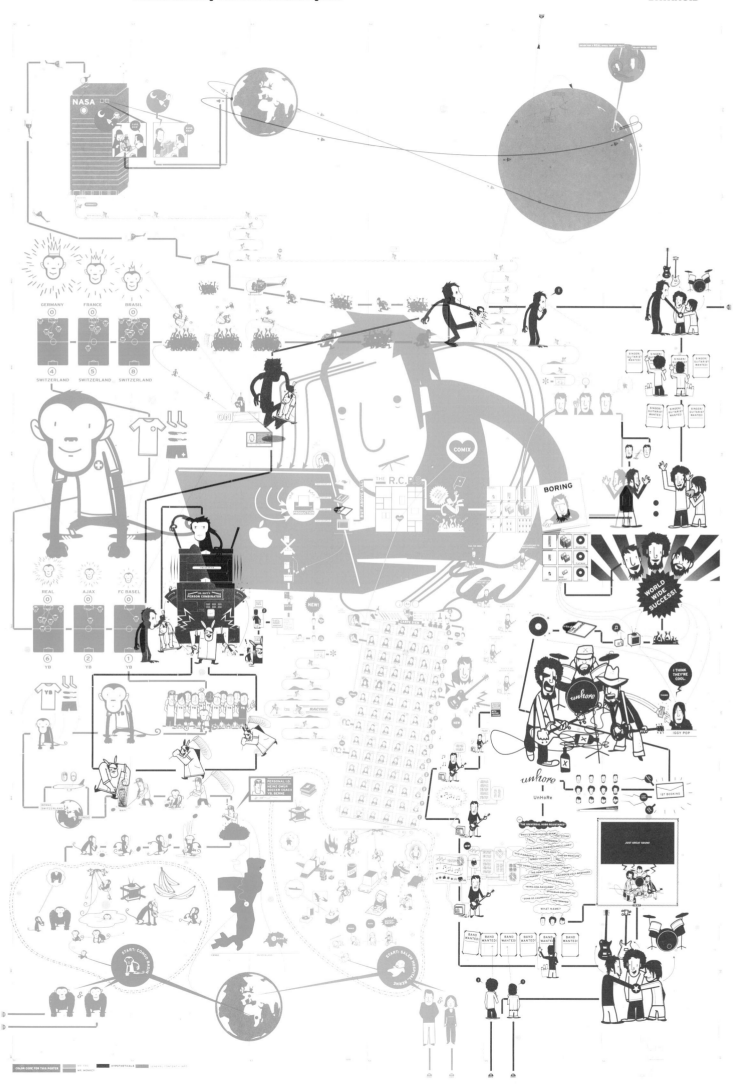

—— **Netzwork/Teamwork** UTA EISENREICH in collaboration with Verena Bachzetsis and the children of her class at Langmatt school, Marco Walser, Valentin Hindermann, Julia Born, Shirana Shahbazi, Niels Schumm — This piece shows how social data is disclosed and used as a basis for deduction in the activity of play. In successive photos, Ute Eisenreich reveals invisible bonds of friendship, envy, and unfamiliarity. Children arranged in a grid use strings to show who they would most like to be like (blue strings), who they would invite to a party (red strings), and who they know least well (yellow strings).   Contained within the confines of a school playground, this experiment becomes a light-hearted reference to the hype and press attention given to social media and the Web 2.0 phenom-

enon. Ultimately, it is all about how people connect with each other. Technology, like distance, is irrelevant. Connection is about emotional, not physical, proximity.
—— **Vocabulary** UTA EISENREICH — The ability to shape and communicate complex concepts is a hallmark of human social evolution. Our ability to communicate—in other words, share meaning—enables us to coordinate and align our efforts, discuss abstract concepts, and consider experiences beyond our lifetime or ability. Ute Eisenreich's installation invites the viewer to appreciate the complex web of meaning created between verbs, nouns, and adjectives. First impressions of a deliberately strictly-arranged photo dictionary soon reveal deeper and richer layers of meaning, as the viewer develops diffuse associations and new interpretations.

—— **Network** WELCOMETO.AS in collaboration with Mikuláš Macháček — The challenge of group thinking affects design students, as their development evolves according to the dominant mindset of their school or university. By using pictograms, Adam Macháček demonstrates this challenge, setting out an alternative. The students' clothing and speech bubbles represent the progression in their thinking. Under the traditional education system they do not change; the message of their school is simply amplified and embellished. But in the networked education system, people bounce off each other like ideas, and individual growth and development are more unexpected and diverse. New, unforeseen ideas pop out from the spaces between people, rather than flowing through a process.

NEXT PAGES —— **All Against Each Other** LEO BURNETT — Geography is defined by conflict. It represents the eternal struggle of mankind against itself, in pursuit of self-determination—a struggle that often ends up as self-defeating. The topology of conflict spreads to every corner of the world in this provocative poster by Leo Burnett for Amnesty International in Portugal. By blending ancient and modern conflicts from all over the globe, it reminds us of the bloody legacy of wars that have led to the rise and fall of once powerful civilisations. Defining moments like Pearl Harbour and Hiroshima merge into an indistinct landscape of flesh and conflict on the broader canvas of human history. National borders are obscured, as are the sources of conflict, emphasising the human cost involved. Only one question still remains: why do we eternally define ourselves through conflict?

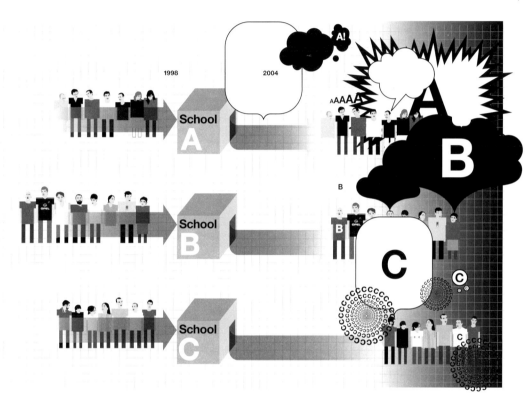

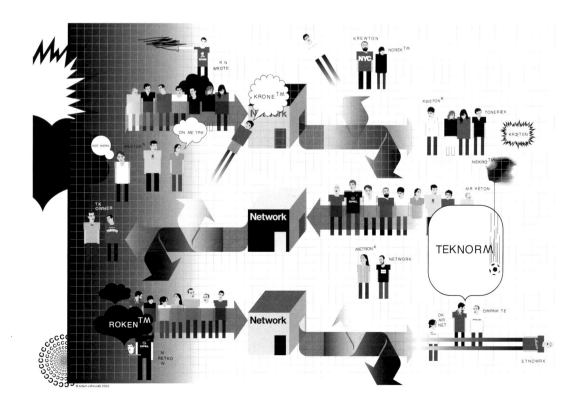

EVERYBODY IS A
SOMEBODY HA

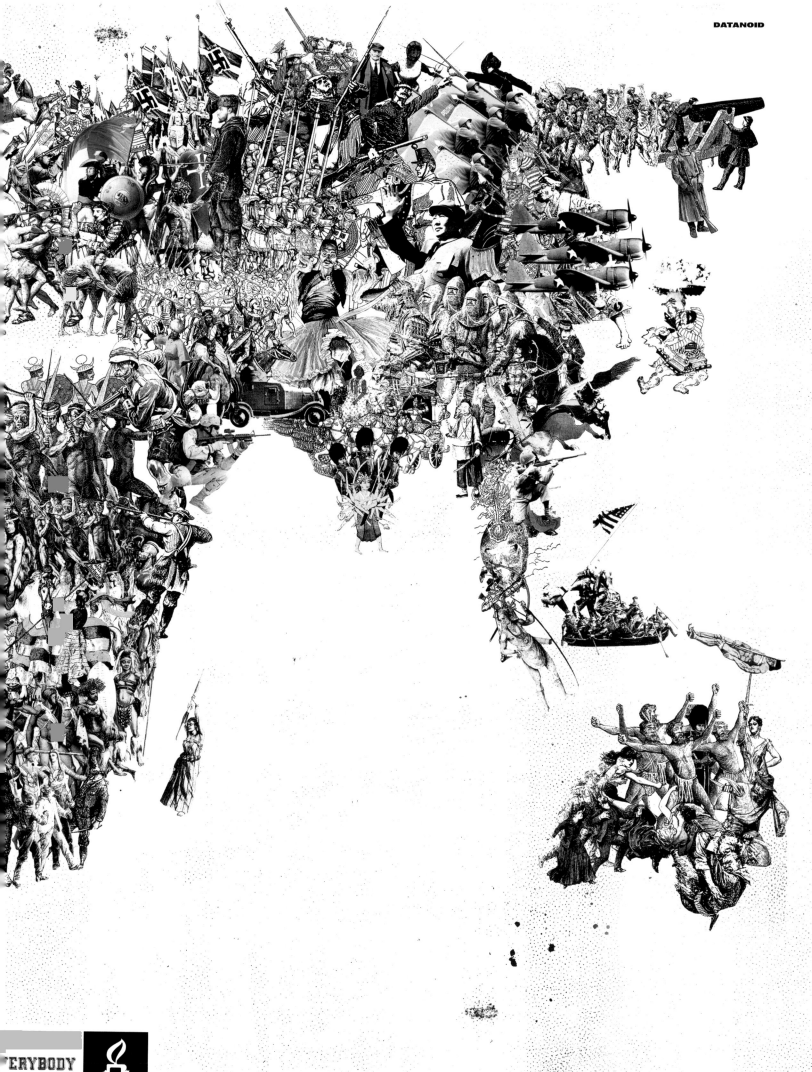

DATANOID

ERYBODY
R THEM

E RIGHTS OF AL

Datalogy

—

Designers can access the entire bandwidth of human perception by investing data with weight, space, and texture. In doing so, they provide sensual experiences of communication, deliciously revealing the richness of complex datasets, so full of meaning and potential interpretations. This is the physical interface of analogy, well suited to the continuous and graduated sensations we derive from our immediate environment.

—

We often fall back on analogy to try and specify the nuances that blunt words cannot accurately convey. 'It's like this, not that, and perhaps a little like those two together', for instance. We combine,

—

'It's like this, not that, and perhaps a little like those two together'

—

juxtapose, and infer diverse concepts to deliver new insight and understanding. When designers attempt to present complex data in graphic form, they can use analogy to build a bridge between the known and the unknown, transforming the familiar through reinterpretation.   The deliberate misuse of everyday objects complements straightforward diagrammatic or schematic visualisation by projecting a world of personal experiences onto a new subject. Cybu Richli's use

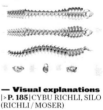

— **Visual explanations**
|>P. 185|CYBU RICHLI, SILO (RICHLI/MOSER)

of gasket seals to uncover the workings of the human spine is both obvious and intriguing. He draws the viewer in, to transfer the known touch and torsion of rubber into the abstract concepts of torsion and flex. How far the analogy goes, or maintains its integrity, is entirely up to the viewer, in his or her application of this new metaphor to physiological analysis.   Moving beyond the direct towards conceptual analogy, Julien Métille's critical examination of the modern music industry operates on various levels to expose degradation and homogenisation. While

— **Unisson** |>P. 199| JULIEN MÉTILLE

Photoshop layers are the direct analogy to the filtering process of the industry, the resultant image—distorted, diminished, and aesthetically perverted—becomes the real direct analogy to the quality of the industry's output. By operating on both a conceptual and a literal level, this analogy becomes complete in its representation of the topic.   The juxtaposition of the known with the unknown provides the tension required for emotional relevance. Xavier Barrade's investigation of the literal translation of verbal metaphors into visual expression relies on the qualitative interpretation of objects to enhance the depic-

tion of the quantitative data. Doughnut sales are shown as a doughnut, house prices as houses. The literal, obvious, and expected suddenly become exciting, as we realise that the photograph is a deliberately constructed datagraph.

— **La représentation des statistiques**
|>P. 200| XAVIER BARRADE

With modern technology providing limitless opportunities to turn familiar objects and ciphers into innovative forms of explanation, the challenge is not one of imagination, but of finely judged relevance. Just as the emotional and historical meaning of objects can enhance understanding, the same objects can also distract and confuse the viewer. Form triumphs over substance, effect over affect. By relying on subjective interpretation and assignation of meaning, the designer ensures that

—

Form triumphs over substance, effect over affect

—

the viewer's cultural context and expertise contribute as much to the quality of the expression as do the composition and design. The weight, space, and sensuality of analogy balance cost with effect.

PREVIOUS PAGE —— **La représen-tation des statistiques** |> P. 200| XAVIER BARRADE, in collaboration with Arnaud Dupont — The subject becomes the object, as buildings are used to depict the rise in house prices. This piece forms part of Xavier Barrade's investigation into unusual, future forms of data presentation.

—— **Anatomie der Datengrafik** |> P. 221| TOBIAS NUSSER & TOM ZIORA — This graphic is part of Tobias Nusser's detailed study 'Anatomy of Datagraphics', discussed in more detail in the Datasphere section. —— Building literally on the theme of water, this part of Tobias Nusser's project 'Anatomy of Datagraphics' uses colour and volume in glasses to depict data. —— **Typical Day Poster** EFFEKTIVE — Rotating numbers — thin metal plates on a digital clock — flip over, marching inexorably through the measure of a day. Displaying the ordinal passage of time, the two human states are coded red or black. In this poster, the time in a typical day becomes a big domineering 'T'.

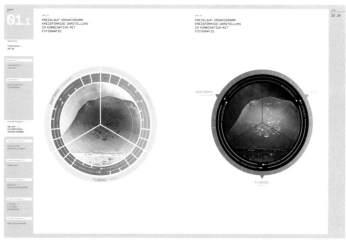

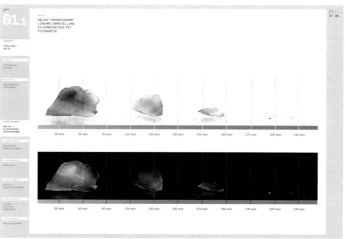

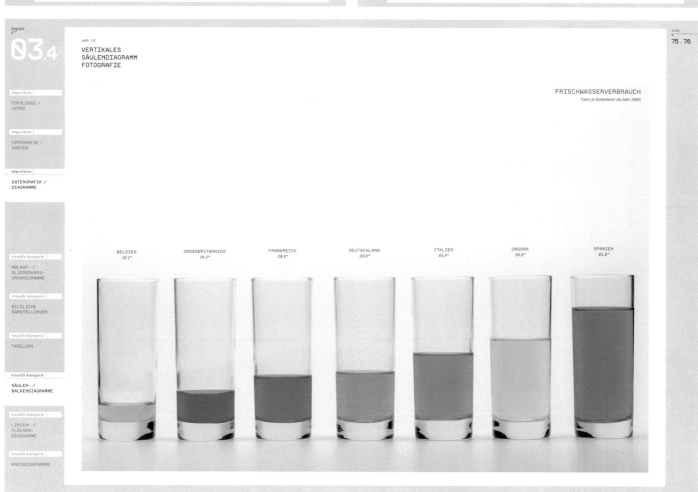

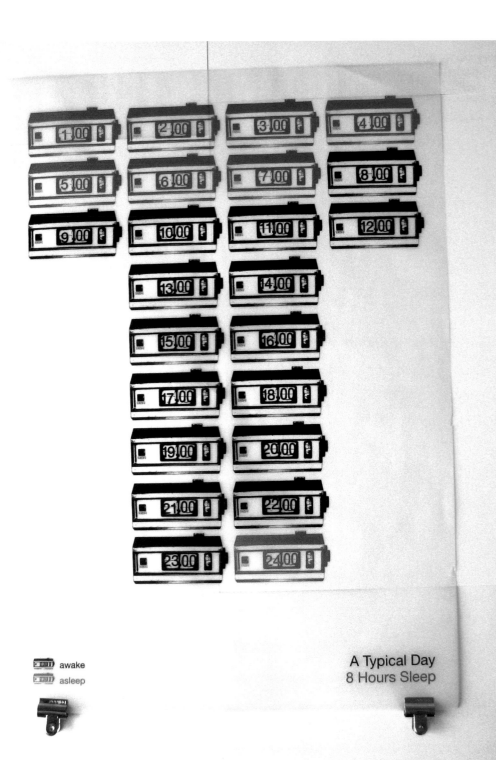

Wachstum einer Avocado

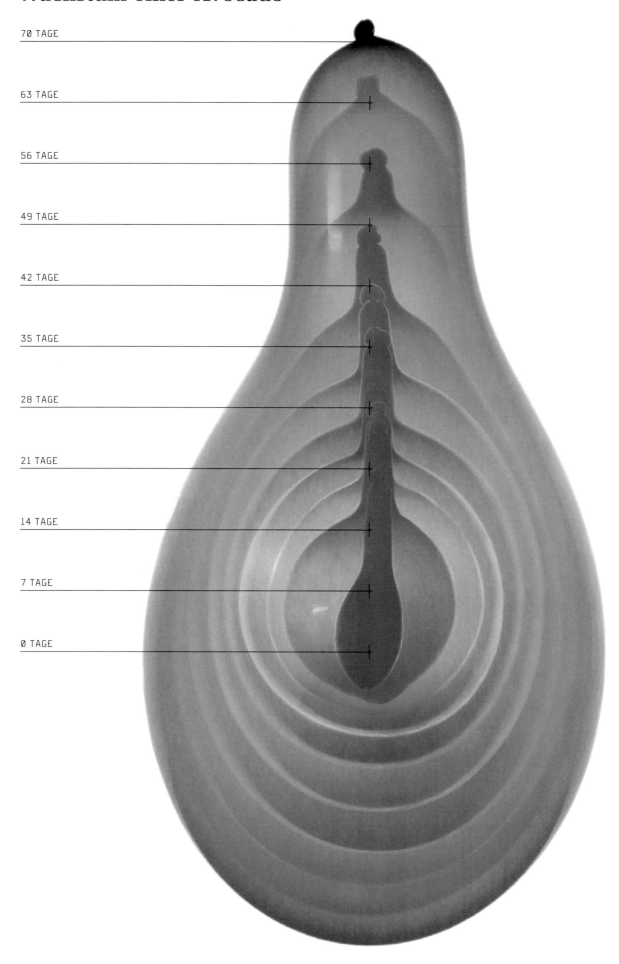

70 TAGE

63 TAGE

56 TAGE

49 TAGE

42 TAGE

35 TAGE

28 TAGE

21 TAGE

14 TAGE

7 TAGE

0 TAGE

Cybu Richli
——Interview

——— You use a lot of analogue technology in developing visual explanations. Do you think this approach changes the way people appreciate the data? ——— Words often don't suffice to explain complex situations. Where words fall short, we intuitively resort to objects from our environment as visual aids. Quickly, the pencil on your desk turns into a street, and the pencil sharpener into a building! Our ancestors used pebbles, notches, or knots in a string long before numerals, as we know them, were developed. To this day, we often rely on our fingers to illustrate numbers. So the use of analogue objects in explanations is a common technique. I believe that familiar objects are good tools for

explaining complex issues. When developing an explanation, however, it's important to realise that not every object is suitable. Each object that is reapplied for a different purpose still has its own characteristics and story that wants to be told. As such, the selected visual aid operates on two levels. In my project 'Visual Explanations', I've used seals from jam jars to represent the structure of a spinal column. They're made of rubber, stretchy and flexible, in bone-white and red. The piece gives the viewer new insight into a complex issue. Abstract and reduced visualisations can easily put distance between the viewer

—

Although aesthetics are taking on an increasingly important role, we must always ensure that visualisations make things easier to understand

—

and the subject. Although aesthetics are taking on an increasingly important role, we must always ensure that visualisations make things easier to understand.

—— **Visual explanations, Growth of an avocado** |▷ P. 188| CYBU RICHLI, Silo (Richli / Moser) — Most people are familiar with the avocado, and have seen its ripe, green, and bulbous form on supermarket shelves. However, the process by which the fruit matures is obscure to most people, as it is grown in far-off lands. By using the familiar metaphor of an inflating balloon, this artwork not only shows the avocado increasing in size over time, but also its resultant increase in volume. Viewers can relate this to their own experiences with inflated water balloons, comparing their recollections of weight and touch with the graphic. The specific characteristics and history of the balloon as an object enhance our understanding of the data being presented. ——
Visual explanations |▷ P. 188| CYBU RICHLI, Silo (Richli / Moser) — One of Cybu Richli's most significant works, this depiction of the human spine is composed entirely of gasket seals. Used white elastic seals are interwoven to produce replicas of the three main types of vertebrae. Red seals are used to represent the spinal cord. This project forms part of a study that investigates the use of familiar objects through easy-to-understand scientific metaphors.

This is the big challenge facing information designers today.

——— I imagine you need to perform many different experiments to find the best way to show the data. How do you approach this process of experimentation? ——— There are always different ways to solve the same problem. I am,

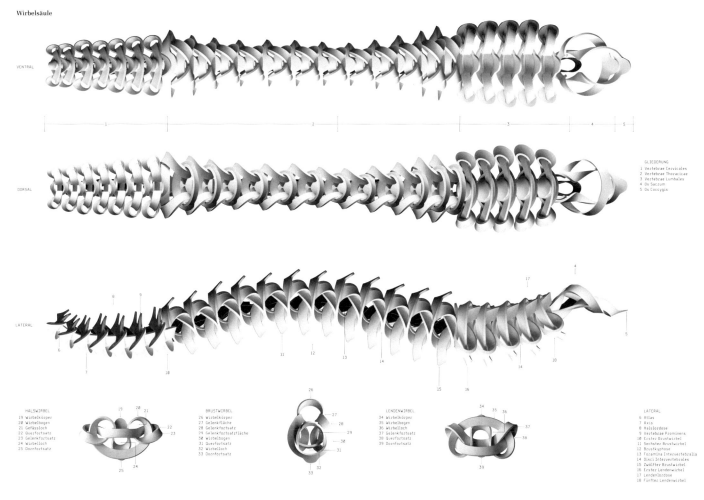

Wirbelsäule

VENTRAL

DORSAL

LATERAL

however, convinced that the path defines the destination. Multiple routes should always be tested in the development of infographics. Usually, I follow an idea that, in my mind, is still diffuse and abstract. With every step, the idea becomes increasingly clear. The best solutions are the ones that are characterised by aesthetic appeal and easy comprehensibility.

—

The data define the shape of the graph. The designer cannot arbitrarily decide to change its shape, as doing so would change the content and meaning

—

—————Do you believe that adding a tactile quality to data presentation changes insight? How does it alter the way people observe or remember the data?—————Adding a tactile dimension to a visual explanation is not a requirement and should depend on the nature of the subject matter. Arbitrarily adding a sensual dimension to an infographic can easily lead to misunderstandings.

—————Does the way data is presented change according to the type of data involved? If so, is it something about the data itself that makes the difference? If not, what drives the choice of visual technique?—————Data is the foundation for the composition and design of infographics. This is especially obvious in graphs. The data define the shape of the graph. The designer cannot arbitrarily decide to change its shape, as doing so would change the content and meaning. This is why it's crucial that we, as designers, grasp or at the very least develop a feeling for the subject matter. This is the only way to ensure that we understand the choices we're making in the design process. Every new subject poses new questions and requires new rules for the design of its infographics. To overcome these challenges, the designer needs the sensitivity and imagination to present a subject sensibly.

—————How do you manage the marriage of science and art? Is this something that can be learnt, or is it a feeling or innate skill?—————Science expressed visually is of particular interest to me. Science needs images for new inventions and

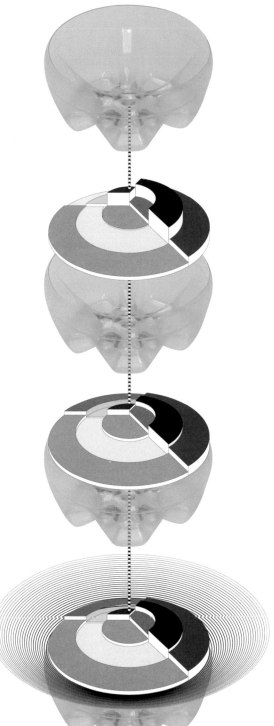

—————— Research in the Visualisation of Financial Data |> PP. 232, 233| CYBU RICHLI, Silo (Richli / Moser) — This model builds on the earlier model of asset allocation. By adding a discrete, segmented layer, specific and minute changes in the portfolio can be shown. —————— **Oil change** CYBU RICHLI — Infographics provide scientists with the unique ability to envision scenarios in a hypothetical environment and to predict future outcomes. This study charts the recovery of a planet from pollution, the rebuilding process being measured by the decrease in air pollution over time. By providing both a micro and a macro view of the scenario, specific effects, as well as the planet's overall development as it travels along a timeline, become more apparent. The deliberate contrast between the ominous dark clouds of pollution resembling an infection, and the clean and symmetrical superstructure, enhances the emotional message of regeneration.

outcomes. In the field of science, there are many phenomena that still cannot be rendered accurately in words. This is why

—

Science needs images for new inventions and outcomes

—

we use images to interpret them or make them accessible visually.

—————Finally, as data sources increase in complexity, the aesthetics of processing are becoming ever more apparent in infographics. How does this influence what we can learn from the data?—————Information graphics provide an impression of complex issues and are thus becoming more important as data become more complex. Without information graphics, much of the data would remain obscure. However, we should always keep in mind that these representations can be manipulated.

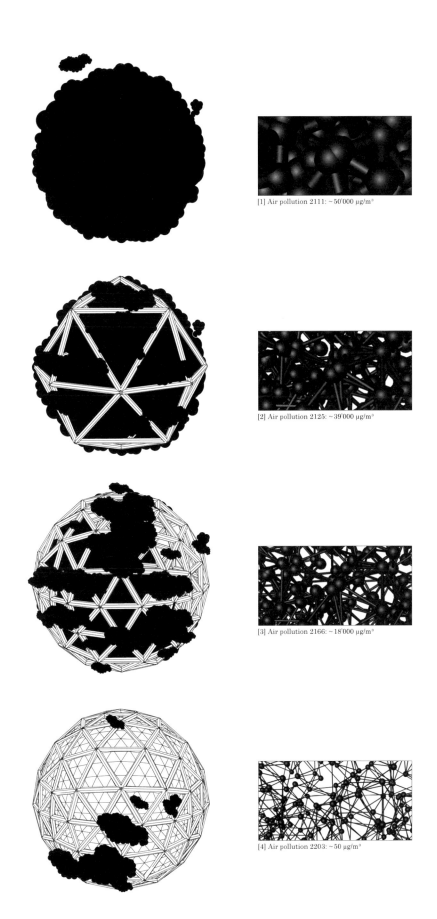

[1] Air pollution 2111: ~ 50'000 µg/m³

[2] Air pollution 2125: ~ 39'000 µg/m³

[3] Air pollution 2166: ~ 18'000 µg/m³

[4] Air pollution 2203: ~ 50 µg/m³

<u>Big Baaaang: snapshots 2111–2203</u>
2111: dirty black clouds; 2125: 1st step of the rebuilt planet; 2166: 2nd step; 2203: new planet.

AUSGANGSLAGE

Schnee entsteht, wenn sich in den Wolken feinste Tröpfchen unterkühlten Wassers an Kristallisationskeimen (zum Beispiel ein Staubteilchen) anlagern und dort gefrieren. Dieser Prozess setzt jedoch in der Regel erst bei Temperaturen unter -10°C ein, wobei noch bis -40°C auch flüssiges Wasser existiert. Die dabei entstehenden Eiskristalle, weniger als 0,1 mm groß, fallen durch ihr zunehmendes Gewicht nach unten und wachsen durch den Unterschied des Dampfdrucks zwischen Eis und

unterkühltem Wasser weiter an. Auch resublimiert der in der Luft enthaltene Wasserdampf, geht also direkt in Eis über und trägt damit zum Kristallwachstum bei. Liegt die Lufttemperatur nahe am Gefrierpunkt, so werden die einzelnen Eiskristalle durch kleine Wassertropfen miteinander verklebt und es entstehen die an einen Wattebausch erinnernde Schneeflocken.

Wo der Schnee auf natürliche Weise nicht oder nicht ausreichend fällt, behilft man sich mit Kunstschnee. Aufgrund der derzeitigen schlechten Wetterprognosen, welche anhaltenden Schneemangel vorhersagen, haben wir uns diesem Problem angenommen und die Entstehung von Schnee untersucht. Wir haben intensiv an der Entwicklung einer Eiskristall-Wachstums-Maschine für den Eigengebrauch gearbeitet.

ANLEITUNG FÜR DIE ERSTELLUNG EINES SCHNEE-GENERATORS

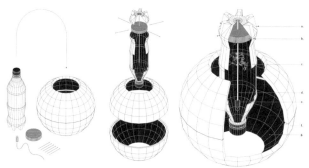

a. Nadeln / b. Schwamm / c. Coca-Cola PET-Flasche / d. Nylonfaden / e. Büroklammer / f. Kühlkessel aus extrudiertem Schaumstoff Polystyrol / g. Kesselhohlraum für gefrorenes Kohlenstoffdioxid

EXPERIMENT-VORBEREITUNGEN

Phase 1: Der Rumpf unserer Eiskristall-Wachstums-Maschine besteht aus einer Coca-Cola PET-Flasche, welche ungefähr 15 mm über dem Boden zweigeteilt ist. In der Mitte des Flaschenbodens wird mittels einer Nadel ein Loch gestochen, weitere fünf Löcher werden auf der Seite benötigt. Durch die fünf seitlichen Löcher ist ein Schwamm mit Nadeln fixiert.

Phase 2: Durch das Loch in der Mitte des Flaschenbodens und den Schwamm hindurch zieht sich ein Nylonfaden, welcher ausserhalb auf dem Flaschenboden fixiert ist. Am anderen Ende des Fadens ist ein Büroklammer befestigt, so dass der Faden bei umgekehrter Haltung der Flasche frei hängt.

Phase 3: Der Kühlkessel besteht aus isolierendem extrudiertem Schaumstoff Polystyrol. Durch eine Öffnung wird die PET-Flasche in umgekehrter Haltung im Kühlkessel stabilisiert.

Phase 4: Der Schwamm wird bewässert und speichert so die erforderliche Feuchtigkeit, die benötigt wird um Schneekristalle zu produzieren.

Phase 5: Der Kühlkessel ist mit gefrorenem Kohlenstoffdioxid (Trockeneis) gefüllt. Die Temperatur im Kessel beträgt rund -60°C. Zur Herstellung von einer kleinen Menge Eiskristallen und daraus resultierenden Schnee werden zirka 7 Kilogramm

Trockeneis benötigt. Die angegebene Menge Trockeneis reicht für einen Kristallisationsprozess von ungefähr 6 Stunden aus.

Resultat: Der Kristallisationsprozess setzt sich in Gang und schon nach wenigen Minuten entstehen erste fraktale Formen. Nach weiteren 20-40 Minuten treten bereits zahlreiche Verästelungen auf.

KRISTALLISATIONSPROZESS

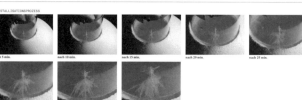

nach 5 min.   nach 10 min.   nach 15 min.   nach 20 min.   nach 25 min.

nach 30 min.   nach 35 min.   nach 40 min.

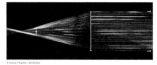

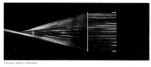

WEITSICHTIGKEIT
Beim Weitsichtigen ist die Brechkraft zu gering, die Lichtstrahlen bündeln sich erst hinter der Netzhaut.

KURZSICHTIGKEIT
Bei unterschiedlichen Krümmungen der Hornhaut in ihren verschiedenen Achsen werden die auftreffenden Lichtstrahlen ungleich gebrochen, das Bild ist zerrissen.

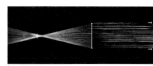

FERNSICHTIGKEIT
Beim Kurzsichtigen bündeln sich die Lichtstrahlen bereits vor der Netzhaut. Hinter diesem Brennpunkt breiten sie sich wieder aus, es resultiert ein verschwommenes Bild.

PRESBYOPIE
Mit zunehmendem Alter verlieren die Augen ihre Brechkraft (aktive Veränderung der Linsenkrümmung): nahe Gegenstände verschwimmen.

Die Sehschärfe

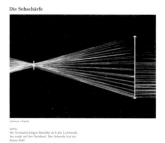

NORMAL
Bei Normalsichtigen bündeln sich die Lichtstrahlen exakt auf der Netzhaut. Die Sehende hat ein klares Bild.

Die Sonne dringt kaum mehr durch

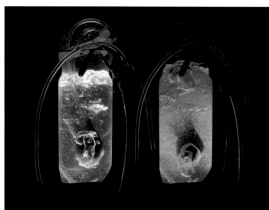

Women	day ∞	1st month	2nd	3st	4th	5th	6th

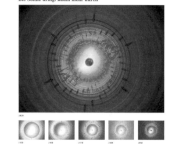

Men	day ∞	1st month	2nd	3st	4th	5th	6th

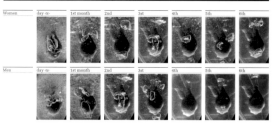

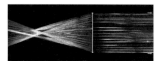

Snow Machine CYBU RICHLI in collaboration with Fabienne Burri — This comprehensive chart not only explains how to manufacture a snow machine; it also demonstrates the process step-by-step. Moreover, it provides a reference section, revealing the machine's inner workings.

With a combination of photography and line diagrams, the designer entices the amateur climatologist into enjoying this slightly alien view of the device, which is shrouded in smoke like a monster, symbolising excitement and the mysteries of nature. **Visual explanations, Optics** CYBU RICHLI, Silo (Richli / Moser) — Umberto Eco famously said that reading glasses were most probably the biggest contributor to the enlightenment of mankind. By extending the intellectually active life of an individual, knowledge could be preserved, improved, and shared with a much larger audience. Using reading glasses meant that the monks of the Middle Ages could continue working on their books into ripe old age. The deterioration of eyesight, and the mechanisms that bring visual acuity, can be simply explained. By stretching and contorting a roll of cling-film across a fixed surface, Cybu Richli creates a potent and accurate illustration of how focus can be distorted and twisted through the lens and cornea of the eye. The researcher then experiments by adding this haptic quality to the behaviour of light, drawing conclusions in new and unexpected ways.

Visual explanations, Ecology CYBU RICHLI, Silo (Richli / Moser) — The atmosphere forms a delicate and fragile shell around Earth, containing the requirements for all known life. Air pollution not only damages life through its direct chemical effects, but also influences the amount of sunlight that can reach the planet, leading to massive climate change.

Stacking plastic cups in an analogy of the increased density of pollution makes its impact graphically and viscerally clear. **Breakup** CYBU RICHLI — Emotions are very real and personal adjuncts to human beings, but their complexity makes them difficult to explain, let alone visualise. Since our emotions are so enmeshed in who we are, it is doubtful that we could ever truly convey their meaning to anyone else. In this installation, the emotions felt by men and women during the six months after the break-up of a relationship are portrayed. A subjective reflection is brought to life through an artificial heart, submerged in a turbulent flow of emotions. Air is pumped through the installation at different rates to convey the sense of personal turmoil. The intention is not to convey an objective and scientifically measurable proof, but to simulate the intuitive level at which emotions are felt. **Breaking Ball** CYBU RICHLI — Apple sauce is a staple culinary accompaniment throughout German-speaking countries, enjoyed with everything from pancakes to potato fritters. The process of making apple sauce is set out in this humorous six-step photomontage.

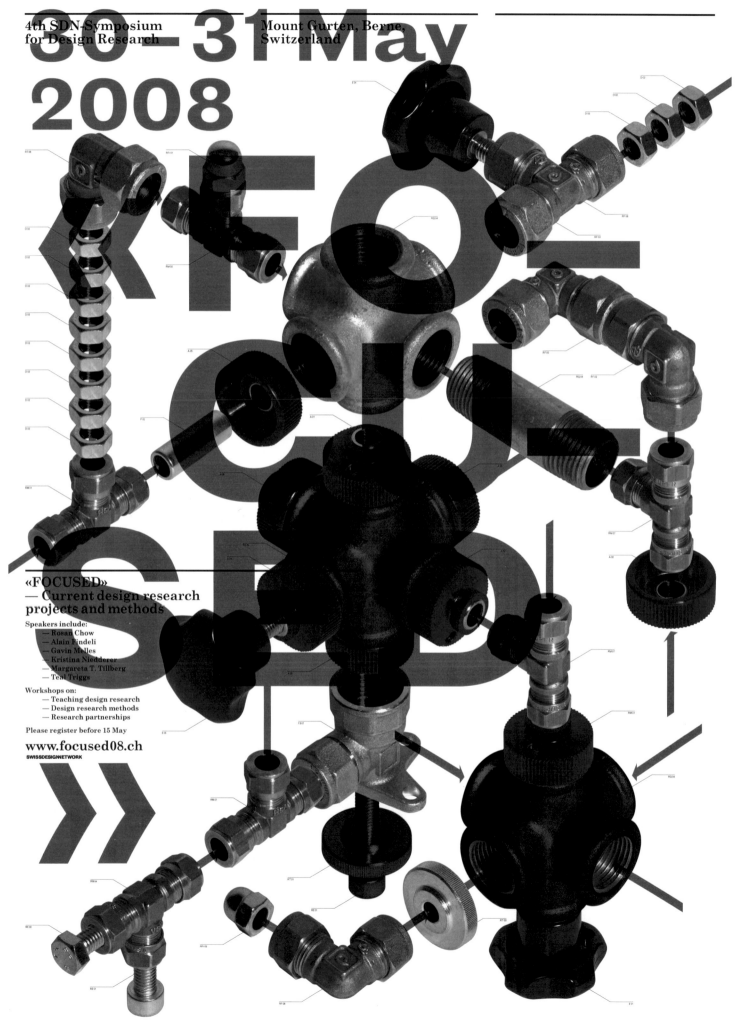

4th SDN-Symposium
for Design Research

Mount Gurten, Berne,
Switzerland

30–31 May
2008

«FOCUSED»
— Current design research
projects and methods

Speakers include:
— Rosan Chow
— Alain Findeli
— Gavin Melles
— Kristina Niedderer
— Margareta T. Tillberg
— Teal Triggs

Workshops on:
— Teaching design research
— Design research methods
— Research partnerships

Please register before 15 May

www.focused08.ch

SWISSDESIGNNETWORK

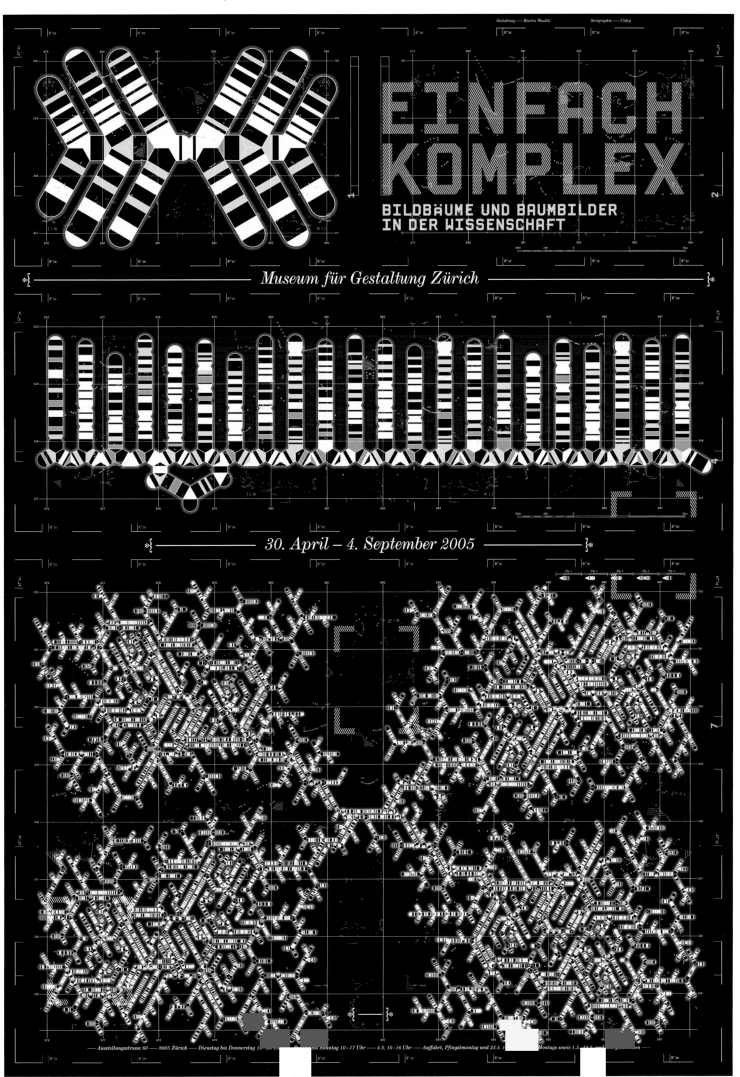

PREVIOUS PAGE ———— **Focused** CYBU RICHLI, in collaboration with Fabienne Burri— At first glance, this exploded view of piping components looks like a random collection of elements, thrown together for visual effect. However, the data labels reveal an intricate network of research objectives, funding, papers, and other elements that combine around the mission of the Swiss Design Network. At once, therefore, the poster identifies and informs the attendee as to what he or she can expect. The components turn into a catalogue of intellectual discourse. ———— **Einfach Komplex** MARTIN WOODTLI — Tree structures are a very popular form of visualisation in scientific infographics. The particular characteristics of tree structures enable them to be applied in cartography, biology, and many other disciplines where relationships and flow need to be set out clearly.   Tree structures can present topological categories in combination with spatial relationships, enabling function and order to be precisely displayed. These qualities are exemplified in Woodtli's use of tree structures in his programme design for the symposium 'Simple/Complex: Tree diagrams and images'.

———— **Einfach Komplex** MARTIN WOODTLI ———— **Étrange** QUENTIN MARGAT — Formal aspects of design are consciously borrowed from science to invest these imaginary shapes—inspired by dissections and elements of the human body—with an apparent validity. The illustrations are not themselves taken from genuine scientific materials, but assume the seriousness and rigour of the discipline through the chosen stylisation.   The formal page structure and use of axonometric projections add to the effect, as loosely referential illustrations are turned into objects of scientific fact.

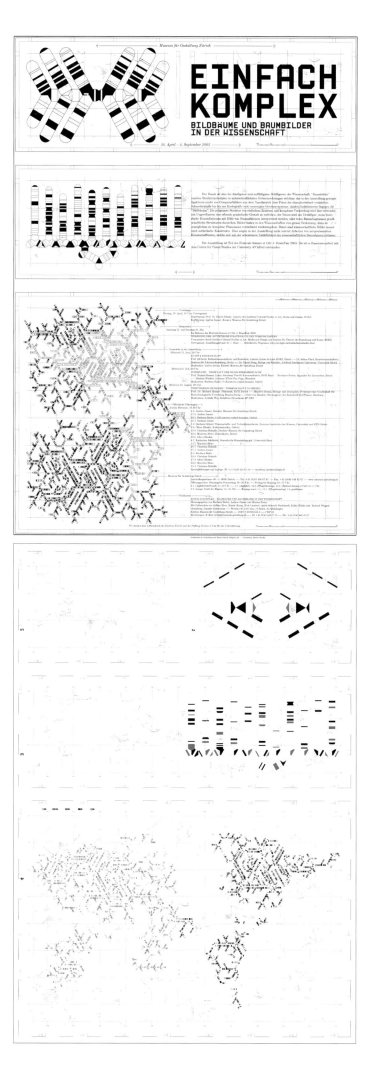

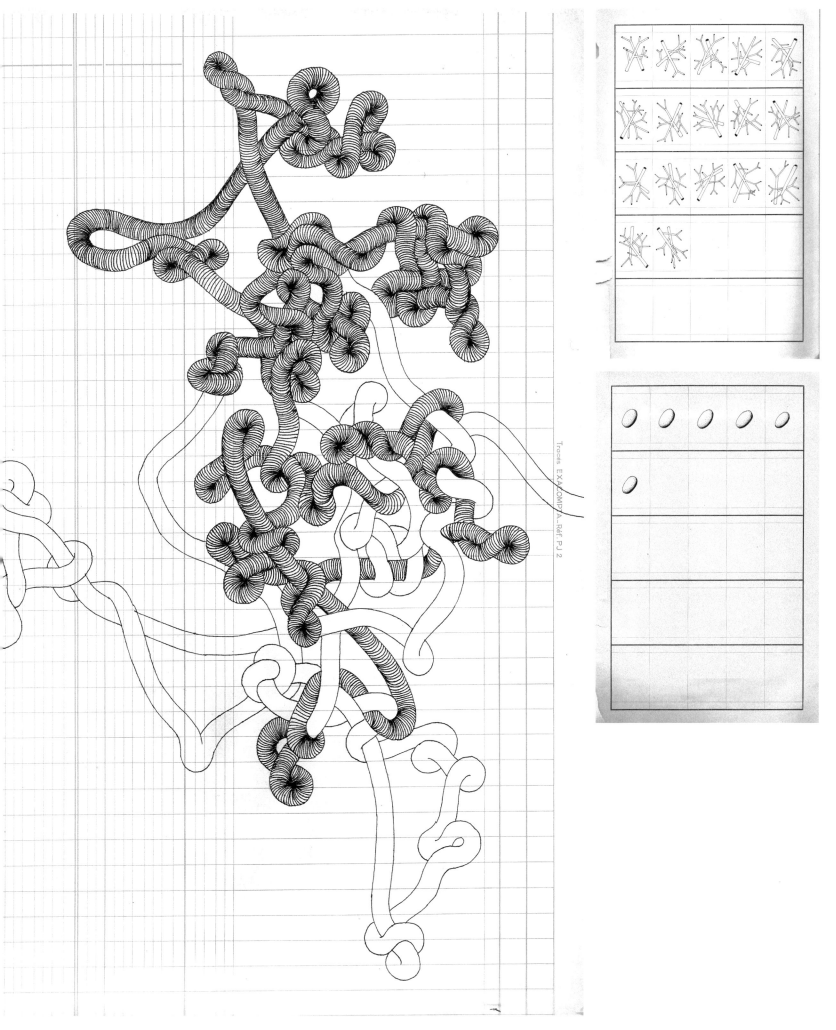

Traces EXACOMPTA - Réf PJ 2

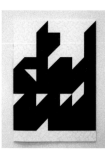

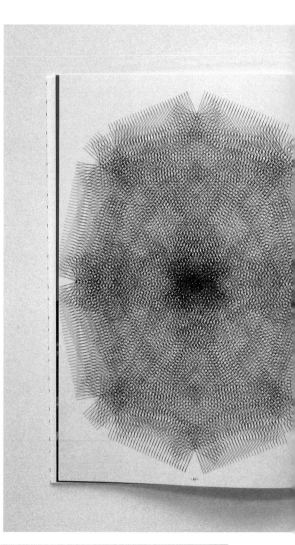

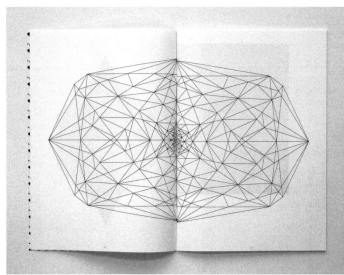

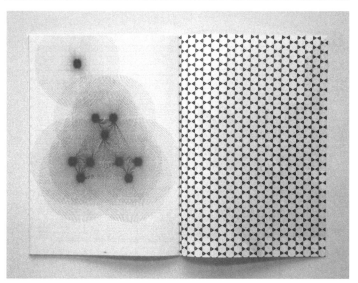

—— **Crystallography** —— **Mineralogy** ONDREJ JÓB — This extensive work by Ondrej Jób deliberately blurs the borders between art and analysis. Using varied and diffuse techniques of subjective and objective analysis, the inner nature and form of crystals are celebrated.

NEXT PAGES —————— **What makes Berlin addictive** MARIA TACKMANN —**'Breathe' Poster** |▷P. 68|STUDIO 8 DESIGN, Matt Willey & Giles Revell, all photographs by Giles Revell — The direct visual link between the branches and bronchial tubes of the human lung reinforces the importance of trees in providing oxygen. The construction of this image as an exact vertical reflection further enhances its message of dependency and connection.

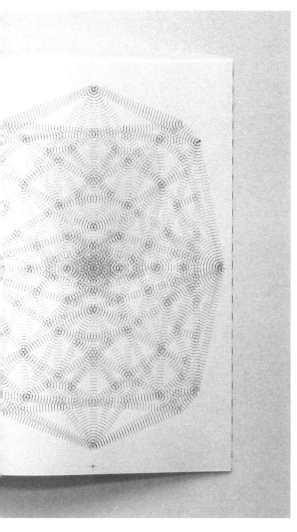

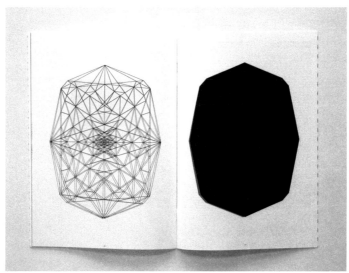

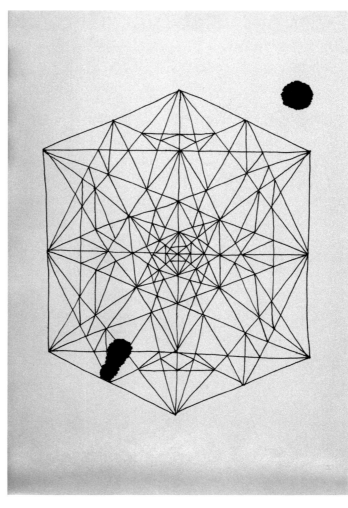

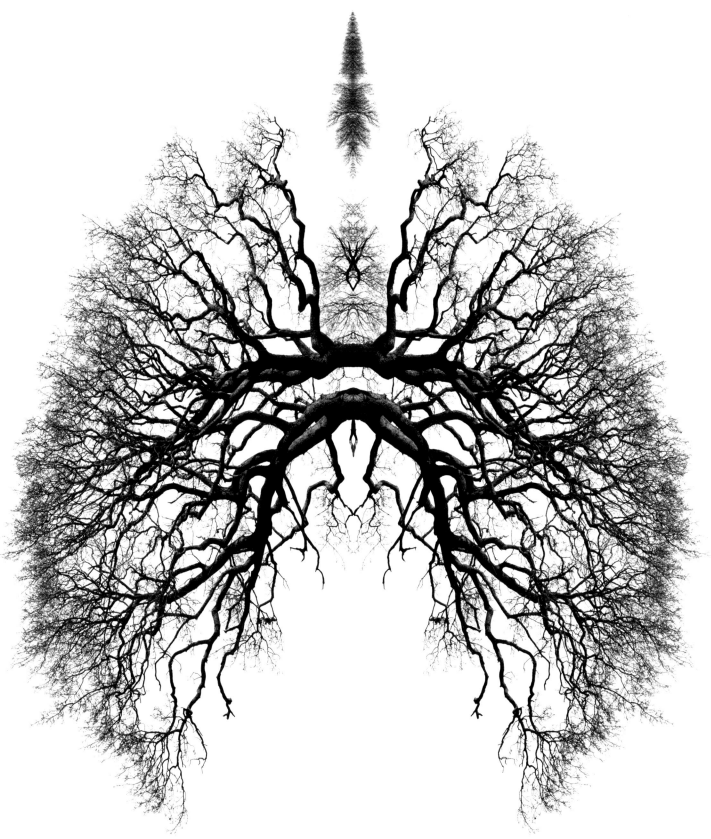

BREATHE

Forests are the lungs of the earth. The destruction of forests has
been a fortifying factor in climate change. With millions of miles of
old growth forests cleared every year, the earth is slowly suffocating
under the increase of greenhouse gases.
www.ran.org

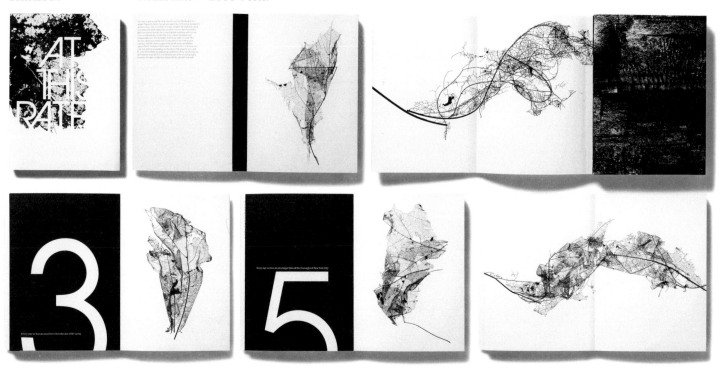

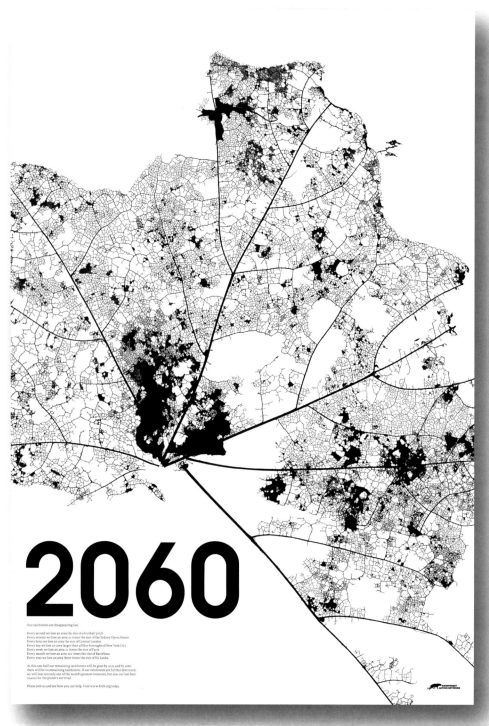

————— **At this Rate** STUDIO 8 DESIGN, Matt Willey & Giles Revell, all photographs by Giles Revell ——**'2060' Poster** STUDIO 8 DESIGN, Matt Willey & Giles Revell, all photographs by Giles Revell — Here, man's destruction of his surroundings is likened to the process of decay in the natural world. Tenuous filaments struggling to maintain the integrity of a once beautiful natural object poignantly reflect the desperate situation of the disappearing rain forests. The veins of a withered leaf are analogous to the urban sprawl that destroys natural forests. As richness, life, and diversity disappear, the hard, lifeless infrastructure of decay is exposed. The two opposing dynamics — life and decay — are made visually obvious as the Rainforest Action Network shows how we are substituting the structures that support life by structures that destroy it. ——— **Unisson** JULIEN MÉTILLE — Modern society's destructive impact on the natural environment has become a well-established theme. Images of forests decimated and disappearing in the name of economic growth have filled magazine and newspaper pages over the decades. But modern society's destructive impact on the cultural ecosphere is less familiar to us, although it is just as devastating. The music industry's profit motive, fuelled by the global distribution imperative, has systematically reduced diversity. In this artwork, the visual processing of an image from the natural world becomes a metaphor for the industrial process of music development and distribution. The layers, acting as filters, show the impact that the demand for immediacy and profit has on raw, natural talent when it comes to delivering the musical end-product. The distorted image becomes pale and is sharply reduced, symbolising the disruptive effects of global industrialisation on our culture. Homogenised and prepackaged mass products have invaded a previously rich and diverse space to remove nuance, subtlety, and self-expression.

——— **La représentation des statistiques** XAVIER BARRADE, in collaboration with Arnaud Dupont — The size of a football pitch is often used as an accessible shorthand to give scale and meaning to surface areas. By graphically showing how many football pitches of rainforest are being eradicated, the message of destruction is brought home in a haunting and devastating way. ——— **England vs. Poland, 12th October 2005**

CHRIS CAMPBELL — England's 2-1 victory over Poland in this game helped secure their berth in the 2006 World Cup finals. Without any overt inscription or text labels on the diagram, the ball possession and movement throughout the entire ninety minutes become a schematic celebration of the beautiful game. The pure passing game is diffused in a dense tangle of stratagems and tactics, as the ball covers every inch of the pitch.

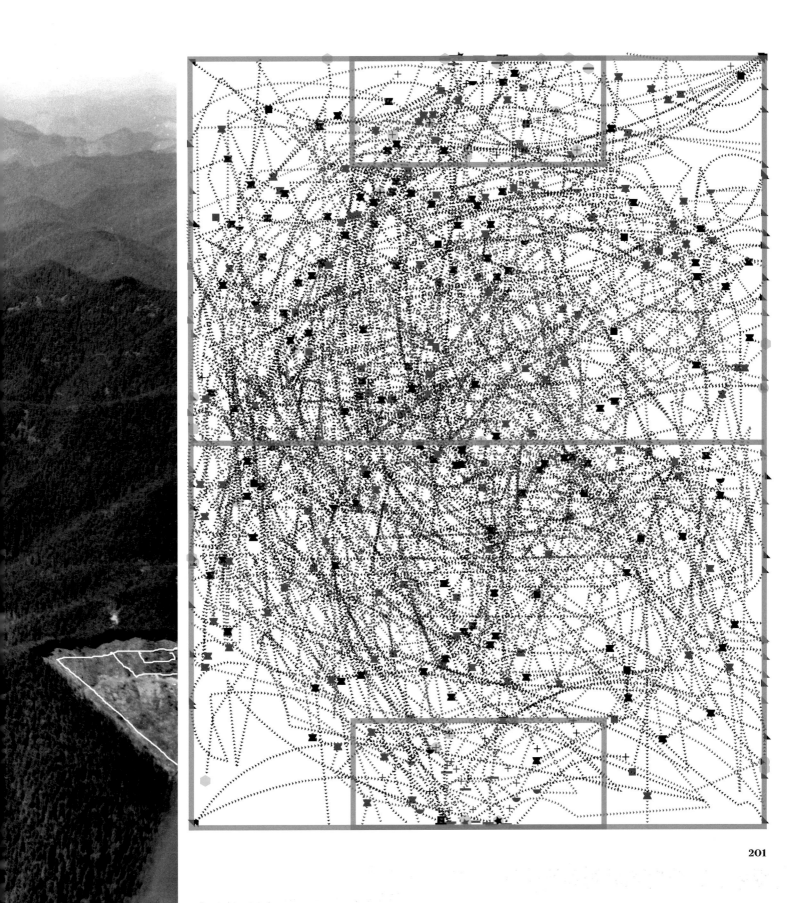

Reykjavík, Iceland 2007

June 15
June 16
June 17
June 18
June 19
June 20
June 21
June 22
June 23
June 24
June 25
June 26
June 27
June 28
June 29
June 30
July 1
July 2
July 3
July 4
July 5
July 6
July 7
July 8
July 9
July 10
July 11
July 12
July 13
July 14
July 15
July 16
July 17
July 18
July 19
July 20
July 21
July 22

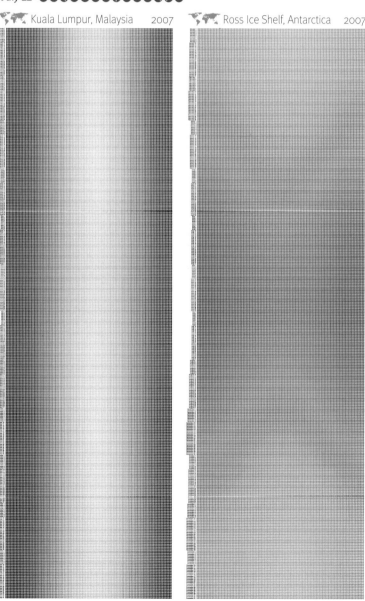

Kuala Lumpur, Malaysia 2007

Ross Ice Shelf, Antarctica 2007

Sunlight Calendar LEE BYRON — A river of light, constructed painstakingly from individual clock faces, reflects the colour of the sky. Each geographic location possesses its own unique solar footprint, with light and darkness streaming across a year of illumination.

The character of each location is captured simply, as we gauge the strength of the seasons, and the rhythms and changes in vitality wrought by the sun's energy awakening human and natural activity. The constant unchanging flow of sunshine in Kuala Lumpur is obviously going to differ from the fluctuating levels of sunlight in Reykjavik.

Light Calendar 2007 ACCEPT & PROCEED, David Johnston & Stephen Heath.

Hours of dark 2007

— Light Calendar 2007

'Light Calendar'
By Accept & Proceed, for Blanka 12/06

©2006 Accept & Proceed
Statistics provided by www.timeanddate.com

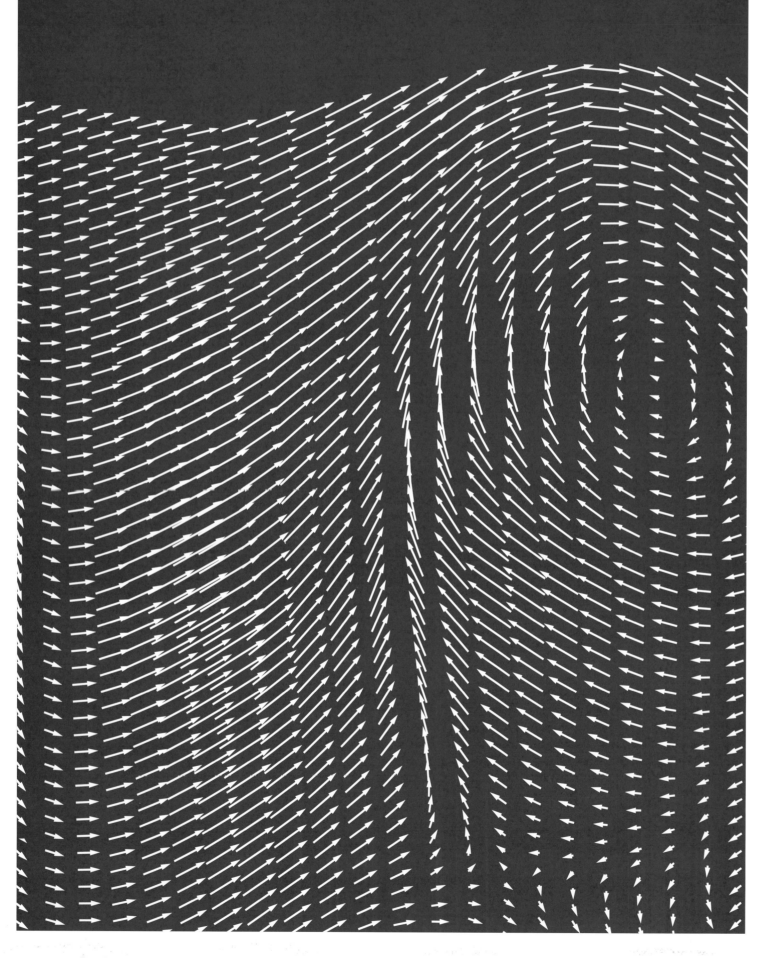

———**Kieler Woche 2008** HEINE/
LENZ/ZIZKA, Peter Zizka & Joel Carneiro
— Kiel Week is considered to be the largest Volksfest in Germany, and is certainly
the biggest sailing event in the world.
Sailing's inextricable relationship with
wind is symbolised by the pattern of ar-
rows forming a textural map on the cover.
The gestalt pattern relies on the contribu-
tions of each individual weather arrow,
in a strong reference to the team nature
of the sport. In this way, the power of the
wind is harnessed by the collective efforts
of the team. ———**Virtual Water,
Water Footprint of Nations** |▷ P. 206|
TIMM KEKERITZ — Water is life. Water
flows through life. The impact that our
daily choices have on water consumption
is not obvious to us. The idea of a carbon
footprint to reflect the impact of energy
consumption on greenhouse gas emissions
has been widely established. Yet there is no
equivalent yardstick for water, the increasingly scarce commodity upon which all life
depends.   The virtual water footprint
of common foodstuffs is a measure of the
fresh water used in their manufacture. The
visual simplicity of the comparison quickly
shocks the viewer into realising the effect
that meat production, for instance, has on
the allocation of scarce resources.

WATER
FOOTPRINTS *of nations*

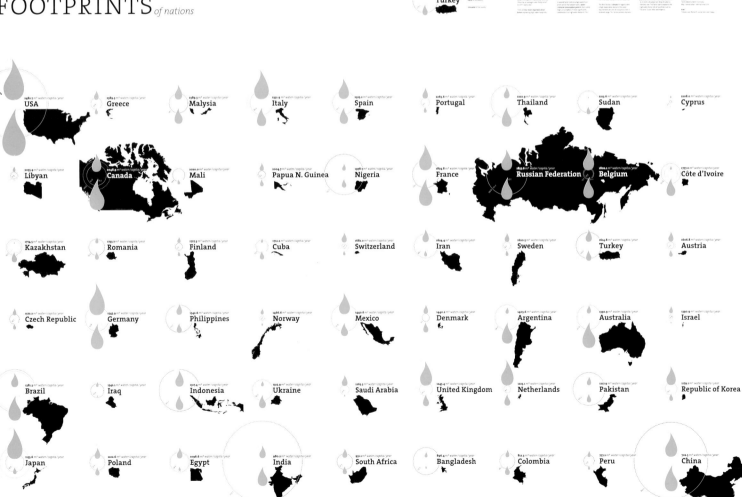

VIRTUAL WATER *inside products*

450 litres of water for
one corb (500 g) of
Corn

Maize consumes about 550 billion m³ of water annually, which is 8 % of the global water use for crop production. About 40 billion m³ of water is used for making maize for export.

500 litres of water for
one pound (500 g) of
Wheat

Wheat consumes about 790 billion m³ of water annually, which constitutes 12 % of the global water use for crop production. International trade in wheat is responsible for 75 billion m³ of virtual water exports annually, which is about 6 % of the total sum of international virtual water flows.

1700 litres of water for
one package (500 g) of
Rice

Paddy rice (the rice as harvested from the field) has consumed 2300 litres of water per kg. One kilogram of paddy rice produces 0.67 kg of milled rice on average. In the shop we buy milled rice in the form of white rice or broken rice. In this form, rice requires 3400 litres of water per kilogram.
The rice fields in the world consume about 1950 billion m³ of water annually, which is 21 % of the global water use for crop production. The sum of virtual water flows between countries related to rice trade is about 75 billion m³ of virtual water per year.

900 litres of water for
one pound (500 g) of
Soybeans

The production of soybeans in the world takes about 290 billion m³ of water annually, which is 4.5 % of the global water use for crop production.

2500 litres of water for
one big piece (500 g) of
Cheese

To produce one kilogram of cheese we need 10 litres of milk.
The volume of water required to produce this milk is 10000 litres. Processing 10 litres of milk also produces 7.3 litres of whey, which generates more or less the same market value as the cheese. Hence, the volume of water to produce 10 litres of milk gets divided into cheese and whey more or less equally.

650 litres of water for
one package (500 g) of
Toast

Producing wheat requires 1300 litres of water per kilogram (global average). One slice of bread has a weight of about 30 g, which implies a water footprint of 40 litres.
If the bread is consumed together with 1 slice of cheese (10 g), then it all together requires 90 litres of water.

90 litres of water for
one pot (750 ml) of
Tea

To produce one kilogram of fresh tealeaves we require 2400 litres of water. One kilogram of fresh tealeaves gives 0.26 kg of made tea, so that one kilogram of made tea (black tea as we buy it in the shop) requires 9200 litres of water. For a standard cup of tea we require three gram of black tea, so that a cup of tea requires 30 litres of water. The water needs for post-harvest processing can be neglected if compared to the water needs for growing the tea plant. The water footprint of tea thus mainly refers to rainwater use.

840 litres of water for
one pot (750 ml) of
Coffee

It costs about 21000 litres of water to produce 1 kilogram of roasted coffee. For a standard cup of coffee we require 7 gram of roasted coffee, so that a cup of coffee requires 140 litres of water. Assuming that a standard cup of coffee is 125 ml, we thus need more than 1100 drops of water for producing one drop of coffee.

1000 litres of water for
one litre of
Milk

Producing a glass of milk (200 ml) requires 200 litres of water. Drinking the same volume of orange juice or apple juice would require 170 and 190 litres of water respectively. Drinking a plain glass of water requires only little more than the water itself.

4500 litres of water for
one steak (300 g) of
Beef

In an industrial beef production system, it takes in average three years before the animal is slaughtered to produce about 200 kg of boneless beef. The animal consumes nearly 1300 kg of grains, 7200 kg of roughages, 24 m³ of water for drinking and 7 cubic meter of water for servicing. This means that to produce one kilogram of boneless beef, we use about 6.5 kg of grain, 36 kg of roughages, and 155 litres of water (only for drinking and servicing). Producing the volume of feed requires about 15300 litres of water in average.

1200 litres of water for
one steak (300 g) of
Goatmeat

In an industrial farming system, it takes 2 years on average before the goat is slaughtered. It will produce 20 kg of fresh goat meat.
During its lifetime the goat consumes about 55 kg of grains, 165 kg of roughages and 3.5 m³ of water for drinking and servicing the farmhouse. This means that to produce one kilogram of goat meat, we use about 2.75 kg of grains and 175 litres of drinking and servicing water. Producing 2.75 kg of feed of this composition takes about 4 m³ of water in average.

1440 litres of water for
one steak (300 g) of
Pork

In an industrial pig farming system, it takes 10 months on average before a pig is slaughtered.
It produces 90 kg of swine carcass, 5 kg of edible offal and 2.5 kg of skin. A pig consumes about 385 kg of grains and 11 m³ of water for drinking and servicing the farmhouse. We need about 10 m³ of water during the slaughtering and cleaning processes. To produce this feed we need 435 m³ of water.

———— **Virtual Water inside**
Products TIMM KEKERITZ

one drop (shown in the illustrations below)
is equivalent to **50 litres of virtual water**
(production-site definition).

The **virtual-water** content of a product (a commodity, good or service) is the **volume of fresh-
water used to produce the product**, measured
at the place where the product was actually
produced. It refers to the sum of the water use
in the various steps of the production chain.

320 litres of water were used to produce the
paper **this poster** (DIN A0) is printed on.
Assuming 160 g / m² paper and that the paper is
produced from wood.

DATA:
Chapagain, A.K. and Hoekstra, A.Y. (2004)
»Water footprints of nations«
Value of Water Research Report Series No. 16.
UNESCO-IHE, Delft, the Netherlands

DESIGN:
Timm Kekeritz, Berlin, Germany
http://www.urban-international.com

FONT:
TheSans and TheSerif, Luc(as) de Groot (1994)

70
litres of water for
one single (100 g)
Apple

In average about 700 litres of water
are needed to produce one kilogram
of apples. The exact amount of water
depends on the origin and breed of
the apple.
One glass of apple juice (200 ml)
requires about 190 litres of water.

50
litres of water for
one single (100 g)
Orange

In average about 500 litres of water
are needed to produce one kilogram
of oranges.
One glass of orange juice (200 ml)
requires about 170 litres of water.

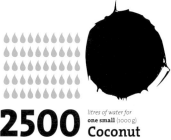

2500
litres of water for
one small (1000 g)
Coconut

Coconut production in the world
consumes about 130 billion m³ of water
annually, which is 2 % of the global
water use for crop production.

720
litres of water for
one bottle (750 ml) of
Wine

Most of the water behind the wine is
for producing the grapes.
The water needed to produce and
recycle the bottle is not included.

150
litres of water for
one bottle (500 ml) of
Beer

Most of the water behind the beer is for
producing the barley.
The water needed to produce and
recycle the bottle is not included.

185
litres of water for
one bag (200 g) of
Potatocrisps

In average about 900 litres of water
are needed to produce 1000 g of potato
flakes. Most of the water behind the
potato flakes is for producing the
potatos.

830
litres of water for
one steak (300 g) of
Sheepmeat

In an industrial sheep farming system,
it takes 18 months on average before a
sheep is slaughtered.
The sheep produces 28 kg of fresh
carcass, 2 kg of edible offal and 4 kg
of skin together with wool. A sheep
consumes about 40 kg of grains and
4 m³ of water for drinking and servicing
the farmhouse. This total volume of
water is distributed over the three
major products based on their relative
market values and product weight
obtained per ton of live sheep.

1170
litres of water for
one breastfilet (300 g) of
Chicken

In an industrial chicken farming system,
it takes 10 weeks on average before the
chicken is slaughtered.
It will produce 1.7 kg of chicken meat. A
chicken consumes about 3.3 kg of grains
and 30 litres of water for drinking and
servicing the farmhouse. This means
that to produce one kilogram of chicken
meat, we use about 2 kg of grains and
20 litres of drinking and servicing water.
Producing two kilograms of feed of
this composition takes about 3.9 m³ of
water in average.

200
litres of water for
one single (60 g)
Egg

As a global average, eggs require about
3300 m³ of water per ton. Most of it is
required for feeding the chickens.

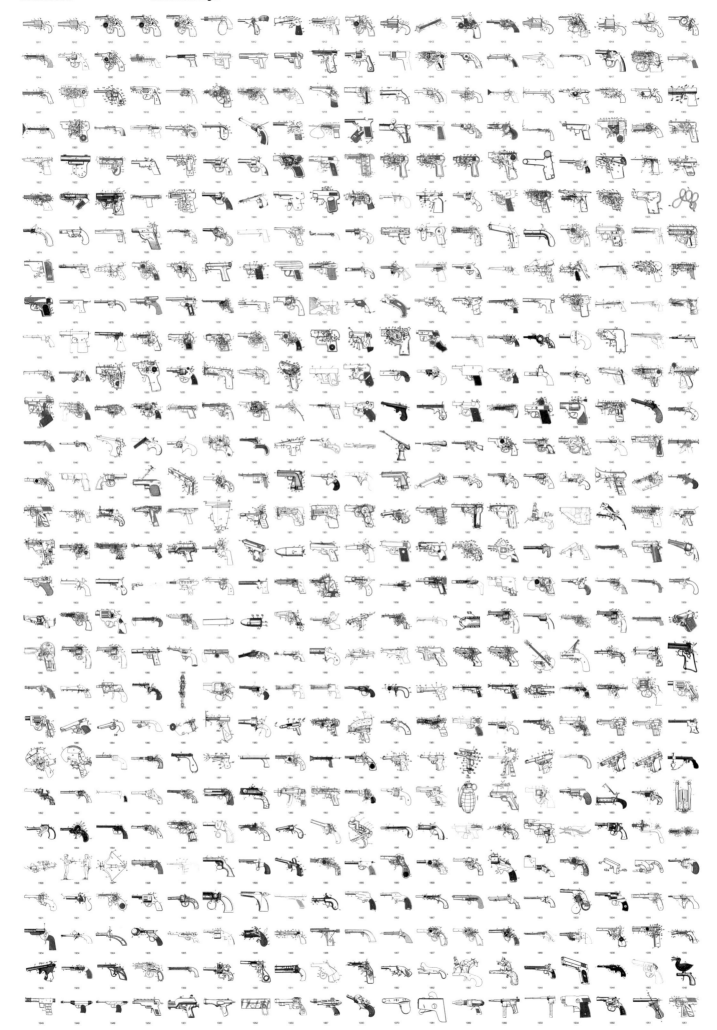

—— **American Toys** CHRISTOPHER BAKER — The United States Patent Office can be viewed as the collective repository of the nation's imagination—a historical database of possible futures. Like the hazy image from an almost-forgotten dream, this imagined toy gun is the residual footprint of all 500 patent applications submitted for the 'toy gun' category since the 1800s. The resultant image becomes a collective expression of the prototypical American toy.

——Spirograf Poster EFFEKTIVE — As children, many of us were fascinated by the elaborate patterns we could make with the Spirograph toy. By switching and combining different cogs, an elegant universe of lines could be created, intersecting in patterns that suggested some scientific experiment. Greig Anderson, from Effective Design, has created posters and badges recalling the patterns associated with the toy, in a modern updated aesthetic.

——Internet statistics ETIENNE CLIQUET — Inverting the onslaught of the paperless office heralded by Internet technology, Etienne Cliquet uses the ancient paper folding art of Origami to display global Internet statistics. Each fold accurately represents the usage statistics of a specific country. By fashioning a metaphor for the living web, using the medium it was intent on replacing, Cliquet creates an ironic allegory and sculptural representation. Negative space, volume, and shape become functional expressions of data in a physical space, mediated by the archaic and fragile vehicle of knowledge—namely, paper.

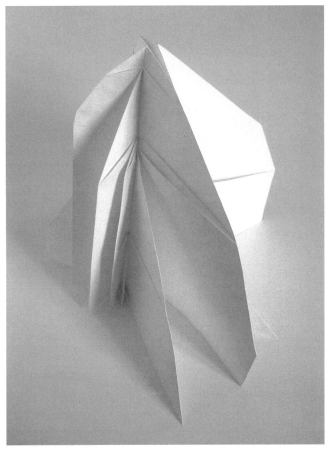

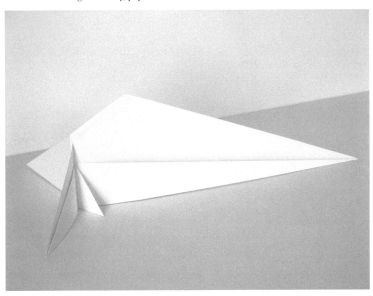

WORLD INTERNET USAGE STATISTICS

Experience NIKKI CHUNG — Guidebooks purvey authoritative accounts of the most desirable places by drawing on the experiences of others. They also provide a sense of reassurance in alien environments. In this series of guidebooks, Nikki Chung quantifies the collective experience of leisure travel by a visual depiction of global tourist movements over one year. Data from the UN World Tourism Organisation was used to create a guidebook for every country in the world, based on the number of tourists who visited in 2005. The number of pages in each book corresponds with the number of tourist arrivals (100,000 arrivals per page). When viewed on a shelf, one year's-worth of 'experience' is presented in a condensed physical bar graph that can be shifted and rearranged in order to infer where tourists travel. Serving as colour-coded data blocks, the guidebooks can be quickly rearranged to express other demographic factors such as GDP, population density, and countries at war. Readers can then browse and compare at multiple levels, according to their own criteria.

—

Datablock

—

—

The implied certainty and substance of rectangular destiny make bar charts and tables a staple of business presentations. The defined borders, clear order, and straightforward comparability of data arranged as blocks complement the power structures implied by using Microsoft PowerPoint™. Those running the seminar are assured that the conversation will proceed within clear constraints. No wonder people refer to a socially inept person as a square.

—

Yet is this stereotype valid? Here, designers remove the confines of the Cartesian grid, allowing blocks to shift into an abstract expression of flow and tension. In Socket's reduced representation of tectonic forces, he plays with visual and formal contrasts to highlight the tension between the blocks. The effect is far more powerful in its abstraction than the expected and more usual literal descriptions. Similarly, Jack Henrie Fisher's analysis of György Kepes's landmark book *Language of Vision*

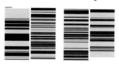

— **Diagrammatic Reading Machine** |▷ P. 231|
JACK HENRIE FISHER

applies the reference to the grid as a matrix for unfolding subtlety and nuance. A visual language is created, ideal for unearthing new insights into the intent and structure of the literary work. Blocks become the basis of non-linear comparison.

In many cases, however, the confines of the printed medium determine the shape of direct visual comparison. The

·The ·Up & Down· of violence in our daily newspaper·

— **World of Violence**
|▷ P. 240| LORENZO GEIGER

lay-out grid becomes an essential aspect—either direct or inferred—of content analysis. Column inches marching over a page are a direct expression of the real-estate dedicated to specific topics. The allocation of space becomes a design choice of editors as a mouthpiece for society. Both Lorenzo Geiger's and Christina Van Vleck's analyses of the news show how blocks of space shape and express opinion. A barometer for mood and sentiment becomes an irregular 'Up and Down' of coloured segments.

The most direct parallel between subject and shape is revealed in catalogtree's analysis of the

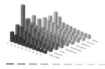

— **PlaNYC** |▷ P. 226|
CATALOGTREE

PlaNYC document, a design for the sustainability of New York City proposed by Mayor Michael Bloomberg. Here, the Manhattan skyline finds itself within a framework of repetition and focus. The planning agenda is revealed according to priorities, with press coverage again dictated by the values of media real-estate. The three-dimensional histogram spells out the shape of things to come. The clean uniformity of data as blocks also imposes simplicity on complex topics. In trying to balance Immofinanz's message of 'complexity made simple', Felix Heienen relies on the discrete and inherent

simplicity of repeated cubes. The underlying message is that the solution is not complex—it is simply hidden in a complex structure, where similarity reduces distinction. By removing layers of clustered cubes, the single solution becomes evident. The basic square structure is then seamlessly applied to the description of work flow and financing options.

—**Immofinanz AG, Annual Report** |▷ P. 218|
BÜRO X WERNER SINGER
FELIX HEINEN

This is all constructed in a self-referential application of buildings as blocks, or in this case, the building blocks of investment. We step inside the blocked-up world of Reto Moser's catalogue of life, to find a rich, complex, and diverse multitude of objects and influences. In this instance, the block becomes an organising force, pressing identity on to an otherwise inscrutable clutter of objects. In the end, it all makes

—**29501 vs. 4714**
|▷ P. 236| RETO MOSER

sense, because it reflects our human need to put things into boxes. The struggle against chaos

—

The clean uniformity of data as blocks imposes simplicity on complex topics

—

and an uncertain universe can be contained, if only for a short while, in the walled certainty of squares.

PREVIOUS PAGE —— **abstract** JACOB
DAHLGREEN, photography by Hendrik
Zeitler

Der Do-it-Yourself-Weg

III. Bestmögliche sektorale Portfolio-Diversifikation

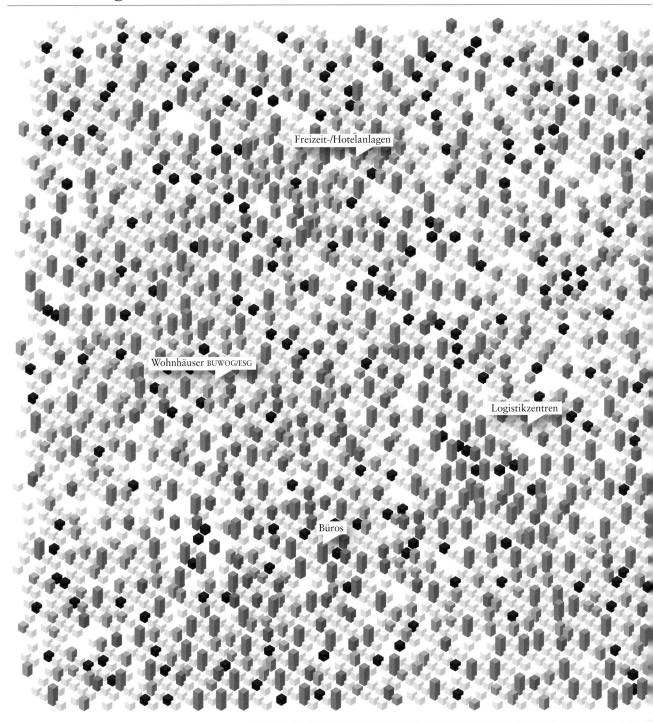

Am besten Sie kaufen Hotels, Wohnungen, Geschäftsgebäude, möglichst ausgewogen!

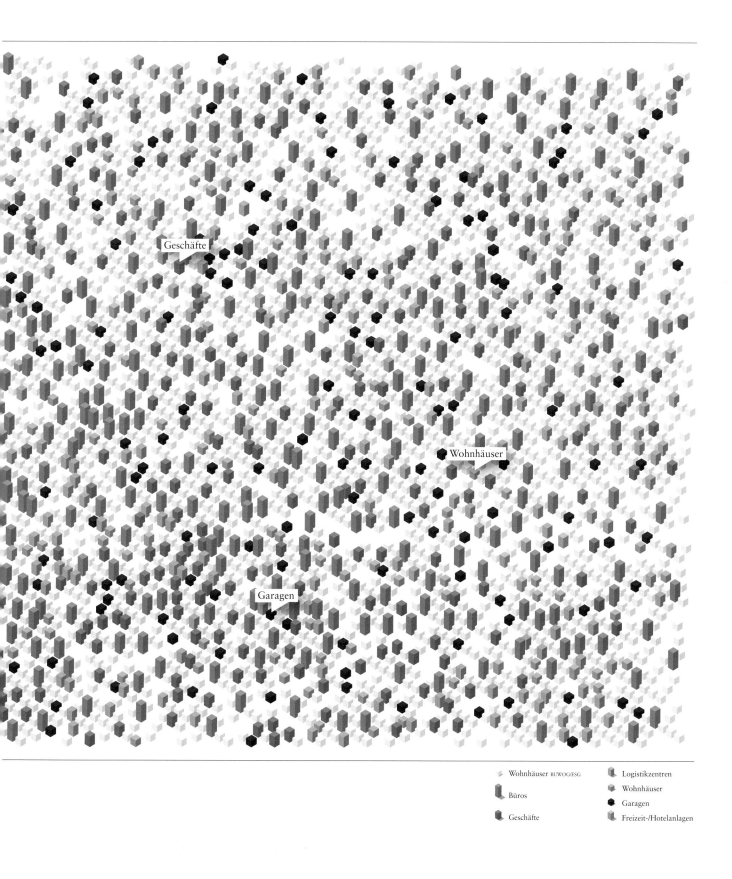

Geschäfte

Wohnhäuser

Garagen

Wohnhäuser BUWOG/ESG   Logistikzentren

Büros   Wohnhäuser

Geschäfte   Garagen

                               Freizeit-/Hotelanlagen

Die Nachfrage nach einzelnen Immobilienkategorien verläuft in Zyklen. Während Wohnungen boomen, können Bürogebäude leer stehen und sich Garagenbesitzer über eine konstante Nachfrage freuen – das Ganze gilt auch in mit umgekehrten Vorzeichen. Die Verteilung des Portfolios auf unterschiedliche Sektoren bildet daher die Basis einer möglichst konstanten Rendite-Entwicklung.

— **Immofinanz AG, Annual Report** BÜRO X WERNER SINGER FELIX HEINEN —Simplicity is shown as a marketing proposition. By contrasting the complexity and risks involved in dilettante property investment compared with the service provided by Immofinanz, Felix Heinen applies simplification and clarification to the data. Complex, inscrutable Excel sheets are scrubbed and parsed, and distilled into clear stories underlining the company's experience and service ethos. The delicate balance between detailing the complexity of the offer, while keeping it easily accessible to the average punter, is maintained as the reader leafs through various data tables designed to express service functionality.

— **Anatomie der Datengrafik**
TOBIAS NUSSER & TOM ZIORA

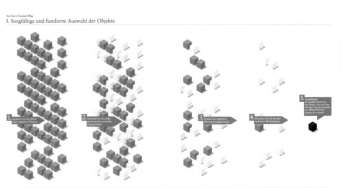

Der Do-it-Yourself-Weg
I. Sorgfältige und fundierte Auswahl der Objekte

Ein Haus zu kaufen ist einfacher als man denkt! Das richtige zu finden hingegen nicht!

Der Do-it-Yourself-Weg
II. Ausgewogene geografische Portfolio-Gewichtung

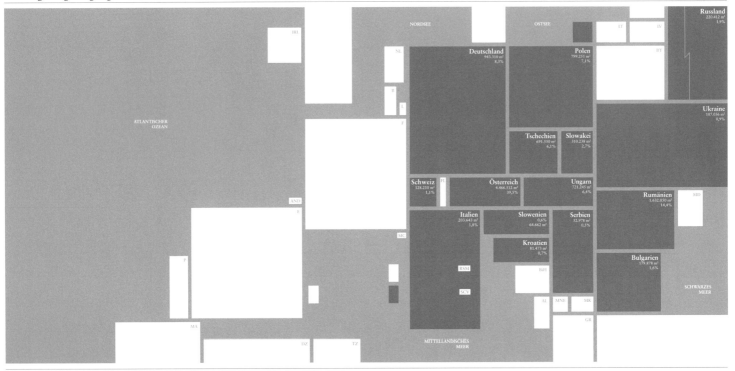

Ein stabiler Kernmarkt bringt Sicherheit – dynamische Wachstumsmärkte Rendite!

Ein Immobilienportfolio gilt dann als ausgewogen, wenn sich die unterschiedlichen geografischen Zyklen ausgleichen. So hat ein temporärer Nachfragerückgang in einem Land keine Auswirkungen auf die Performance Ihres Gesamtportfolios, sofern durch einen anderen florierenden Markt ausgeglichen wird. Um feststellen zu können welcher Markt sich nun wie entwickelt und wann der richtige Zeitpunkt für ein Investment ist, braucht es Erfahrung und genaue Kenntnis der lokalen Gegebenheit. Am besten Sie gehen auf Reisen und planen Lehrgeld mit ein.

Der Do-it-Yourself-Weg
V. Optimale Finanzierung

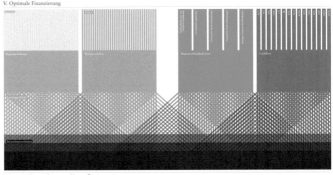

Fremd- oder selbstfinanziert – oder beides? Aber wie und in welchem Verhältnis?

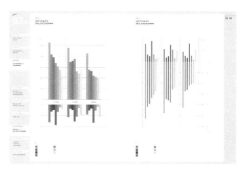

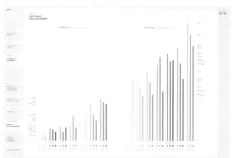

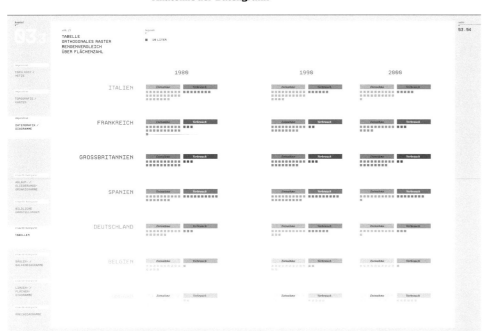

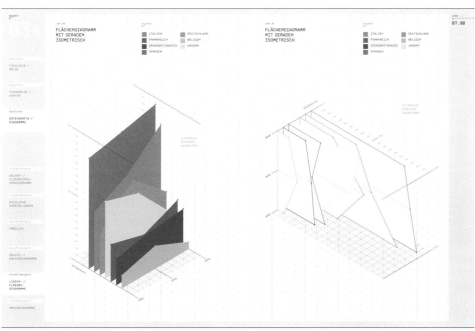

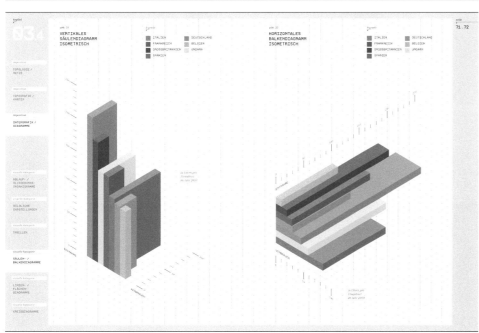

——— **Werkbeiträge: Ausschreibung 2008** CYBU RICHLI — Applying the theme and identity developed for a public competition, the figures for cultural income and investment are sampled and resampled to produce an aesthetic, referential expression of Lucerne's cultural finances. The ongoing 'W' motif forms the background for the abstracted bar charts.

—— **Universal Growth & Decline (2/2)** ABI HUYNH — This work is a study in using the omnipresent bar chart to show various increasing and declining values. Bars are constructed using the same number of overlapping squares, either compacted or expanded to fill the vertical axis. The effect is of a tonal and spatial gradation, increasing the comparative effect.

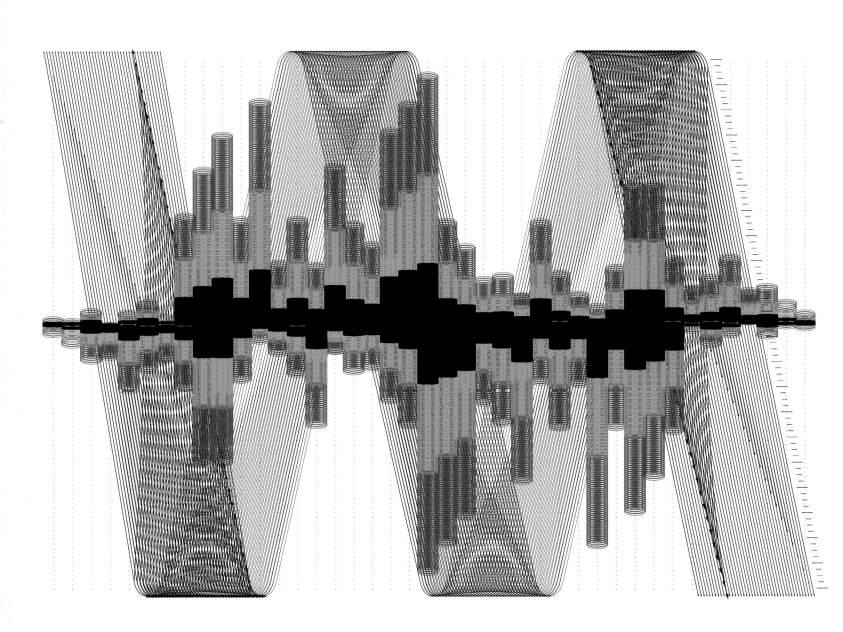

Fig 1. --
Universal Decline

Depicts general universal
trend towards unlimited potential for decline.

Fig 1. --
indicates inevitable
decline in the areas /
values in chart C.1

Note: this graph is not limited
to these values, the value of
the graph is the representation of "General Growth" thereby
value can be substituted for any
positive or negative values as
there is always potential.

C.1 Possible Values:
Gross Domestic Product, Personal
Net Worth, Urban Development,
Multi-Level Marketing Potential,
Population, Real Estate Value,
Consumer Electronic Production,
Quality of Education, Romantic
Comedy Film Gross, Gross World
Product, Conflict Resolution
Through Peaceful Means, Age, Re-
ligious Understanding, Consumer
Spending, Countries Visited,
All Industrial Sectors, Gross
National Product, Professional
Athelete Salaries, Guiness World
Records, Number of Love Songs,
Global Justice, Social Rela-
tions Index, Equality, Strategic
Marketing Growth, Applied Inno-
vation, Belief, Happiness, World
Commodity Values, Tourism, Re-
search & Development, Advertis-
ing Spending, Growth Indicators,
Investor Confidence, Faith,
Independent Music Industry,
Manufacturing, General Under-
standing, Citizenship, Economic
Prosperity ...and more!

TROPHY SIZE MATTERS

LEGEND

- SPORTS
- ENTERTAINMENT
- POLITICS

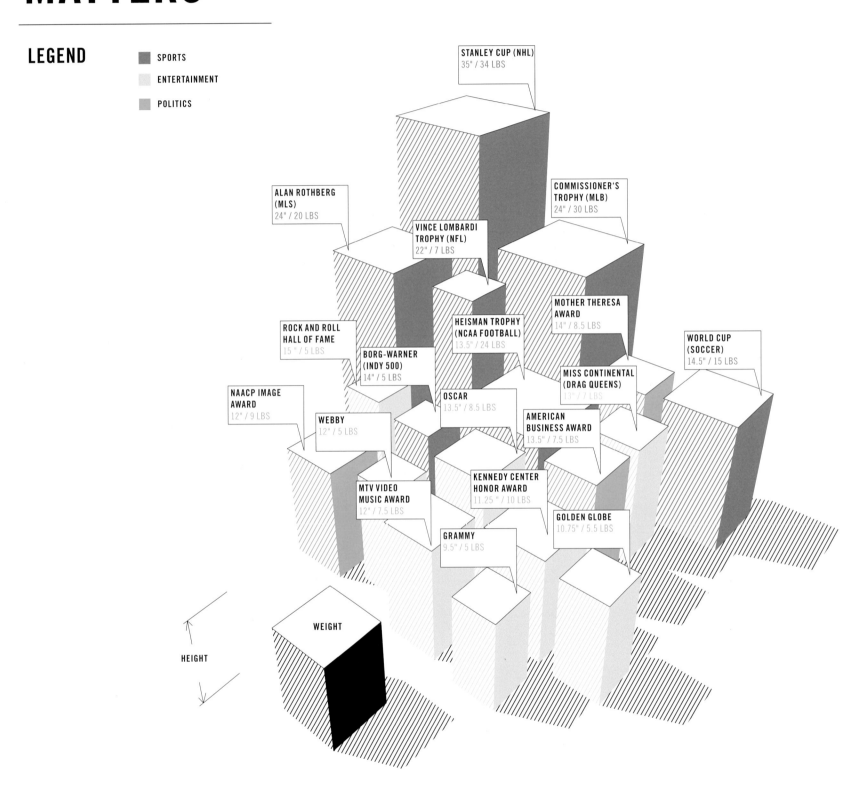

STANLEY CUP (NHL)
35" / 34 LBS

ALAN ROTHBERG
(MLS)
24" / 20 LBS

COMMISSIONER'S
TROPHY (MLB)
24" / 30 LBS

VINCE LOMBARDI
TROPHY (NFL)
22" / 7 LBS

MOTHER THERESA
AWARD
14" / 8.5 LBS

ROCK AND ROLL
HALL OF FAME
15 " / 5 LBS

HEISMAN TROPHY
(NCAA FOOTBALL)
13.5" / 24 LBS

WORLD CUP
(SOCCER)
14.5" / 15 LBS

BORG-WARNER
(INDY 500)
14" / 5 LBS

MISS CONTINENTAL
(DRAG QUEENS)
13" / 7 LBS

NAACP IMAGE
AWARD
12" / 9 LBS

OSCAR
13.5" / 8.5 LBS

WEBBY
12" / 5 LBS

AMERICAN
BUSINESS AWARD
13.5" / 7.5 LBS

MTV VIDEO
MUSIC AWARD
12" / 7.5 LBS

KENNEDY CENTER
HONOR AWARD
11.25 " / 10 LBS

GOLDEN GLOBE
10.75" / 5.5 LBS

GRAMMY
9.5" / 5 LBS

WEIGHT

HEIGHT

Catalogtree
—Interview

————Does Catalogtree have a house style or special approach to infographics? ————We believe that form equals behaviour. We ask the content to behave in a certain way rather than telling each word or data point exactly what to do. An infographic should be a data-driven image, not an illustration of the data. By behaving in a manner proposed by us, the data shapes itself into an intriguing picture.

—

An infographic should be a data-driven image, not an illustration of the data

—

————What is the particular motive that drives your experimentation and use of infographics as a form of expression? How would you apply this sense of experimentation to a client brief? ————We're fascinated by the idea that by just going about our daily routines, we become part of a large and unseen ornament. Without realising it, we're hardly ever alone in behaving the way we as individuals behave. The traces we leave and the patterns we make are just too vague and big and intertwined for us to see them clearly. We catch a glimpse of this when scientists begin to compile data sets on social behaviour. The possibility of showing what behaviour looks like is a very strong driving force behind our self-initiated projects. We believe that our approach to design decisions is communicated to the reader on a subliminal level. This leaves us no choice but to be sincere.   Apart from this, we both share a curiosity for technical innovation. We use theoretical projects to test new techniques for use in commercial applications.

————How have the expectations and opportunities surrounding infographics changed over the past ten years? ————The flow of dynamic content in newer media and the wide availability of large data sets have brought generative design into being, but to the detriment of hand-drawn layouts and illustration. With the amount of content being processed, this is a necessity rather than a sign of progress. We do feel, however, that this new way of working opens up fresh new perspectives, just as it places new demands on designers, such as the ability to program.

————Does working on infographics destined for a global audience change your approach to shaping the viewer's experience of the data? ————So far it hasn't changed the process. Our approach to developing infographics depends strongly on the subject matter and client. It certainly helps that most of the work we've done so far has been abstract, showing the data in a quantitative rather than illustrative way.

PERCENTAL CHANGE IN HOUSE-PRIZES IN CHICAGO, MIAMI AND NEW YORK FOR 2005-2006

———— **Trophy Size Matters**
CATALOGTREE — The ostentatious nature of victory celebrations is shown as a simple formula of weight times height. Jostling with each other as if on the winner's podium at a sporting event, the columns are colour-coded to indicate sport, politics, or entertainment as the areas of competitive reward. American sport clearly stands head and shoulders above other fields, taking first prize when it comes to awarding enormous trophies to recognise victory. —— **Housing Prizes** CATALOGTREE — 'Little boxes made of ticky tacky, little boxes on the hillside, little boxes all the same.' Like the 1960s song lampooning the spead of suburbia, this depiction highlights the weakness in the sub-prime market—a major cause of the global financial crisis that started in 2007. The downward trend in New York and Chicago stands in stark contrast with the positive returns experienced in Miami. The percentage change in values, shown as piles of boxes rather than smooth bars, reinforces the hollow nature of risky investments in unsecured mortgages.

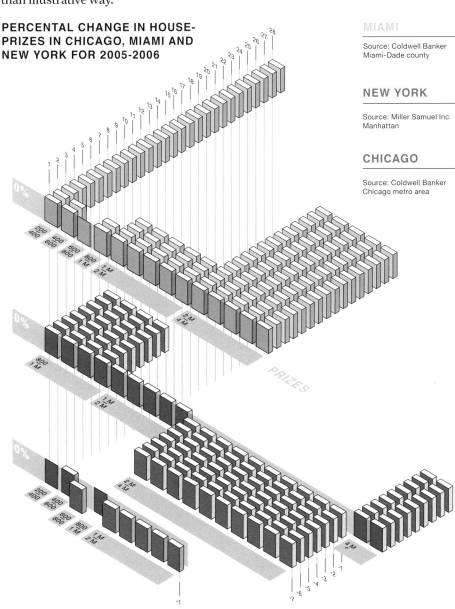

MIAMI

Source: Coldwell Banker
Miami-Dade county

NEW YORK

Source: Miller Samuel Inc
Manhattan

CHICAGO

Source: Coldwell Banker
Chicago metro area

———How should designers deal with their own cultural bias when approaching an infographics project? ———Our own cultural bias is embedded in every graphic, so it's hard to disentangle the various details. That said, the cultural bias of the client is even more significant. Infographics for men's magazines, for instance, are based on different sources and have undergone different editorial choices than infographics published in the *Times*.

———What role does art play in informing the aesthetics of infographics? ———We see a strong overlap in approach when it comes to generative, computational art or live cinema, although the aim is different. With our work for magazines, our primary goal is to inform, and thus our approach is shaped by the rules of graphic design and not art.

———How do you find the balance between simplicity and complexity when designing a specific visual representation of data? ———Information density, as Edward Tufte describes it, is a key factor in our work. Oddly enough, fitting a few data points into a large space is more difficult than fitting many data points into a small space. Maybe this is because we're used to the information density of a book spread and feel uncomfortable when we have to cope with less data than you'd see on a nicely filled page layout.

———Do you think technology is changing the way people look at data and diagrams? If so, where do you think this is leading us in terms of design? ———Today's technology allows designers to process larger quantities of data than ever before. However, we're leaning towards a way of working that reveals the process of production. For this reason, we favour techniques like silk-screening, which—with all of its limitations – allows the viewer to understand how a piece was made.

—

Our primary goal is to inform, and thus our approach is shaped by the rules of graphic design and not art

—

———What was your most challenging design brief, what made it so challenging, and how did you approach the challenge? ———We usually receive content and sizes—the bigger the data set, the better it gets. The challenge lies in the number of dimensions contained within the data, and in the contrast between separate data points. With the Iraq-Afghanistan graphic we made for *GOOD* magazine, we had to cope with a broad range of different data: some companies received more than 700 times more money than others. Because of this contrast and the limited space at our disposal, we weren't able to represent the data using conventional formats like column graphs or pie charts. Instead, we had to create a modular and hyphenated column graph running in multiple rows over two pages. The large number of data points in the set also meant that we had to computer generate the entire image.

———With data sources growing in complexity, the aesthetics of processing are becoming all the more apparent in infographics. How does this influence what we can learn from the data? ———When the aim is to inform, data has to be subjected to editorial interpretation before a design is generated. If you skip this step, the infographic will turn out to be an exact reproduction of the raw data. We like our working process to be visible—probably out of an urge to be accountable. But whatever the reason, it should never be a process for the process's sake; rather, it should be an aid in creating an image that tells a certain story.

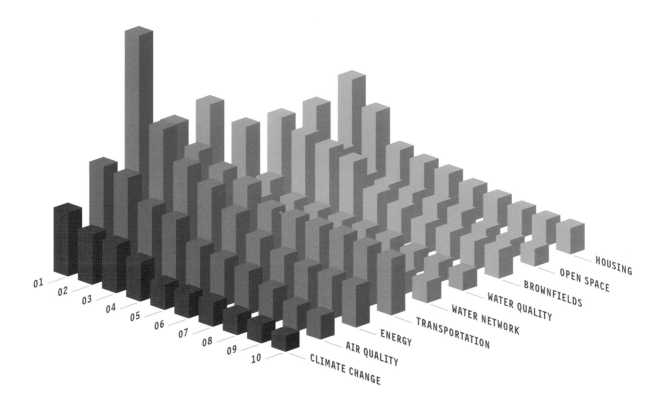

	CLIMATE CHANGE		AIR QUALITY		ENERGY		TRANSPORTATION		WATER NETWORK		WATER QUALITY		BROWNFIELDS		OPEN SPACE		HOUSING
01	86×	CITY	131×	CITY	290×	ENERGY	155×	CITY	165×	WATER	119×	WATER	115×	SITE	114×	PARK	133×	HOUSING
02	68×	CHANGE	127×	EMISSION	176×	CITY	130×	TRANSIT	72×	TUNNEL	58×	CITY	102×	STATE	66×	SPACE	101×	CITY
03	65×	CLIMATE	99×	AIR	137×	NYC	115×	NYC	62×	CITY	42×	NYC	96×	PROGRAM	43×	OPEN	61×	NYC
04	53×	NYC	93×	VEHICLE	120×	POWER	107×	CONGESTION	49×	SYSTEM	40×	STORM	89×	CITY	42×	FIELD	55×	UNIT
05	34×	EMISSION	68×	FUEL	96×	BUILDING	86×	SERVICE	43×	RESERVOIR	38×	SYSTEM	58×	CLEANUP	42×	CITY	52×	LAND
06	33×	PLAN	63×	QUALITY	74×	PLANT	85×	TRANSPORTATION	36×	NYC	38×	WATERWAY	49×	NYC	40×	NYC	45×	AREA
07	33×	BUILDING	58×	NYC	63×	ELECTRICITY	85×	MANHATTAN	35×	SUPPLY	36×	SEWER	40×	LAND	39×	PLAYGROUND	41×	NEIGHBORHOOD
08	28×	PLANNING	45×	DIESEL	58×	GAS	85×	SUBWAY	32×	DELAWARE	30×	QUALITY	40×	REDEVELOPMENT	28×	SITE	37×	BUILDING
09	26×	ENERGY	34×	YEAR	57×	SUPPLY	81×	TRAFFIC	29×	CROTON	27×	TREE	39×	COMMUNITY	24×	STREET	35×	TRANSIT
10	22×	IMPACT	32×	TREE	56×	DEMAND	76×	TIME	29×	AQUEDUCT	25×	PLANT	39×	REMEDIATION	24×	NEIGHBORHOOD	35×	GROWTH

— PlaNYC CATALOGTREE, in collaboration with Lutz Issler — How do you drive the agenda for a greener New York? In this chart, the skyline of attention is clearly shown. Frequency turns into landmarks in this histogram reflecting the number of references to specific subjects in Mayor Michael Bloomberg's planning document. From 'climate change' to 'housing', the attention given to each topic in each chapter of the PlaNYC is shown, creating a virtual cityscape of development intention. **— Meta Rankings** CATALOGTREE — Is it form, or substance? Catalogtree developed this perceptive and surprisingly simple representation of search results from the news database LexisNexus. By comparing search results for famous architects, it shows news as space or volume. For each individual, the colour-coding differentiates between stories that are related to architecture, and those that are not. This is a very powerful and elegant way of seeing how famous each architect is in relation to the others, using coverage as a proxy for fame. It is equally informative in showing how much of the news and media hype surrounding certain architects actually results from their work. **— The Cost of Nation (Re)building** CATALOGTREE — Both topical and controversial in its subject matter, this graphic shows the number of contracts won by different companies for wartime reconstruction projects. The large-scale difference between companies leads to the modular and hyphenated column graph running in multiple rows, across pages—a reminder of the huge scale and ongoing challenge of rebuilding a nation.

——— **Where do you start in terms of selecting a specific form of expression? Do you rely on rough sketches or reference books?** ——— We have a blackboard in our studio that we use for sketching. To preserve important sketches, we make digital photos.

——— **How would you describe your personal style in infographics?** ——— We follow a certain approach that precedes any stylistic decision. It's never the other way around. The stylistic choices we make are highly subjective and influenced by mood swings, fashion, feasibility, and opportunism.

ARCHITECTURE'S TOP NEWSMAKERS   SOURCE: LEXISNEXIS

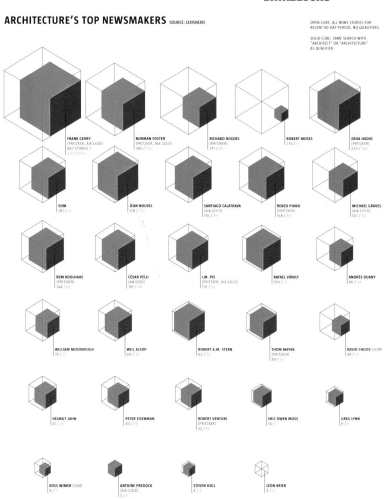

OPEN CUBE: ALL NEWS STORIES FOR RECENT 90-DAY PERIOD, NO QUALIFIERS.

SOLID CUBE: SAME SEARCH WITH "ARCHITECT" OR "ARCHITECTURE" AS QUALIFIER.

THE COST OF NATION (RE)BUILDING

VALUE OF U.S. GOVERNMENT CONTRACTS AWARDED IN IRAQ AND AFGHANISTAN (OCT '03–SEP '06)

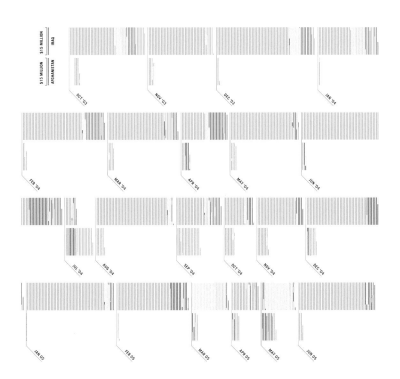

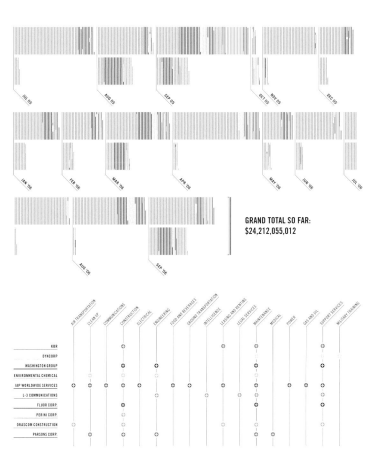

GRAND TOTAL SO FAR: $24,212,055,012

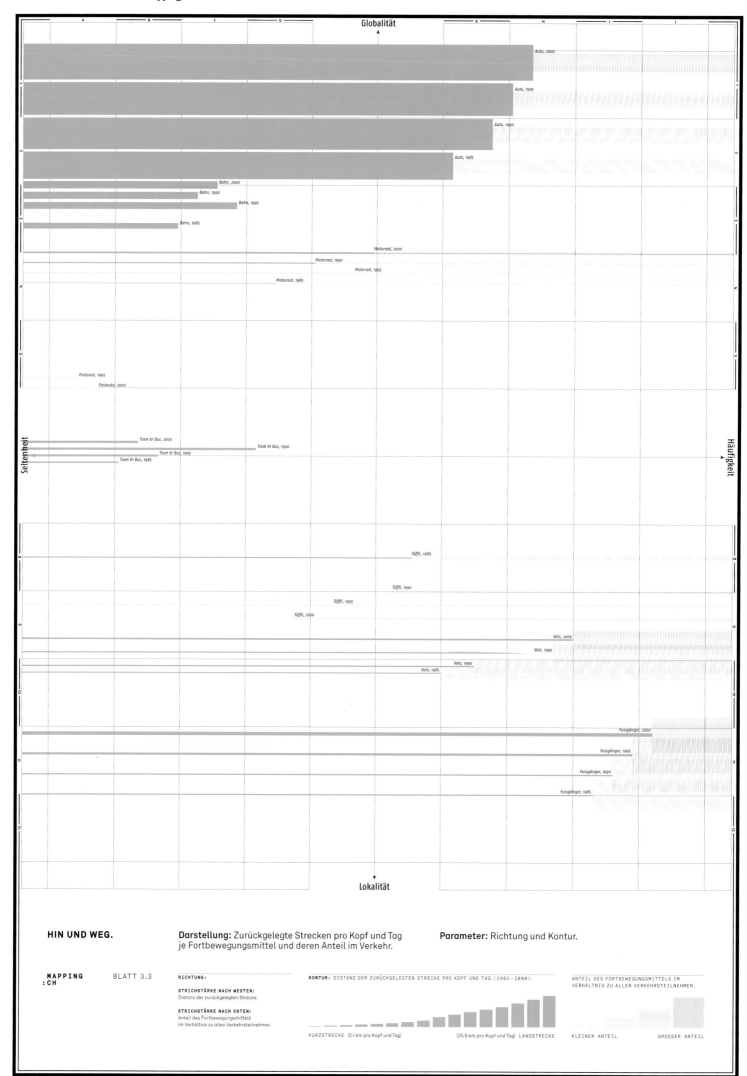

— **mapping:ch** LORENZO GEIGER
— **Diagrammatic Reading Machine: A visual index of Language of Vision** JACK HENRIE FISHER, University of Illinois at Chicago — This is a further visual study in Jack Fischer's analysis of György Kepes's landmark book *Language of Vision*. The project's importance is discussed in more detail in the Datanets section.

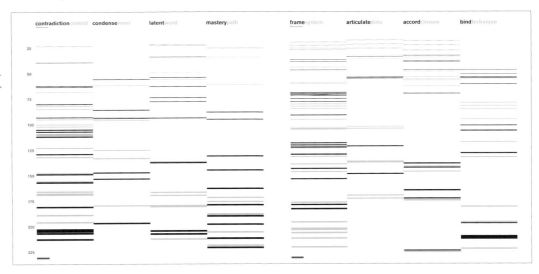

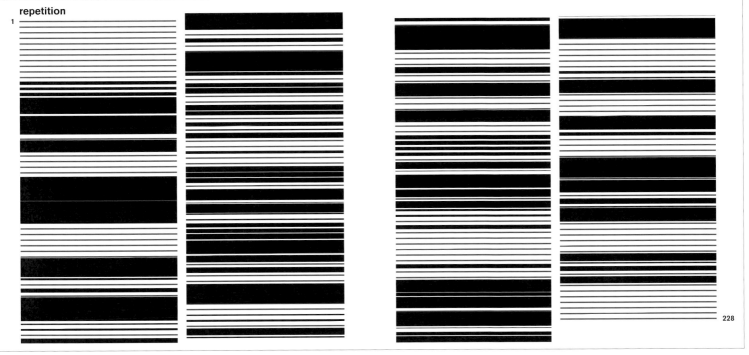

— Research in the Visualization of Financial Data CYBU RICHLI, Silo (Richli / Moser) — Part of the series described in the Datalogy section, this chart uses the arrangement of monotone blocks in a predefined, outlined space to compare the actual versus target allocation in an portfolio of shares. ———— This work uses space and colour to differentiate between industry sector allocations of shares in a portfolio.

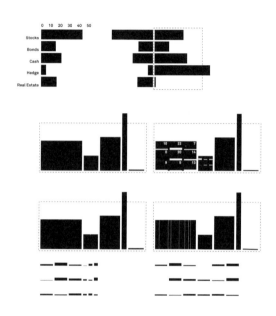

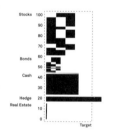

INVESTMENT STYLE CHANGES OVER TIME

	31.03.02	30.06.02	30.09.02	31.12.02	31.03.03	30.06.03	30.09.03	31.12.03	31.03.04	30.06.04
LV	7.0	7.6	9.4	7.3	0.9	8.1	8.6	11.1	16.1	10.8
LC	22.8	25.6	23.6	25.1	23.7	27.5	33.0	34.3	36.6	33.7
LG	50.2	46.7	49.5	51.8	54.7	53.7	43.9	36.1	26.4	21.1
MV	0.0	0.0	0.0	0.5	0.3	0.0	0.4	2.9	2.7	5.4
MC	2.0	2.7	2.6	1.0	1.4	1.5	5.2	7.8	12.6	20.1
MG	16.9	16.7	13.2	12.9	10.4	9.0	7.5	5.8	3.2	4.0
SV	0.0	0.0	0.0	0.0	0.0	0.0	0.2	0.6	0.8	
SC	0.0	0.0	0.0	0.0	0.0	0.0	1.3	1.3	2.9	
SG	1.1	0.7	1.4	1.3	0.6	0.3	0.4	0.6	0.5	1.3

V – VALUE C – CORE G – GROWTH L – LARGE M – MEDIUM S – SMALL

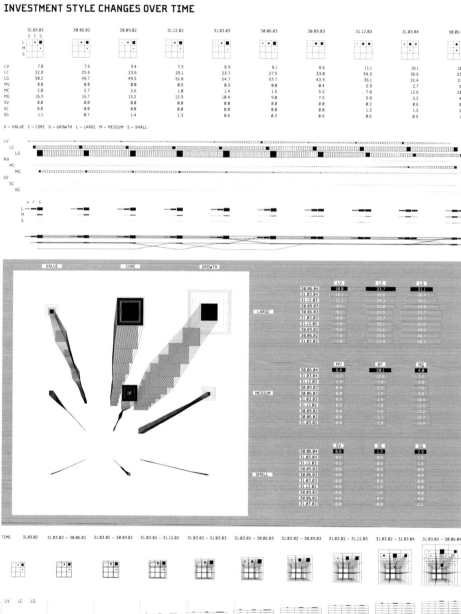

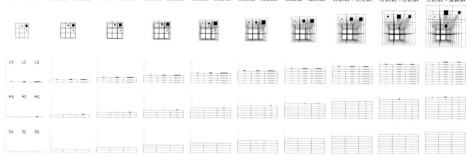

STOCK SECTOR

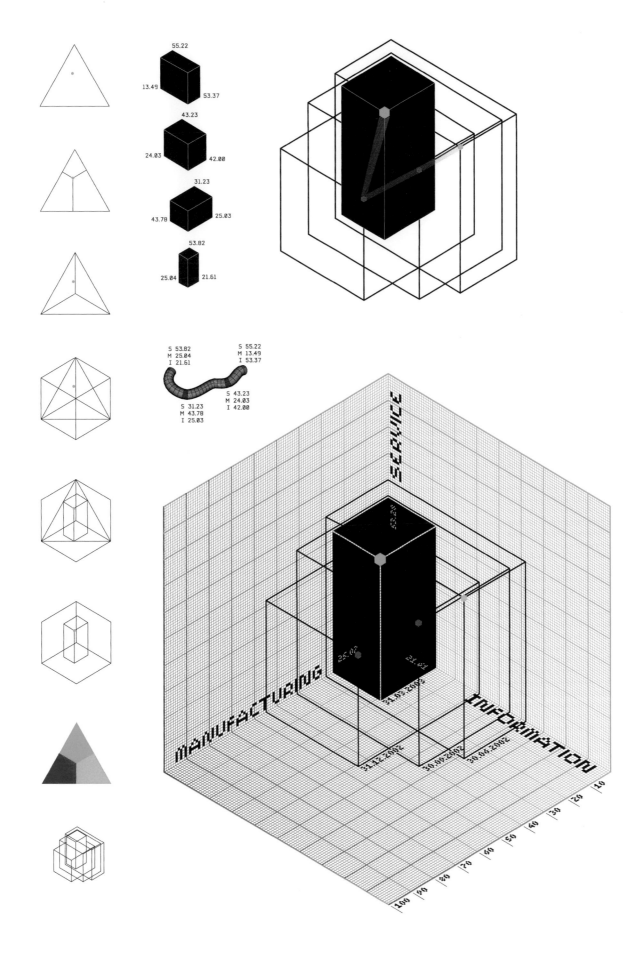

SOCKET STUDIOS

EARTH SYSTEMS
NUMBER 002: FAULT LINE

SOCKET STUDIOS

Bevolking

Prognose 2004	2005	2010	2015
0 t/m 4 jaar	30400	30600 ■	30200 ■
5 t/m 14 jaar	52800	55400 ■	56800 ■
15 t/m 19 jaar	26700 ■	27800 ■	28000 ■
20 t/m 44 jaar	192900 ■	199800 ■	197600 ■
45 t/m 64 jaar	109400 ■	120200 ■	125500 ■
65 t/m 79 jaar	43300 ■	43500 ■	49100 ■
80 jaar of ouder	20900 ■	18700 ■	16800 ■
Totaal	476400	496000	504000

Bron: DSO/Beleid/Onderzoek

fig. DSO.06 / Bevolkingsprognose

Wonen

Woningvoorraad	1996	2001	2002	2003
aantal woningen	206823	215570	221716	226156

Bron: CBS

Woningvoorraad naar soort woning	%	%	%	%
% eengezinswoning	-	14,9 ■	17,4 ■	18,5 ■
% meergezinswoning	-	84,4 ■	81,9 ■	80,8 ■

Bron: CBS
(bewerking DSO/Beleid/Onderzoek)

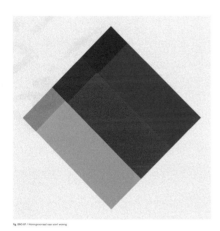

fig. DSO.07 / Woningvoorraad naar soort woning

Wonen

Corporatiewoningen (1 juli)	aantal	gemiddelde huur (euro)	Woningzoekenden voor Haags aanbod	1996	2000	2001	2002
■ 2000	78218	310	totaal aantal	35397	46303	53362	56343
■ 2001	81022	320	w.v.				
■ 2002	81972	332	doorstromer	16219	19555	20251	21733
■ 2003	82345	345	starter	19166	26739	33108	34598

Bron: corporatiebestanden
(bewerking DSO/Beleid/Onderzoek)

w.v. naar inkomensgroep		
doelgroep	28463	30483 34216 36162
niet-doelgroep	6711	14675 17986 19883

Bron: aanbodmarkt
(bewerking DSO/Beleid/Onderzoek)

fig. DSO.11 / Ontwikkeling gemiddelde huur corporatiewoningen

fig. DSO.11 / Ontwikkeling gemiddelde huur corporatiewoningen

— Earth Systems 002 - Fault Line SOCKET STUDIOS — This work depicts the tension between uneven tectonic forces colliding. The dramatic powers of nature are rendered simply as a fault line in the visual structure. **—— The Hague in facts and figures** TOKO — The cultural significance of The Hague featured strongly in the brief for this annual report on the city. The ambition to transform data into works of art led to the conscious choices of composition and colour. Layered shades and hues emphasise the aesthetic considerations of the city fathers in terms of improving the inhabitant's experience of the city. Showing these 'works of art' on canvas brings conceptual closure to the inherent message.

NEXT PAGES ——— **29501 vs. 4714** RETO MOSER — The self is seen here as a database. All the contents in the designer's computer and room are blended into a massive 'folder'. The files are arranged by extension type, going from left to right, and top to bottom. By avoiding the traditional file tree structure and rejecting any hierarchy, all the data is brought to the same level and validity in expressing the designer's individual lifestyle and personality. The mp3 catalogue is an expression of musical taste, while images and photos are used as references to physical aesthetic choices.

Economie

Winkels in Den Haag naar type	2002	2003
■ vrije tijd	385	350
■ in & om huis	1022	973
■ mode & luxe	1047	1033
■ dagelijkse boodschappen	1174	1135
■ detailhandel overig	249	251
■ leegstand	572	630
totaal aantal verkooppunten	4449	4372

Bron: Locatus

Kerncijfers kantorenmarkt	m² bvo
voorraad op 1-1-2004	4196800
nieuwbouw in 2003	113700
functiewijziging in 2003	-23300
groei voorraad in 2003	90400
in aanbouw op 1-1-2004	119500
aanbod op 1-1- 2004	314700
opname in 2003	209300

Bron: DSO/Beleid/Onderzoek

fig. DSO.17 / Winkels in Den Haag naar type, 2003

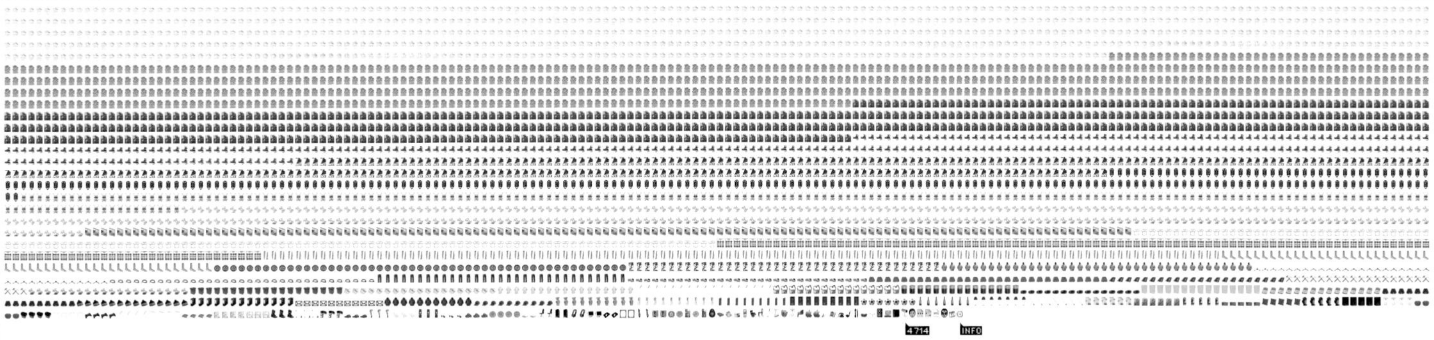
4714
INFO

—— **Atlas of Electromagnetic Spectrum** BESTIARIO in collaboration with Jose Luis de Vicente and Irma Vilà — The aim of this project was to build a clear and intelligible explanation of how the electromagnetic spectrum works in scientific terms, how it is regulated, and the relationship between common technologies like radio, TV, WiFi, mobile telephony, and many others. The atlas also creates a crucial archive of the different interventions that artists, designers, social pioneers, activists, hackers, and other groups have made in Hertzian space. The social and cultural potential of these technologies has been enriched

beyond their designated uses by alternative readings and perspectives, as well as by the policies that regulate them. In essence, these interventions are an expression of how civilians are reclaiming their role in a participative political environment, via directives which govern these invisible forces of information, dissemination, and control.

—— **World/Spectrum/Archive** LUST — When read in a traditional manner, the news provides information about a specific topic, but what does that information add up to? World/Spectrum/Archive is an investigation into the wider implications of world news, viewed on a macro scale. By

evaluating the positive and negative connotations of each country's headlines, a montage is created, summarising the state of the world on a given day. Using Google as the base reference for the predominant semantic disposition, a surprising and overwhelming positive bias is revealed in Western countries. —— **The 24/7 Alibi** BARBARA HAHN & CHRISTINE ZIMMERMANN — In our surveillance society, we have all become impenetrable waves of blind data in the blocks of official tracking files. The blunt instruments used by governments to track and monitor their citizens often lead to unintended consequences.

After showing up on the FBI's so-called Terrorist Watch List, the American art professor Hassan Elahi was forced to endure many intrusions into his privacy and the inconvenience of repeatedly having to prove his innocence. In this visualisation of Professor Elahi's alibi, Barbara Hahn and Christine Zimmermann have captured both the blurred definition of privacy and the confusing regulations to which everyday citizens are increasingly being subjected. In addition to photos of toilets, data pertaining to phone calls and expenses serve as proof of a individual's physical location, their layers presented here behind slanted bars.

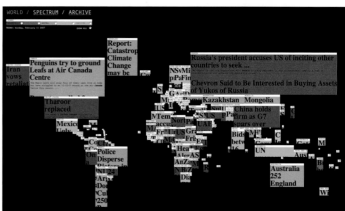

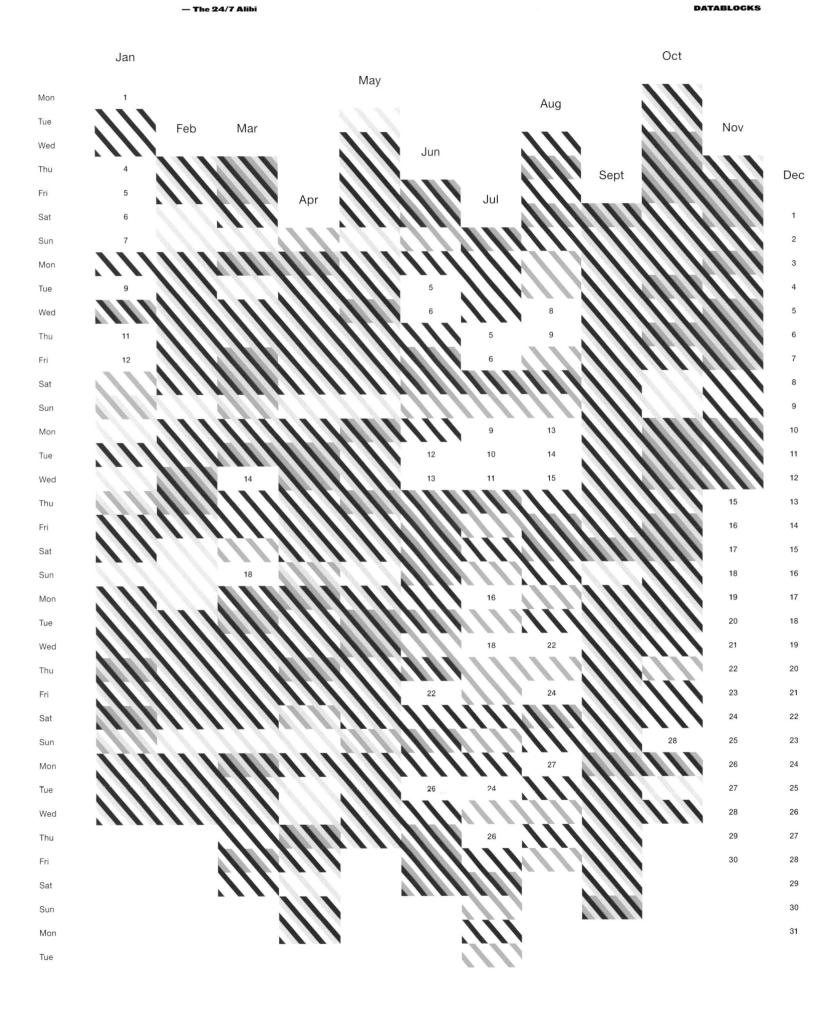

dated photos of toilets   dated expenses   dated telephone calls

Data source: http://trackingtransience.net

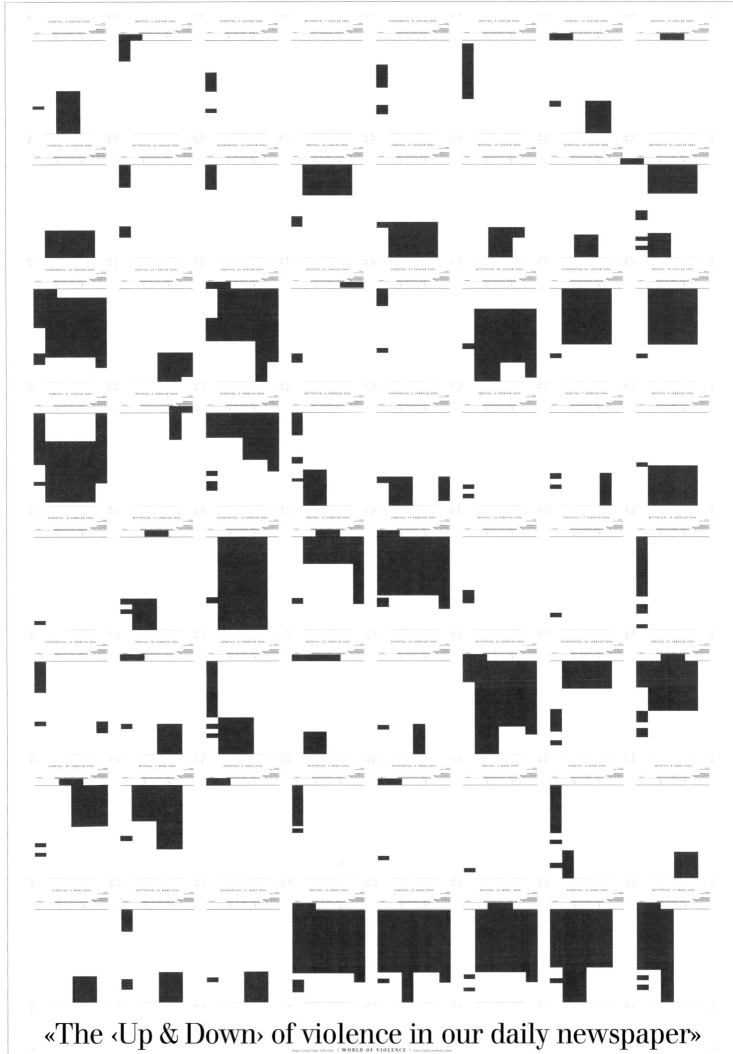

«The ‹Up & Down› of violence in our daily newspaper»

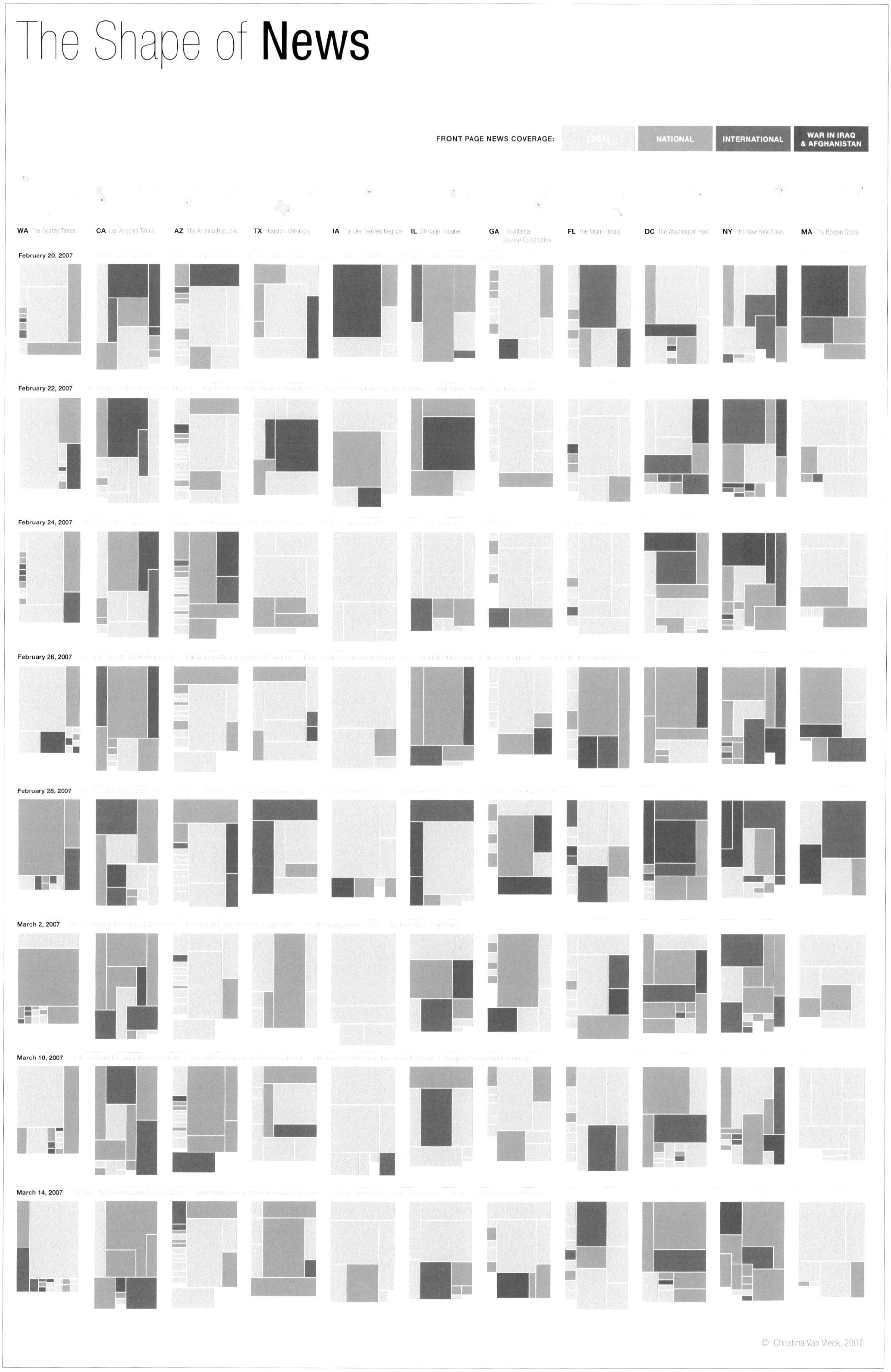

The Shape of News

FRONT PAGE NEWS COVERAGE: LOCAL NATIONAL INTERNATIONAL WAR IN IRAQ & AFGHANISTAN

| WA The Seattle Times | CA Los Angeles Times | AZ The Arizona Republic | TX Houston Chronicle | IA The Des Moines Register | IL Chicago Tribune | GA The Atlanta Journal-Constitution | FL The Miami Herald | DC The Washington Post | NY The New York Times | MA The Boston Globe |

February 20, 2007

February 22, 2007

February 24, 2007

February 26, 2007

February 28, 2007

March 2, 2007

March 10, 2007

March 14, 2007

© Christina Van Vleck, 2007

PREVIOUS PAGES ———————— **World of Violence** LORENZO GEIGER—This work catalogues the coverage of violence over a year. The front pages of the newspaper *Der Bund* were analysed and the space containing stories about violence marked red. 'Up and Down' are the inferred values of the fluctuating number of column inches committed to the subject. —— **The Shape of News: Front Page News Coverage Across the Country** CHRISTINA VAN VLECK — This chart is similar to Lorenzo Geiger's analysis of newspaper title pages. Rather than examining one specific topic, this study uses various colours to express a multivariate mapping of news interest. The arrangement according to US states provides the viewer with insight into the way public opinion was formed during the Iraq War. Was it hyper-localism, nationalism, or factual reporting? The tenor of regional reporting is revealed over a period of two months.

—— **Overnewsed but uninformed** STEFAN BRÄUTIGAM — This chart forms part of the study into news ownership and distribution. 'Overnewsed but uninformed' aims to clarify the metastructure of media, enabling readers to find sources they can trust. The coverage of a specific incident on the front pages of newspapers is identified, abstracted, and colour-coded according to the paper's ultimate parent company. —— **Von Schwarmfischen, Haien und Delphinen - Visualisierte Führungsverständnisse im Medizinmanagement** BARBARA HAHN & CHRISTINE ZIMMERMANN — Here, management in medicine is shown as figures of speech. Schools, sharks, and dolphins are some of the metaphors used by doctors to describe their management style. Head physicians were interviewed at length to get an understanding of their approach to management, and the styles they adopt. Their responses were then reduced to a compact visual semantic, with size, order, and orientation providing a shorthand table of contents. The interview data serve not only to inform the reader of the content, but also to provide a framework for assimilating the report. —— **90 Minuten** URSINA VÖLLM, CHRISTIAN DICK AND HANNES GLOOR — The challenge was to produce five artworks, defined by the terms 'Exile, Now, Assembly, Play' and, most importantly, 'Football'. The entire commentary of a top league match between Schalke 04 and AC Milan is transcribed in a newspaper format. The text is complemented with a photomontage of Barcelona's fan club in Zurich, terrace chants, and stickers in team colours.

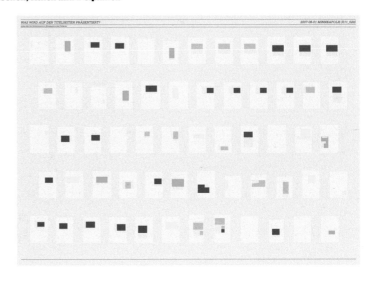

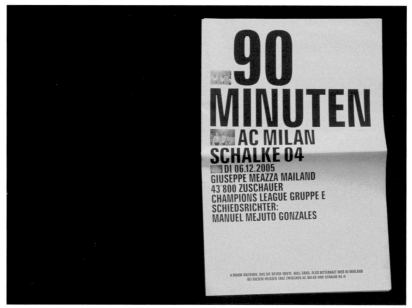

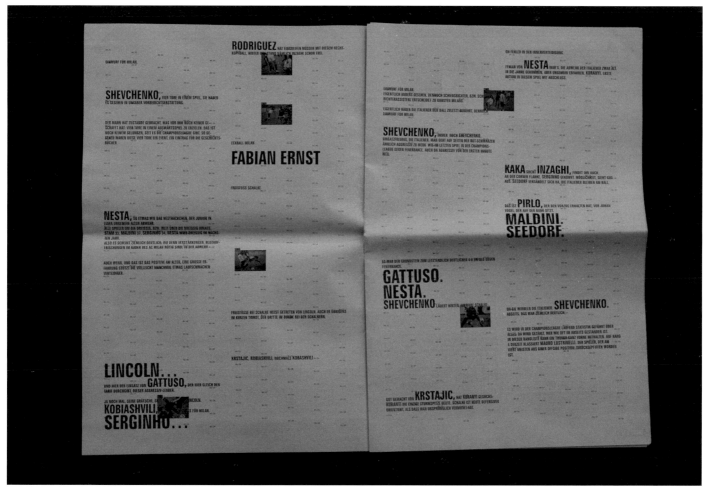

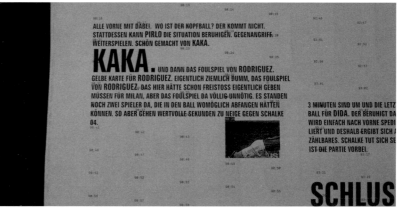

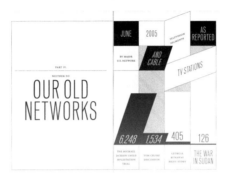

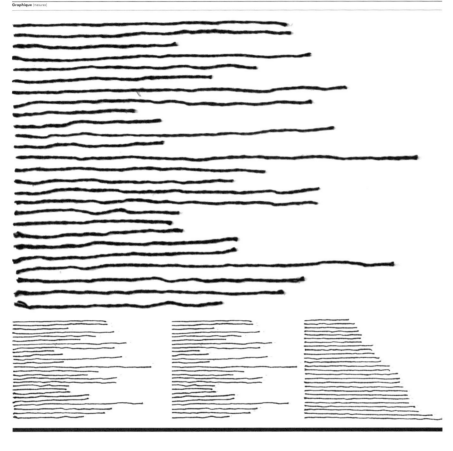

CODE TYPOGRAPHIQUE

Le procédé:

Impression de la police Souvenir, Light, en bas de casse, corps 1000 pt. A l'aide de fils de laine, relevé des dimensions de chaque caractère en suivant l'ossature de la lettre. Les fils sont ensuite mesurés pour déterminer la longueur de chaques lettres de l'alphabet.

Graphique (mesuré)

We Tell Stories: Hard Times
NICHOLAS FELTON, Matt Mason (author), Jeremy Ettinghausen (publisher), Adrian Hon (producer) — Piracy and copyright issues are woven into this interactive means of storytelling by Nicholas Felton. The artwork references *Hard Times*, the weekly serial that Charles Dickens wrote for *Household Words* magazine. Hard times are again with us, as the data reveals a bleak picture of modern-day America. Blocks of data are juxtaposed, intersected, and arranged in a difficult and poignant narrative. Each page of dense and complex datagraphics is contrasted with simple slogans, revealing deeper motives and insights concerning the social relevance of the observations. — **Typographic Code** BENOIT LEMOINE — Here, a cipher is transmuted to an alphabet. The outline of a font is traced using wool. The resultant lengths of wool are then displayed as the new alphabet, creating a typographic, machine-readable code based on distances and proportions. The columns, which at first glance represent a bar chart, are in fact the words in a sentence. — **Information's Anatomy** ELODIE MANDRAY — This is a formal study of the content presented in a local newspaper. The text has been subjected to various analyses and is presented in graphical form. In this image, the length of the content is shown as bar charts. The exact length, as opposed to word count, is provided, treating the newsprint as retail space that can be divided into square inches and filled with words. The newspaper's layout grid is obliquely suggested, as breaks in the bars indicate column widths and paragraph breaks.

Figure 8, longueur de l'information.

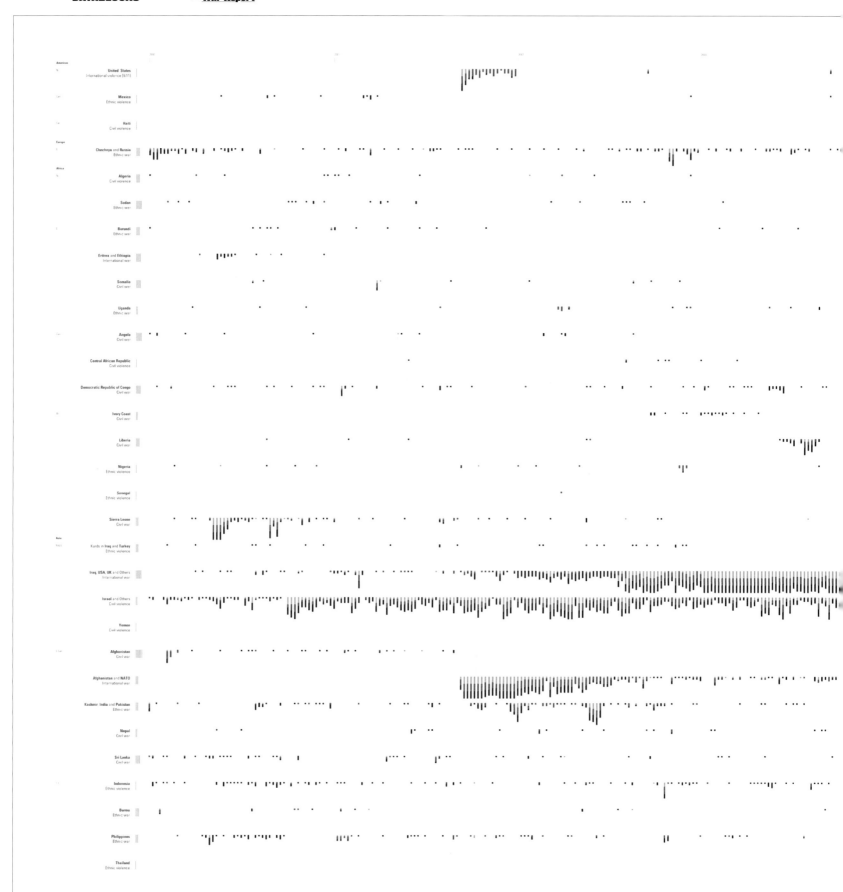

Weekly newspaper coverage of major global conflicts, 2000–2005

A system was developed for analysing level of coverage, which was then
applied to approximately **15,000 articles** on active global conflicts published
by the **Daily Mail** [·], **The Sun** [•] and **The Guardian** [•] between 2000–2005.

All articles were ranked according to word count and position in relation to
the newspapers' page order. To obtain a time line of coverage for all major
conflicts weekly averages were calculated to provide the above data.

Weekly level of coverage

1 low coverage (mainly one short article per week)
2 medium-low coverage
3 medium coverage (mainly 3–4 short articles or 2–3 long
articles per week)
4 medium-high coverage
5 high coverage (5 + long articles per week, including front pages)

Conflict magnitude

A scaled indicator of the destructive impact of a conflict from low to high
intensity. It reflects multiple factors including: area destruction; population
displacement; and episode duration. It was developed by the Center for
Global Policy, based at George Mason University.

low intensity   high intensity   conflict: start   end

— **War Report** CHRIS CAMPBELL

— *War Report* is a broadsheet-sized book presenting the results of an analysis of coverage of world conflicts by three British national newspapers: the *Guardian*, *Daily Mail*, and *Sun*. The presentation of this data gives a detailed, day-by-day insight into the three newspapers' attention to world conflicts: what events are covered; which regions are given preference; how coverage changes over time; and whether a war's intensity influences the level of coverage it receives. 15,000 articles on global conflicts, published by the three newspapers between 2000 and 2005, were analysed. All articles were ranked according to word count and position in terms of the newspapers' page order.   The form of the datagraphics corresponds to the subject matter, as the colour palette is deliberately constrained to the CMYK colours of the broadsheet press.

Americas
United States	International violence (9/11)
Mexico	Ethnic violence
Haiti	Civil violence

Europe
| Chechnya and Russia | Ethnic war |

Africa
Algeria	Civil violence
Sudan	Ethnic war
Burundi	Ethnic war
Eritrea and Ethiopia	International war
Somalia	Civil war
Uganda	Ethnic war
Angola	Civil war
Central African Republic	Civil violence
Democratic Republic of Congo	Civil war
Ivory Coast	Civil war
Liberia	Civil war
Nigeria	Ethnic violence
Senegal	Ethnic violence
Sierra Leone	Civil war

Asia
Kurds in Iraq and Turkey	Ethnic violence
Iraq, USA, UK and Others	International war
Israel and Others	Civil violence
Yemen	Civil violence
Afghanistan	Civil war
Afghanistan and NATO	International war
Kashmir, India and Pakistan	Ethnic war
Nepal	Civil war
Sri Lanka	Civil war
Indonesia	Ethnic violence
Burma	Ethnic war
Philippines	Ethnic war
Thailand	Ethnic violence

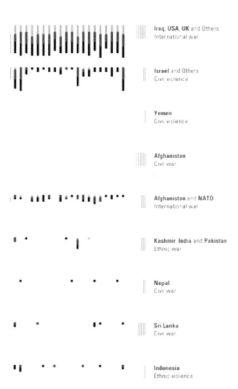

Iraq, USA, UK and Others	International war
Israel and Others	Civil violence
Yemen	Civil violence
Afghanistan	Civil war
Afghanistan and NATO	International war
Kashmir, India and Pakistan	Ethnic war
Nepal	Civil war
Sri Lanka	Civil war
Indonesia	Ethnic violence

————— **Datenvisualisierung jenseits von Kuchen- und Balkendiagrammen** BARBARA HAHN & CHRISTINE ZIMMERMANN — **Names** CATALOGTREE — This project ranks and codes the ethnic distribution of the top 100 surnames in the United States. Each ethnic group is signified by a specific triangle. The patriarchal orthography would reveal a perfect hexagon if a surname were equally distributed between the various ethnic groups. Instead, reality shapes into a multitude of tangram-like forms, revealing the distinct ethnic association of each surname.

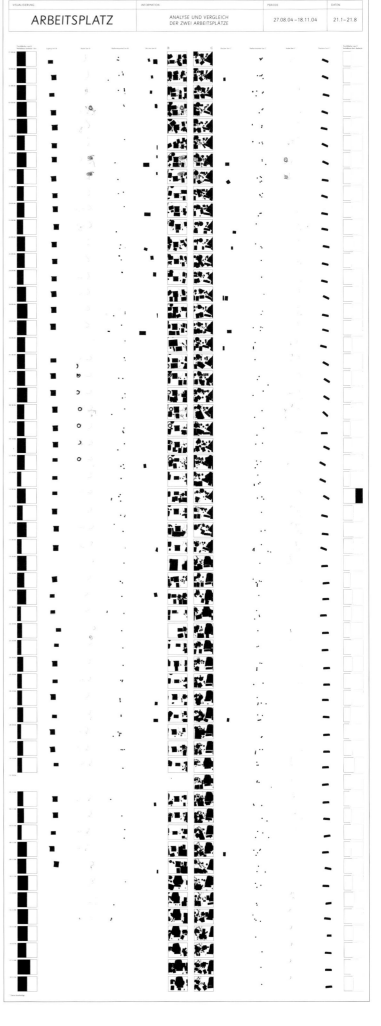

#		#		#		#		#	
1	SMITH	201	CARROLL	401	PAUL	601	NASH	801	WALLS
2	JOHNSON	202	HUDSON	402	MANNING	602	DICKERSON	802	BOYLE
3	WILLIAMS	203	DUNCAN	403	GARNER	603	BOND	803	MAYER
4	BROWN	204	ARMSTRONG	404	MCGEE	604	WYATT	804	ZUNIGA
5	JONES	205	BERRY	405	REESE	605	FOLEY	805	GILES
6	MILLER	206	ANDREWS	406	FRANCIS	606	CHASE	806	PINEDA
7	DAVIS	207	JOHNSTON	407	BURGESS	607	GATES	807	PACE
8	GARCIA	208	RAY	408	ADKINS	608	VINCENT	808	HURLEY
9	RODRIGUEZ	209	LANE	409	GOODMAN	609	MATHEWS	809	MAY
10	WILSON	210	RILEY	410	CURRY	610	HODGE	810	MCMILLAN
11	MARTINEZ	211	CARPENTER	411	BRADY	611	GARRISON	811	CROSBY
12	ANDERSON	212	PERKINS	412	CHRISTENSEN	612	TREVINO	812	AYERS
13	TAYLOR	213	AGUILAR	413	POTTER	613	VILLARREAL	813	CASE
14	THOMAS	214	SILVA	414	WALTON	614	HEATH	814	BENTLEY
15	HERNANDEZ	215	RICHARDS	415	GOODWIN	615	DALTON	815	SHEPHERD
16	MOORE	216	WILLIS	416	MULLINS	616	VALENCIA	816	EVERETT
17	MARTIN	217	MATTHEWS	417	MOLINA	617	CALLAHAN	817	PUGH
18	JACKSON	218	CHAPMAN	418	WEBSTER	618	HENSLEY	818	DAVID
19	THOMPSON	219	LAWRENCE	419	FISCHER	619	ATKINS	819	MCMAHON
20	WHITE	220	GARZA	420	CAMPOS	620	HUFFMAN	820	DUNLAP
21	LOPEZ	221	VARGAS	421	AVILA	621	ROY	821	BENDER
22	LEE	222	WATKINS	422	SHERMAN	622	BOYER	822	HAHN
23	GONZALEZ	223	WHEELER	423	TODD	623	SHIELDS	823	HARDING
24	HARRIS	224	LARSON	424	CHANG	624	LIN	824	ACEVEDO
25	CLARK	225	CARLSON	425	BLAKE	625	HANCOCK	825	RAYMOND
26	LEWIS	226	HARPER	426	MALONE	626	GRIMES	826	BLACKBURN
27	ROBINSON	227	GEORGE	427	WOLF	627	GLENN	827	DUFFY
28	WALKER	228	GREENE	428	HODGES	628	CLINE	828	LANDRY
29	PEREZ	229	BURKE	429	JUAREZ	629	DELACRUZ	829	DOUGHERTY
30	HALL	230	GUZMAN	430	GILL	630	CAMACHO	830	BAUTISTA
31	YOUNG	231	MORRISON	431	FARMER	631	DILLON	831	SHAH
32	ALLEN	232	MUNOZ	432	HINES	632	PARRISH	832	POTTS
33	SANCHEZ	233	JACOBS	433	GALLAGHER	633	ONEILL	833	ARROYO
34	WRIGHT	234	OBRIEN	434	DURAN	634	MELTON	834	VALENTINE
35	KING	235	LAWSON	435	HUBBARD	635	BOOTH	835	MEZA
36	SCOTT	236	FRANKLIN	436	CANNON	636	KANE	836	GOULD
37	GREEN	237	LYNCH	437	MIRANDA	637	BERG	837	VAUGHAN
38	BAKER	238	BISHOP	438	WANG	638	HARRELL	838	FRY
39	ADAMS	239	CARR	439	SAUNDERS	639	PITTS	839	RUSH
40	NELSON	240	SALAZAR	440	TATE	640	SAVAGE	840	AVERY
41	HILL	241	AUSTIN	441	MACK	641	WIGGINS	841	HERRING
42	RAMIREZ	242	MENDEZ	442	HAMMOND	642	BRENNAN	842	DODSON
43	CAMPBELL	243	GILBERT	443	CARRILLO	643	SALAS	843	CLEMENTS
44	MITCHELL	244	JENSEN	444	TOWNSEND	644	MARKS	844	SAMPSON
45	ROBERTS	245	WILLIAMSON	445	WISE	645	RUSSO	845	TAPIA
46	CARTER	246	MONTGOMERY	446	INGRAM	646	SAWYER	846	BEAN
47	PHILLIPS	247	HARVEY	447	BARTON	647	BAXTER	847	LYNN
48	EVANS	248	OLIVER	448	MEJIA	648	GOLDEN	848	CRANE
49	TURNER	249	HOWELL	449	AYALA	649	HUTCHINSON	849	FARLEY
50	TORRES	250	DEAN	450	SCHROEDER	650	LIU	850	CISNEROS
51	PARKER	251	HANSON	451	HAMPTON	651	WALTER	851	BENTON
52	COLLINS	252	WEBER	452	ROWE	652	MCDOWELL	852	ASHLEY
53	EDWARDS	253	GARRETT	453	PARSONS	653	WILEY	853	MCKAY
54	STEWART	254	SIMS	454	FRANK	654	RICH	854	FINLEY
55	FLORES	255	BURTON	455	WATERS	655	HUMPHREY	855	BEST
56	MORRIS	256	FULLER	456	STRICKLAND	656	JOHNS	856	BLEVINS
57	NGUYEN	257	SOTO	457	OSBORNE	657	KOCH	857	FRIEDMAN
58	MURPHY	258	MCCOY	458	MAXWELL	658	SUAREZ	858	MOSES
59	RIVERA	259	WELCH	459	CHAN	659	HOBBS	859	SOSA
60	COOK	260	CHEN	460	DELEON	660	BEARD	860	BLANCHARD
61	ROGERS	261	SCHULTZ	461	NORMAN	661	GILMORE	861	HUBER
62	MORGAN	262	WALTERS	462	HARRINGTON	662	IBARRA	862	FRYE
63	PETERSON	263	REID	463	CASEY	663	KEITH	863	KRUEGER
64	COOPER	264	FIELDS	464	PATTON	664	MACIAS	864	BERNARD
65	REED	265	WALSH	465	LOGAN	665	KHAN	865	ROSARIO
66	BAILEY	266	LITTLE	466	BOWERS	666	ANDRADE	866	RUBIO
67	BELL	267	FOWLER	467	MUELLER	667	WARE	867	MULLEN
68	GOMEZ	268	BOWMAN	468	GLOVER	668	STEPHENSON	868	BENJAMIN
69	KELLY	269	DAVIDSON	469	FLOYD	669	HENSON	869	HALEY
70	HOWARD	270	MAY	470	HARTMAN	670	WILKERSON	870	CHUNG
71	WARD	271	DAY	471	BUCHANAN	671	DYER	871	MOYER
72	COX	272	SCHNEIDER	472	COBB	672	MCCLURE	872	CHOI
73	DIAZ	273	NEWMAN	473	FRENCH	673	BLACKWELL	873	HORNE
74	RICHARDSON	274	BREWER	474	KRAMER	674	MERCADO	874	YU
75	WOOD	275	LUCAS	475	MCCORMICK	675	TANNER	875	WOODWARD
76	WATSON	276	HOLLAND	476	CLARKE	676	EATON	876	ALI
77	BROOKS	277	WONG	477	TYLER	677	CLAY	877	NIXON
78	BENNETT	278	BANKS	478	GIBBS	678	BARRON	878	HAYDEN
79	GRAY	279	SANTOS	479	MOODY	679	BEASLEY	879	RIVERS
80	JAMES	280	CURTIS	480	CONNER	680	ONEAL	880	ESTES
81	REYES	281	PEARSON	481	SPARKS	681	PRESTON	881	MCCARTY
82	CRUZ	282	DELGADO	482	MCGUIRE	682	SMALL	882	RICHMOND
83	HUGHES	283	VALDEZ	483	LEON	683	WU	883	STUART
84	PRICE	284	PENA	484	BAUER	684	ZAMORA	884	MAYNARD
85	MYERS	285	RIOS	485	NORTON	685	MACDONALD	885	BRANDT
86	LONG	286	DOUGLAS	486	POPE	686	VANCE	886	OCONNELL
87	FOSTER	287	SANDOVAL	487	FLYNN	687	SNOW	887	HANNA
88	SANDERS	288	BARRETT	488	HOGAN	688	MCCLAIN	888	SANFORD
89	ROSS	289	HOPKINS	489	ROBLES	689	STAFFORD	889	SHEPPARD
90	MORALES	290	KELLER	490	SALINAS	690	OROZCO	890	CHURCH
91	POWELL	291	GUERRERO	491	YATES	691	BARRY	891	BURCH
92	SULLIVAN	292	STANLEY	492	LINDSEY	692	ENGLISH	892	LEVY
93	RUSSELL	293	BATES	493	LLOYD	693	SHANNON	893	RASMUSSEN
94	ORTIZ	294	ALVARADO	494	MARSH	694	KLINE	894	COFFEY
95	JENKINS	295	BECK	495	MCBRIDE	695	JACOBSON	895	PONCE
96	GUTIERREZ	296	ORTEGA	496	OWEN	696	WOODARD	896	FAULKNER
97	PERRY	297	WADE	497	SOLIS	697	HUANG	897	DONALDSON
98	BUTLER	298	ESTRADA	498	PHAM	698	KEMP	898	SCHMITT
99	BARNES	299	CONTRERAS	499	LANG	699	MOSLEY	899	NOVAK
100	FISHER	300	BARNETT	500	PRATT	700	PRINCE	900	COSTA
101	HENDERSON	301	CALDWELL	501	LARA	701	MERRITT	901	MONTES
102	COLEMAN	302	SANTIAGO	502	BROCK	702	HURST	902	BOOKER
103	SIMMONS	303	LAMBERT	503	BALLARD	703	VILLANUEVA	903	CORDOVA
104	PATTERSON	304	POWERS	504	TRUJILLO	704	ROACH	904	WALLER
105	JORDAN	305	CHAMBERS	505	SHAFFER	705	NOLAN	905	ARELLANO
106	REYNOLDS	306	NUNEZ	506	DRAKE	706	LAM	906	MADDOX
107	HAMILTON	307	CRAIG	507	ROMAN	707	YODER	907	MATA
108	GRAHAM	308	LEONARD	508	AGUIRRE	708	MCCULLOUGH	908	BONILLA
109	KIM	309	LOWE	509	MORTON	709	LESTER	909	STANTON
110	GONZALES	310	RHODES	510	STOKES	710	SANTANA	910	COMPTON
111	ALEXANDER	311	BYRD	511	LAMB	711	VALENZUELA	911	KAUFMAN
112	RAMOS	312	GREGORY	512	PACHECO	712	WINTERS	912	DUDLEY
113	WALLACE	313	SHELTON	513	PATRICK	713	BARRERA	913	MCPHERSON
114	GRIFFIN	314	FRAZIER	514	COCHRAN	714	LEACH	914	BELTRAN
115	WEST	315	BECKER	515	SHEPHERD	715	ORR	915	DICKSON
116	COLE	316	MALDONADO	516	CAIN	716	BERGER	916	MCCANN
117	HAYES	317	FLEMING	517	BURNETT	717	MCKEE	917	VILLEGAS
118	CHAVEZ	318	VEGA	518	HESS	718	STRONG	918	PROCTOR
119	GIBSON	319	SUTTON	519	LI	719	CONWAY	919	HESTER
120	BRYANT	320	COHEN	520	CERVANTES	720	STEIN	920	CANTRELL
121	ELLIS	321	JENNINGS	521	OLSEN	721	WHITEHEAD	921	DAUGHERTY
122	STEVENS	322	PARKS	522	BRIGGS	722	BULLOCK	922	CHERRY
123	MURRAY	323	MCDANIEL	523	OCHOA	723	ESCOBAR	923	BRAY
124	FORD	324	WATTS	524	CABRERA	724	KNOX	924	DAVILA
125	MARSHALL	325	BARKER	525	VELASQUEZ	725	MEADOWS	925	ROWLAND
126	OWENS	326	NORRIS	526	MONTOYA	726	SOLOMON	926	LEVINE
127	MCDONALD	327	VAUGHN	527	ROTH	727	VELEZ	927	MADDEN
128	HARRISON	328	VAZQUEZ	528	MEYERS	728	ODONNELL	928	SPENCE
129	RUIZ	329	HOLT	529	CARDENAS	729	KERR	929	GOOD
130	KENNEDY	330	SCHWARTZ	530	FUENTES	730	STOUT	930	IRWIN
131	WELLS	331	STEELE	531	WEISS	731	BLANKENSHIP	931	WERNER
132	ALVAREZ	332	BENSON	532	HOOVER	732	BROWNING	932	KRAUSE
133	WOODS	333	NEAL	533	WILKINS	733	KENT	933	PETTY
134	MENDOZA	334	DOMINGUEZ	534	NICHOLSON	734	LOZANO	934	WHITNEY
135	CASTILLO	335	HORTON	535	UNDERWOOD	735	BARTLETT	935	BAIRD
136	OLSON	336	TERRY	536	SHORT	736	PRUITT	936	HOOPER
137	WEBB	337	WOLFE	537	CARSON	737	BUCK	937	POLLARD
138	WASHINGTON	338	HALE	538	MORROW	738	BARR	938	ZAVALA
139	TUCKER	339	LYONS	539	COLON	739	GAINES	939	JARVIS
140	FREEMAN	340	GRAVES	540	HOLLOWAY	740	DURHAM	940	HOLDEN
141	BURNS	341	HAYNES	541	SUMMERS	741	GENTRY	941	HAAS
142	HENRY	342	MILES	542	BRYAN	742	MCINTYRE	942	HENDRIX
143	VASQUEZ	343	PARK	543	PETERSEN	743	SLOAN	943	MCGRATH
144	SNYDER	344	WARNER	544	MCKENZIE	744	MELENDEZ	944	BIRD
145	SIMPSON	345	PADILLA	545	SERRANO	745	ROCHA	945	LUCERO
146	CRAWFORD	346	BUSH	546	WILCOX	746	HERMAN	946	TERRELL
147	JIMENEZ	347	THORNTON	547	CAREY	747	SEXTON	947	RIGGS
148	PORTER	348	MCCARTHY	548	CLAYTON	748	MOON	948	JOYCE
149	MASON	349	MANN	549	POOLE	749	HENDRICKS	949	MERCER
150	SHAW	350	ZIMMERMAN	550	CALDERON	750	RANGEL	950	ROLLINS
151	GORDON	351	ERICKSON	551	GALLEGOS	751	STARK	951	GALLOWAY
152	WAGNER	352	FLETCHER	552	GREER	752	LOWERY	952	DUKE
153	HUNTER	353	MCKINNEY	553	RIVAS	753	HARDIN	953	ODOM
154	ROMERO	354	PAGE	554	GUERRA	754	HULL	954	ANDERSEN
155	HICKS	355	DAWSON	555	DECKER	755	SELLERS	955	DOWNS
156	DIXON	356	JOSEPH	556	COLLIER	756	ELLISON	956	HATFIELD
157	HUNT	357	MARQUEZ	557	WALL	757	CALHOUN	957	BENITEZ
158	PALMER	358	REEVES	558	WHITAKER	758	GILLESPIE	958	ARCHER
159	ROBERTSON	359	KLEIN	559	BASS	759	MORA	959	MUELLER
160	BLACK	360	ESPINOZA	560	FLOWERS	760	KNAPP	960	TRAVIS
161	HOLMES	361	BALDWIN	561	DAVENPORT	761	MCCALL	961	MCNEIL
162	STONE	362	MORAN	562	CONLEY	762	MORSE	962	HINTON
163	MEYER	363	LOVE	563	HOUSTON	763	DORSEY	963	ZHANG
164	BOYD	364	ROBBINS	564	HUFF	764	WEEKS	964	HAYS
165	MILLS	365	HIGGINS	565	COPELAND	765	NIELSEN	965	MAYO
166	WARREN	366	BALL	566	HOOD	766	LIVINGSTON	966	FRITZ
167	FOX	367	CORTEZ	567	MONROE	767	LEBLANC	967	BRANCH
168	ROSE	368	LE	568	MASSEY	768	MCLEAN	968	MOONEY
169	RICE	369	GRIFFITH	569	ROBERSON	769	BRADSHAW	969	EWING
170	MORENO	370	BOWEN	570	COMBS	770	GLASS	970	RITTER
171	SCHMIDT	371	SHARP	571	FRANCO	771	MIDDLETON	971	ESPARZA
172	PATEL	372	CUMMINGS	572	LARSEN	772	BUCKLEY	972	FREY
173	FERGUSON	373	RAMSEY	573	PITTMAN	773	SCHAEFER	973	BRAUN
174	NICHOLS	374	HARDY	574	RANDALL	774	FROST	974	GAY
175	HERRERA	375	SWANSON	575	SKINNER	775	HOWE	975	RIDDLE
176	MEDINA	376	BARBER	576	WILKINSON	776	HOUSE	976	HANEY
177	RYAN	377	ACOSTA	577	KIRBY	777	MCINTOSH	977	KAISER
178	FERNANDEZ	378	LUNA	578	CAMERON	778	HO	978	HOLDER
179	WEAVER	379	CHANDLER	579	BRIDGES	779	PENNINGTON	979	CHANEY
180	DANIELS	380	BLAIR	580	ANTHONY	780	REILLY	980	MCKNIGHT
181	STEPHENS	381	DANIEL	581	RICHARD	781	HEBERT	981	GAMBLE
182	GARDNER	382	CROSS	582	KIRK	782	MCFARLAND	982	VANG
183	PAYNE	383	SIMON	583	BRUCE	783	HICKMAN	983	COOLEY
184	KELLEY	384	DENNIS	584	SINGLETON	784	NOBLE	984	CARNEY
185	DUNN	385	OCONNOR	585	MATHIS	785	SPEARS	985	COWAN
186	PIERCE	386	QUINN	586	BRADFORD	786	CONRAD	986	FORBES
187	ARNOLD	387	GROSS	587	BOONE	787	ARIAS	987	FERRELL
188	TRAN	388	NAVARRO	588	ABBOTT	788	GALVAN	988	DAVIES
189	SPENCER	389	MOSS	589	CHARLES	789	VELAZQUEZ	989	BARAJAS
190	PETERS	390	FITZGERALD	590	ALLISON	790	HUYNH	990	SHEA
191	HAWKINS	391	DOYLE	591	SWEENEY	791	FREDERICK	991	OSBORN
192	GRANT	392	MCLAUGHLIN	592	ATKINSON	792	RANDOLPH	992	BRIGHT
193	HANSEN	393	ROJAS	593	HORN	793	CANTU	993	CUEVAS
194	CASTRO	394	RODGERS	594	JEFFERSON	794	FITZPATRICK	994	BOLTON
195	HOFFMAN	395	STEVENSON	595	ROSALES	795	MAHONEY	995	MURILLO
196	HART	396	SINGH	596	YORK	796	PECK	996	LUTZ
197	ELLIOTT	397	YANG	597	CHRISTIAN	797	VILLA	997	DUARTE
198	CUNNINGHAM	398	FIGUEROA	598	PHELPS	798	MICHAEL	998	KIDD
199	KNIGHT	399	HARMON	599	FARRELL	799	DONOVAN	999	KEY
200	BRADLEY	400	NEWTON	600	CASTANEDA	800	MCCONNELL	1000	COOKE

FREQUENTLY OCCURING AMERICAN SURNAMES — TOP 1000

VISUALIZATION: Catalogtree, 2008

SOURCE: http://www.census.gov/genealogy/www/freqnames2k.html

HISPANIC / WHITE / BLACK / PACIFIC / INDIAN / ALASKAN / AMERICAN / >2 RACES

—**Extruded Expanded** MICHELLE
ALLARD, photography by the Macdonald
Stewart Art Centre ——— **Flourish I**
MICHELLE ALLARD.

Index

—

Data Flow
Visualising Information
in Graphic Design

—

Edited by Robert Klanten, Nicolas Bourquin,
Thibaud Tissot, Sven Ehmann
Text editor and foreword by Ferdi van Heerden

—

Project management by Julian Sorge for Gestalten
Design by onlab, Thibaud Tissot
Typefaces: Farnham, Bureau Grot

—

Cover photography by Andrea Galvani © 2006,
La morte di un'immagine #7
C-Print on aluminium, wood frame, perspex, 118 x 148 cm
Private collection, Imola, Italy. Edition of 5 in different
format. Courtesy Galleria Artericambi, Verona, Italy.

—

Production management by Martin Bretschneider
for Gestalten
Copyediting by Matthew Gaskins
Printed by SIA Livonia Print, Riga
Made in Europe

—

Published by Gestalten, Berlin 2008
ISBN 978-3-89955-217-1

3rd printing, 2009

Bibliographic information published by the
Deutsche Nationalbibliothek.
The Deutsche Nationalbibliothek lists this publication in
the Deutsche Nationalbibliografie;
detailed bibliographic data is available on the internet at
http://dnb.d-nb.de.

—

None of the content in this book was published in exchange
for payment by commercial parties or designers; Gestalten
selected all included work based solely on its artistic merit.

—

This book was printed according to the internationally
accepted FSC and ISO 14001 standards for environmental protection, which requirements for an environmental
management system.

Mixed Sources
Product group from well-managed
forests and other controlled sources
www.fsc.org Cert no. SGS-COC-3005
© 1996 Forest Stewardship Council
FSC

Gestalten is a climate neutral company and so are our products. We collaborate with the non-profit carbon offset provider
myclimate (www.myclimate.org) to neutralize the company's
carbon footprint produced through our worldwide business
activities by investing in projects that reduce CO_2 emissions
(www.gestalten.com/myclimate).

myclimate
Protect our planet